INTRODUCTION

I tell thee that although it is a long time on the road, it is on the road and coming....

Charles Dickens

Because of time pressures, complexity, rapid change, and global competition, many of today's organizations are teaming with other organizations and individuals, creating new forms of enterprise called "virtual organizations." These relationships differ in significant ways from traditional partnerships or alliances: they generally are product and project focused, flexible and short lived. They are based primarily on competencies rather than historical relationships or cost. They are complex, with organizations often finding themselves in networks of worldwide virtual alliances that include customers and competitors as well as organizations that provide research, design, manufacturing, marketing, and support competencies.

In the best of situations, such relationships are difficult to maintain, and even more difficult to turn to value. What's needed is a set of business processes based on information and communications technologies that can support these flexible, far reaching, information intensive virtual organizations. Few organizations have those processes and technologies in place today. The resulting tension between the new demands of virtual work and traditional business processes is creating stress and even chaos.

Going Virtual extends the scope of "virtual" beyond the *nature* of virtual relationships, to include these new processes and technologies. Our subject is not how the organizations look, but how virtual teams actually work; how they use networked electronic information and communications systems as the infrastructure for their teaming processes. We call this capability to "work together apart," *virtual operations*. The virtual organization and, in a few cases, the virtual operations model has been validated by leading edge innovators in both domestic and international situations. But wider acceptance seems to be primarily theoretical–more energy is consumed in agreeing that virtual is good than in actually attempting to reengineer one's organization to the virtual model This is due in large part to the stresses organizations are experiencing in just trying to remain afloat in today's globally competitive economy. It has been suggested that reengineering your organization is like trying to perform open heart surgery on yourself while running a marathon. Reengineering for virtual operations seems like an overwhelming task, best left to the adventurous few.

It is very tempting, less risky–safer–to settle for continuous improvement rather than to try to break through to step, stairway, or elevator functions of improved performance. However, that safety is an illusion, since all around us continuous improvement initiatives achieve diminishing, or even destructive returns. Rates of improvement often trail the rates of change, initiating small fixes that may obscure more significant threats.

This phenomenon is noticeable across industries ranging from professional sports to product manufacturing. For example, for the past few years, professional football teams in the US have been perfecting their "kicking game," continuously increasing both accuracy and distances from which their specialists can kick field goals. This trend has been based on coaches' underlying belief that three sure points are more desirable than six risky ones. Over the past two or three seasons, however, with accuracy high and many game scores consisting entirely of field goal successes, audiences have become bored with the game and attendance has dropped. The league has responded with rule changes that make field goals riskier, and teams are shifting back to more exciting and entertaining touchdown oriented tactics.

In this example, the continuous field goal improvement satisfied the teams, whose goals were putting winning scores on the board, but obscured what the spectators wanted: entertainment. The implication here is that the *value* generated by the enterprise of professional football is entertainment, not victorious sport performance. Maybe the consumers of the product should have been stakeholders in the strategic decision to build up the kicking game.

A manufacturing example, based on a real situation, is a bit closer to our virtual operations focus. A manufacturing organization, after downsizing, naturally was forced to develop its supplier bases, looking for economies in purchasing worldwide. The organization focused its continuous improvement by gradually automating its centralized purchasing-supply system. What it ultimately discovered was that the now automated system, after some increases in efficiency, did not improve the effectiveness of the overall manufacturing process. It got points on the board but really didn't provide the performance improvements the situation demanded.

What was really needed was redesign and decentralization of the entire enterprise system: bringing suppliers and other stakeholders into virtual partnering relationships, having supplier partners handle ordering as well as order fulfillment, and implementing electronic processes and technologies that would support the virtual processes and teams. When processes were redesigned on a decentralized, stakeholder-participation model, dramatic new levels of overall effectiveness, not just spot efficiencies, were achieved.

The Main Agenda

Going Virtual sets forth what we think is a persuasive case for such virtual reengineering, suggests a strategy for making the transition to virtual operations, and provides guidelines for redesign of fundamental virtual processes. The book is intended to be:

1. A call to action to companies, organizations, and groups that may be languishing in the organizational doldrums of last-generation assumptions, processes, roles, and technology; either unaware of or resistant to the emerging virtual imperative. What these organizations and individuals need to get in the game and play it well, both as leaders and partners, is commitment and guidance. *Going Virtual* aims to stimulate this commitment, support proselytizing, and provide direction for transitioning to this new way of doing business.

2. A handbook giving guidance and support for organizations which have entered the virtual playing field and are immersed in the contest, but aren't really sure of the rules. The book will help them optimize their investments in the path they've already chosen, reduce their risk in process innovation, build a foundation for training, and develop a common ground for working in virtual alliances.

3. A guide for organizations and individuals considering a transition to telecommuting. The principles of virtual operations can

help the telecommuter be a presence in the teaming of office staff and other telecommuters, not merely a remote individual contributor pounding out spreadsheets and documents to be sent about the system by E-mail.

The Approach

Going Virtual moves from concept to action to results. Through interviews, commentary, and exposition, the first three Parts of the book present the case for and principles of virtual operations. The last two Parts consist of action-level guidelines for progressing through the strategic and tactical stages of the virtual transition cycle. *Going Virtual* culminates in a series of step-by-step checklists that lead the reader through the transition from his or her current situation to an operational, virtual future.

The "current situation" is the focus of the Epilogue. Here we recognize that many readers will have experienced what Herman Melville called a "shock of recognition" while reading this book. They will identify with many of the situations described here, because their organizations are already engaged in the virtual environment. Their challenge is not to begin strategically planning for the future, but to dynamically and gracefully transition into the virtual operations paradigm that will help them better accomplish the work they have underway today.

One organization involved in this process is the Ameritech Cellular Services unit, part of Ameritech Mobile Communications, Inc., headquartered just outside Chicago. In a significant way, the book is structured around a current virtual initiative led by Cellular Services.

Ameritech is developing a market leadership position based on breakthrough mobile, wireless networking and the combined knowledge and products of several world-class information processing and software applications contributors. The Cellular Services case is one of an organization thrust into the virtual environment, seeking to transition from the four-walls organizational model to the networked, distributed, competency-based virtual model, supported by virtual operations.

However, the virtual arena in many ways belongs to small companies who understand their real competencies and can't afford to overreach them, rather than huge corporations who are used to bringing the competencies they need "into the organization." These smaller enterprises are becoming more and more significant in industry: They will not replace the larger corporations, but provide essential virtual competencies to them and to each other. Major corporations are in no small way learning from entrepreneurial success and spinning off their own organizations in that model. We address both kinds of enterprise in this book.

Our Readers

Most readers will bring to this book expertise in one or another of its primary focus areas: business process redesign, organizational transformation, design of communication and learning processes, individual and teaming skills, and computer and telecommunications technology. The intent of *Going Virtual* is not to develop competencies in these areas, but to offer a new synthesis, in this case a virtual paradigm into which the readers can integrate their valuable knowledge and skills. Active reading required!

Going Virtual is addressed specifically to:

- Organizational decision makers and influencers who are considering or already committed to meeting the challenge of working in the *de facto* virtual environment
- Those who plan, design, lead, and manage value-adding, non-collocated work processes
- Contributors to virtual teams, including those leading virtual initiatives as well as their partners -- formerly known and treated as suppliers, competitors, and customers
- Senior executives, middle line and process managers, product champions,   process reengineering experts, IS and network managers, MBA curriculum designers, distance learning professionals, teachers, and students.

An audience of particular interest is middle-management, an endangered species whose ranks are being squeezed out of productive roles by downsizing and the resultant collapse of organizational pyramids. The best middle managers are extremely competent in evaluating contributors' capabilities and managing relationships—key skills in virtual work. This book could help middle-managers extend their existing skills to provide an attractive set of credentials for the 1990s and beyond.

Another group that should be especially receptive to these ideas is human resource and training professionals. For training provides the leverage for transitioning to virtual operations. Training and learning, both of which will be addressed in some detail in the book, catalyze the change process. Training professionals have the responsibility—and the opportunity—to create and extend the competencies required to sustain and evolve virtual operations.

Similarly, higher education -- academia -- should take heed of the virtual phenomenon. The unprecedented needs for continuous, specialized learning can provide these beleaguered institutions with the opportunity to take on a new and exciting role: that of the "learning stakeholder" in virtual operations. But they will themselves need to learn to be players, to move beyond dependence on curriculum and faculty, and to deliver the capability for virtual workers to easily access the competencies that can add value to a continuous learning situation. This will be a challenge, but one that promises great rewards for those who succeed.

With this, in Part I we'll begin the virtual odyssey by defining what we mean by virtual.

ACKNOWLEDGEMENTS

This book is a result of a virtual effort by two on-line writers and many stakeholders. Because virtual operations is an emerging discipline, our work was more search than research. Search we did and found people out there in a myriad of organizations, engaged in a variety of virtual activities. That these folks were eager to share their ongoing experiences bodes well for a collaborative, virtual future.

First and foremost our thanks to Greg Oslan and the Ameritech Cellular Data project team, who were willing to share their learning from successes and failures in the Ameritech Cellular Services virtual project. We hope they find things in this book that will help them a bit the next time around.

We also extend thanks to our many virtual contributors, who through phone conferences, E-mail, computer conferencing and yes, face-to-face meetings gave us stories, insights, and cautions about virtual work. This forward thinking and acting cadre includes Bill (BJ) Johnson of IBM, Ray McCann and Barry Nelson of Management Research Associates, Larry Walker and Dawn Rohrbacher of Digital Equipment Corporation, Richard Manganello of the Windmill Group, and Jim McClellan of the McClellan organization. Also in this number are the "gang of many" at AT&T Global Information Solution's virtually working Enterprise Design and Development Group (ED&D): Hans Gyllstrom, Ulf Fagerquist, and their partner, John Gundry of Knowledge Ability, U.K. Key contributions in the virtual learning sector came from Frank Medeiros of San Diego State University, and Steve Eskow, who runs the Electronic University Network, which delivers virtual courses over America On-line.

We thank Patti Bisano and Jake Landry at CDC for sharing their knowledge of audioconferencing and other interactive applications, and

Michael Schrage for finding time in his schedule to comment on our manuscript.

Finally, we wish to thank Mike Meehan, our editor at Prentice Hall for his efforts in advancing our manuscript, from concept to draft, through the administrative hoops, and Lisa Garboski, our production editor, for editing and managing the text through the end game.

Ray Grenier and George Metes

BIOGRAPHIES

George Metes is President of Virtual Learning Systems, Inc., and a partner in Grenier & Metes Associates. Over the last 15 years he has worked with a variety of industrial, educational, and public organizations in the areas of human systems integration, virtual work, and distance learning. With Ray Grenier, he is co-author of *Enterprise Networking: Working Together Apart* (Digital Press, 1992). He holds an A.B. from Dartmouth College and a Ph.D. in literature and linguistics from the University of Wisconsin.

Ray Grenier is a partner in Grenier & Metes Associates. He has over 35 years experience in telecommunications systems operations as a career officer in the USAF, and as an executive with several organizations including General Telephone and Digital Equipment Corporation. Most recently his work has focused on the design of interactive work processes that combine voice, data, and image technologies to support the needs of widely dispersed management and virtual teams. He holds degrees and professional certificates from MIT, Boston University and the Air Force Institute of Technology.

THE ARGUMENT
FOR VIRTUAL
OPERATIONS

Chapter 1: The Virtual Situation

Chapter 2: Trip Report -- A Tour of the Virtual
Future

Chapter 3: The Ameritech Story

In this first Part we will examine virtual operations from
three perspectives. Chapter 1 establishes the setting for virtual operations by taking the large view of today's virtual
environment, from global business pressures to the opportunity for virtual work. In Chapter 2 we look into the future at an
idealized, fictitious situation in which organizations achieve a
high level of performance by recognizing the virtual environment and transitioning to virtual operations. As a reality
check, in Chapter 3 we engage in a dialogue with the
leader of an actual virtual initiative, the Ameritech Cellular
Services virtual "one-stop-shopping" initiative to bring to market wireless data solutions.

The varied approaches here are intended to provide a
holistic sense of the scope, complexity, opportunity, difficulty,
and value of virtual operations in today's -- and tomorrow's --
organizational environments.

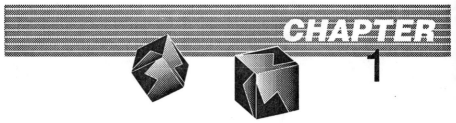

THE VIRTUAL
SITUATION

Lois: Virtual reality. You know what virtual means?
Honey: Ah. Sort of.
Lois: It's like really real. So virtual reality is practically, totally real,
*   but not.*
**   Short Cuts, The Screen Play.**[1]

Virtual reality, virtual classrooms, virtual surgery, virtual offices, virtual corporations, virtual car lots, virtual-you-name-it. Every day another familiar activity or place suddenly, "goes virtual." This incredibly fast moving final decade of the twentieth century is bringing us into virtual realms that will forever change the way we work, learn, govern, shop, and entertain ourselves.

The term "virtual" traditionally has implied a flip-flop between appearance and reality: something appears to be what it really isn't, as in, "the meeting room was a virtual circus," or, "Boxen Corporation had been given virtually no chance to pull off the deal." (Obviously, Boxen did pull it off!) Today the meaning of "virtual" has been extended to suggest

- Greatly enhanced effects or actions
- Physical behavior of non-physical (often electronic) entities
- The use of telecommunications and computing technologies.

Virtual reality is a case in point. We've all seen the human subjects encased in gloves, helmets, recliners, and other sorts of technological wombs, participating in activities they electronically construct, feeling as if

---

[1]*Short Cuts,* directed by Robert Altman. The screenplay by Robert Altman and Frank Barhydt. Based on the writings of Raymond Carver. Fineline Features in Association with Spelling Films International, 1994.

2

they are physically involved in real, intense situations. Years ago we saw the "orgasmatron" of Woody Allen's Sleeper; today our virtual travelers fly jet aircraft, crawl through human cells, walk on the moon, or stroll through Bangkok with full (or greater) sensory apprehension of time, place, and motion. The effects of reality are felt, although the usual physical causes have been replaced by electronic simulations and stimulations.

Common threads run through the phenomena we call virtual. Most involve human participants in carefully designed complex systems, supported by sophisticated electronic information and communications technologies. For example, virtual medicine is practiced today, with teams of medical specialists consulting and guiding on-site staff in the treatment of difficult cases. All data about patients is available electronically; through video and links, the patient, hospital staff, and remote team can work together to address the patient's needs. In the not-so-distant future we're promised virtual surgery, with an operation performed on a patient by a medical team whose members are physically located at hospitals thousands of miles apart; the team communicates through video hookups, monitors life processes through data networks, slices through tissue with remotely controlled laser and robotically manipulated instruments. The effects are local -- the patient is treated -- but the performance of the surgery is enhanced by the "telepresence" of physically distributed experts, who use carefully planned procedures supported by computer and telecommunications technologies.[2]

Virtual activities are becoming so much a part of our culture that we've begun to accept virtuality as part of everyday reality. Consider the virtual, or electronic mall, which permits us to leisurely shop by TV, virtually cruising aisles of boutiques to consume without leaving our armchairs.

And what about those extremely popular MTV, TV-watching personalities, Bevis and Butthead. These animated lads entertain our youth by giving running commentaries on music videos, which present performers lipsynching recorded electronic music. It brings to mind the words of Glenn Gould, the renowned pianist who avoided concerts in favor of the recording studio. "The ideal relationship between performer and audience," said Gould, "is one-to-none."[3] Going far beyond Gould's dictum, the virtual entertainment effect of the B & B hour is at least four electronic dimensions away from the reality of concert hall or recording studio performance. Count 'em.

Exciting innovations such as these will surely influence the way we live in the twenty-first century. However, in Going Virtual our focus is on a specific virtual phenomenon, one that we feel has enormous economic, cul-

---

[2]Gary Taubes, "Surgery in Cyberspace," Discover, December 1994, pp. 84-94.

[3]Glenn Gould, in 32 Short Films about Glenn Gould. Directed by Francois Girard. Screenplay by Francois Girard and Don McKellage, Canada: Max Films, 1993.

tural, and social implications: the potential of virtual operations for today's business organizations.

The Virtual Business Situation

"Here we are teaming with engine, airframe, electronics makers and suppliers, customers, even competitors...spread all over the place....We're trying to learn how to work together under these conditions: to share design and management information, to develop and sustain parallel engineering efforts across distances and between organizations....We need to figure out how to manage our functional, philosophical, and cultural differences -- to share just enough of our design and manufacturing processes to get the work done faster without giving away the store."

Senior Executive, Aerospace Industry

The business world has begun recognizing the potential of the "Virtual Organization," or "Virtual Corporation," as the enterprise model most likely to be up to the complex challenges of the 1990s and beyond. Those challenges include unprecedented customer expectations and alternatives, global competition, time compression, complexity, rapid change, and ubiquitous technology. In the virtual model, as it's typically defined, a lead organization creates alliances with a set of other groups, both internal and external, that possess the best-in-world competencies to build a specific product or service in a very short period of time.

Such an alliance is "virtual" in that it is really not one homogeneous organization, but a hybrid of groups and individuals from different companies, even industries, that includes competitors, customers, and suppliers, whose purpose is not longevity, but bringing a specific, highest quality product or service to market as quickly as possible. Indeed, the alliance is temporary, with extremely short concept-to-delivery cycles.

For example, a half-dozen or so companies form an alliance to bring to market quickly a new pharmaceutical product. Each company provides stakeholders in the virtual team with specific competencies: research and development; chemistry; physiology; marketing; testing; distribution, and support. As soon as the mission is accomplished, the alliance breaks up, and the organizations involved look for new teaming possibilities. This pseudo-organization certainly qualifies as a virtual entity; it is a complex system that produces enhanced effects: high quality products and services in record times and at reduced overall costs.

Increasingly, such alliances are forming, adapting, and learning how to turn this situation into a powerful competitive advantage.

Changes of this magnitude are not new. In their book *The Virtual Corporation,* William Davidow and Michael Malone help us see the long view of process evolution through a study of Beretta, the Italian arms manufacturing firm. They trace the company's response to historical, industrial paradigms that have driven the evolution of process design and changed the role of information and knowledge work. Each new industrial paradigm that characterized Beretta's growth was signaled by breakthroughs that forced change. In developing this case study, the authors focus on the physical and mechanical processes used to create value. It's also interesting to observe the gradually shifting influence from mechanical to information based processes, and to consider how individuals adapted to the increasing role of information and information processing systems.[4]

• The English System (1800) -- Replaced hand building with a processes that focused on using generic tools that could be used to build any product. Information was drawn from personal knowledge, experience, and skills of craftsmen. Learning occurred through mentors and hands on experience.

• The American System (1850) -- High volume production and the use of interchangeable parts. Work became mechanized, and workers became specialists within a formalized production system. Information still represented by individual experience, but critical information now focused on the production process. Learning occurred through several mentors who, as specialists, represented different skills; hands on experience still required.

• Taylor Scientific Management (1900) -- Time and motion analysis focused on the activities of individual workers and defined roles and responsibilities needed to optimize productivity. New categories of information were created that abstracted various aspects of work. Value now influenced by information concerning better and faster processing techniques. Learning included observation and analysis techniques to supplement mechanical skills.

• Statistical Process Control (1945) -- The return of worker involvement. The beginning of quality control as a technique to manage long-term production. Information included statistical data compiled.

[4]William H. Davidow & Michael S. Malone, *The Virtual Corporation: Structuring and Revitalizing the Corporation for the 21st Century* (New York: Harper Business, 1992), pp. 25-30. This pioneering work remains one of the best studies of virtual organizations, their circumstances and their value.

over time. More information needed to make decisions and manage risks. Learning became more complex and covered more disciplines not directly related to the value creating process.

• Numerical Control (1976) -- The introduction of information processing into the value producing equation. Companies transitioned into information based organizations where information became a tool and information workers began to have major influence. Quantum jump in information volume and the number of information processing techniques. Data based on quantification techniques distributed to every part of the organization. Learning was specialized, complex, and required constant updating.

• Computer-Integrated Manufacturing (1987) -- The organization is linked into an information infrastructure capable of feeding information to machines that complete work processes. This phase created the ability to respond to market opportunities worldwide -- virtual operations! Information, specifically electronic information, becomes the coin-of-the-realm. Learning expands to include techniques for working in the information environment, and the requirement is for continuous learning -- for everyone.

Through each of these phases Beretta managed the changes that were required to take advantage of the emerging tools, processes, and competencies. Each phase matured through continuous improvement until a new breakthrough opened the door for innovators to make major improvements in time, quality, and cost management. Using the breakthroughs, Beretta became more efficient in business, survived negative business cycles, and kept their company at the leading edge of their industry -- for over three hundred years!

Now, at the start of the breakthrough to virtual operations, we can posit this scenario:

• Virtual operations (1994) -- The integration of work processes with a ubiquitous electronic information infrastructure that enables the optimum teaming of world class competencies to create value. The era of teams of knowledge workers able to use electronic systems to support knowledge and information worldwide. Interactions are in real time and designed to use all available telecommunications facilities. Learning is continuous, collaborative, and acquired through the information infrastructure.

Virtual Teams

Of course, the virtual organization is just a starting point. Value is created not by the organization's existence, but by the accomplishments of virtual teams: product development teams, management teams, executive teams. These teams engage in the following activities:

• Create value by bringing together stakeholders who have the competencies needed to deliver a product or service, regardless of where physically, or in what organization the competency resides.

— Ameritech, a leading provider of telecommunications products and services has put together a network of telecommunications product and service providers to deliver mobile office solutions in record times.

— Virtual teams combine multi-organizational competencies to conduct biomedical product R & D, perform surgical procedures, and write proposals to government agencies. No longer anomalies, virtual teams are rapidly becoming mainstream.

• Produce information-based products or services by accessing, sharing, and processing electronic information, and by building collaborative knowledge through electronic communications: networks, shared databases, groupware applications, and so forth.

— Digital Equipment Corporation has been "virtually" developing computer systems for years, using shared databases, simulation and modeling systems, as well as audio-, computer- and videoconferencing to support dialogue. Worldwide competencies in circuit design, video technologies, chip design, and manufacturing "stay home" while collaboratively building products based on electronic information.

— Universities, such as those constituting the BESTNET consortium in California and Mexico, use computer conferencing across the Internet to collaboratively teach courses in Spanish and English, thereby addressing the needs of the border communities, where language, not nationality governs accessibility to learning.

• Ground their product and service design and development processes, as well as all other key business processes (marketing, sales, management, continuous learning) in the capabilities of robust, networked information and communications infrastructures. These organizations live, learn, and work in the network; the infrastructure is the virtual office, lab, and shop floor.

– One division of a leading global telecommunications giant is located, virtually, in a worldwide network. With designers, technicians, and consultants distributed around the world, the team meets continuously through computer conferencing in the network, at intervals through desktop videoconferencing, and occasionally in person at a customer's site. Their product is the design of similar organization and work models for their customers.

Virtual teaming is an optimal way to work in the current environment of time compression, distributed resources, increasing dependency on knowledge-based input, the premium on flexibility and adaptability, and availability of electronic information and communication through networks. The way teams create value in the virtual environment is through virtual operations.

Virtual Operations

We've already mentioned that virtual organizations, or teams, generate value through their operations, not their existence. These *virtual operations* are *processes designed to optimize the potential of competencies and technologies in the virtual environment.*
The basic elements of virtual operations are

• Virtual Work Processes, or Tasks
• Virtual Teaming
• Virtual Communications
• Virtual Learning.

It's important to keep in mind that these categories exist only for convenience; the operations themselves are tightly interrelated, recursive, and often inseparable. For example, at the heart of virtual work tasks are virtual communications processes and technologies, which work only if there is a sound teaming culture. This culture is not innate, but must be learned by the teaming partners. The learning, in turn, takes place through communications that are integral to the value adding work processes. There is, then, a positive feedback loop linking productive virtual work to virtual teaming, through learning processes based on communications. For clarity, however, we will look at each of these threads of virtual operations separately and in order. Here, we will merely introduce the key operations, as each will receive full coverage in Parts V and VI.

• Virtual Work Tasks - In projects supported by virtual work tasks, participation has less to do with location, or even organization, than it does with competency. A senior manager may have responsibility for projects whose people are distributed all over the world, connected through electronic networks: seeing them at work isn't likely. Nor is observation worth a great deal, since the value of virtual work is in the result, not the activity.

Virtual processes are typically designed for simultaneous electronic information access, not serial information flow. That is, people can see the work developing through the sharing of online information. In the network they can perceive the whole work process and accomplish their work in simultaneous sub-processes. This holistic view of the project enables participants to anticipate problems and negotiate solutions while the work is still upstream, eliminating costly back to the drawing board loopbacks. For example, in a major consulting engagement, consultants could use the electronic information and network infrastructure to track and evaluate colleagues' technical recommendations for, say, an inventory management application, while designing the client's training plan. The two tasks can evolve simultaneously even though they are going on at different physical locations. Moreover, the client's evolving business plan, being developed back at headquarters, can be referred to continuously, keeping time and money constraints before the whole team at all times.

This emphasis on accepting the primary role of electronic information is critical to virtual operations. The tradition of publishing information on paper is a long one. There is a sense of closure, completion, permanence, and professionalism embodied in the formatted, crisply printed page. But in the virtual environment the goal is to collaboratively create electronic "information objects," not to generate attractive, permanent reports, specifications, or even designs. Until the information and knowledge takes its final form imbedded in a product or service, there is no point to fixing information on paper: not for sharing, not for distribution, not for management.

• Virtual Teaming - For virtual teams to be effective, they need to design and develop certain beliefs, skills, and cultural foundations. Virtual work depends on an extremely high level of communications, and therefore trust. Teams must develop the capabilities to

work with information and communications technologies in stressful situations, with a variety of competencies in people from several
locations and organizations. This requires a variety of personal and
collective changes in attitudes and behaviors, not to mention knowledge and skills.

• Virtual Communications - In the virtual context the focus is on
primarily electronic interpersonal communications, involving the
building, exchange, access, use, distribution, recording, change, and
sharing of information and knowledge in support of all work and
learning processes. Communication is regarded as work, not as an
adjunct, or support function for work. Because of its complex, critical
role in virtual operations, communications must be designed; communication will not just happen, any more than the complicated work of
building an oil rig, law brief, or TV set will fortuitously come together.

• Virtual Learning - Virtual learning is a designed, collaborative,
continuous process through which individuals, teams of individuals,
and organizations build the knowledge, skills, perspectives, and experience -- the competencies -- they need to

1. Build a teaming culture

2. Sustain organizational and cross-organizational virtual operations

3. Build the higher levels of specialty and virtual operations capabilities needed to meet the increasing work demands of the virtual
   future.

Virtual learning is largely based on the belief that in virtual situations, learning best occurs in the same environment (the network),
with the same tools (electronic communications), by learners performing actual work.

Virtual Technologies - Of course, technology is not a virtual operation, but a font of potential that makes virtual operations possible.
There can be no virtual operations without technology: Indeed, the
greatest stresses in organizations today can be traced to their striving
to succeed in a virtual business environment without the benefits of
virtual processes and technologies.

Technologies can be found to support most virtual processes.
Work tasks, teaming, communications, and learning operations are
built on an infrastructure of networks, information systems, communications applications (groupware), modeling and simulation software, file transfer, and database access capabilities. Wireless

communications and a worldwide telephone system now make access to a team's network ubiquitous. Advances in scanning technologies mean that virtually all information can be digitized, brought in to the virtual infrastructure. Multimedia communications and presentation applications provide bandwidth that supports everything from ASCII characters to full motion 3D graphics and video.

Technology, in spite of vendor claims, will not provide virtual solutions, but is instrumental to those solutions. The technology challenge organizations face today is to continuously redesign their virtual processes to productively utilize the most robust technologies that are available. There will be no plateau in the evolution of virtual operations, certainly none for technology.

Barriers to Making the Virtual Transition

Most of us, regardless of our position in an organization, are thoroughly immersed in the today's virtual environment. We have come to accept the electronic information and new information technologies as an integral part of our environment. Millions of people have become network junkies, joining information services such as CompuServe and America Online. They surf the Internet, playing games, communicating with each other, and playing interactive games. Most children have access to computers in schools and many know more about their home computers than do their parents. With all this exposure to the reality of electronic networked information, it is not surprising that many of us have become blasé about technology, making it difficult to appreciate the role technology can play in reaching the breakthrough performance of virtual operations.

One challenge, then, is to be able to appreciate virtual operations as more than business as usual. Our approach in *Going Virtual* will be to isolate key processes in any work situations and overlay what we call the "virtual spin" on the redesign, or reengineering of these activities to support virtual work. When we speak of information and networking technologies it will be in terms of their potential to support these virtual operations, not as a general presence in our 1990s society.

There are other barriers to making the virtual transition. Most companies are already over their heads in the complexity and pressures of today's competitive business environment. Many are downsizing, creating alliances, and reengineering their operations to get greater efficiencies. They are unwilling to take the risk or expend the energy to undertake yet more transformation.

Our response here is to propose a transition process that involves individuals from all levels of the organization in both strategic and tactical design efforts. This work leads into prototype projects that move the organizations into virtual operations in a structured, controlled and focused way. Organizations can introduce virtual operations into their culture with minimal disturbance of ongoing work and economic use of people and technology resources.

Final Comments

We think that our industries, domestic and multinational, have no choice but to reengineer for the virtual future in order to survive. The pathway to healthy economic future for business is through transitioning to virtual operations. Continuous improvement will not do it. Executive musical chairs will not do it. Alleged technology solutions will not do it. What is needed is an appreciation of the new realities of the virtual marketplace and a systematic approach to redesigning work - processes, people skills, technologies - to meet those realities. We hope what follows in *Going Virtual* will provide that appreciation and deliver guidelines and ideas for transitioning to this new level of capability.

As the poet Chaucer said about the pressures of the medieval environment:

> Since here-against no creature alive,
> Of any kind, can successfully strive.
> Then it is wisdom, it seems to me,
> To make virtue of necessity.
>   from "The Knight's Tale," *The Canterbury Tales*

The pressures of the virtual environment are today's reality; and the virtual operations opportunity is a necessity, not a choice. As the poet said, wisdom lies in making a virtue of that necessity.

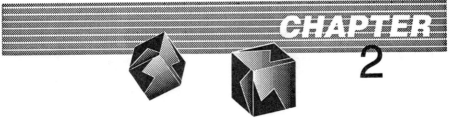

TOURING THE VIRTUAL FUTURE

All this is true, even if it never happened.
Chief Broom, in *One Flew Over the Cuckoo's Nest*,
Ken Kesey[1]

I'm Mary Dixon the VP of New Product Development at a mid-sized hospital supply company in San Diego. A few weeks back our CEO came to my office and handed me a printed invitation to a morning long seminar at the ZYX corporation headquarters in La Jolla. The topic of the seminar was: *Virtual Operations: Continuous Transitions to the Future.* "Here Mary, you're the one who's always looking into the future....might be a good show to check out." Right. Hint, hint. So I punched the date into my PC scheduler and a couple weeks later there I was, in a huge auditorium that looked more like the flight deck of the Starship Enterprise than a place to hear what I expected to be a traditional presentation.

A hundred or so guests were settling into deep, sculpted seats, each provided with a very high-tech computer monitor and printer, and a very low-tech coffee holder. What follows is an account of what went on that morning, drawn primarily from a video tape of the proceedings that was later made available to everyone. As each presenter spoke, terse, bulleted slides appeared on our personal monitors and were quietly printed out as the next slide appeared. So I have a pretty good permanent record of what went on.

From stage right entered the introductory speaker, briskly striding to the podium, stage left, past a large, movie-house sized projection screen and several smaller monitors and speakers. He gave the mike a couple non- tech taps, was satisfied with the echo and began.

[2]Ken Kesey, *One Flew Over the Cuckoo's Nest*, (New York: Penguin, 1976), p. 8.

"Good Morning, Ladies and Gentlemen, my name is John Harris. I'm Director of Public Relations here at ZYX Corporation and I've been asked to take you folks on a virtual tour of our company. Our CEO, Harry Harrison, will be launching the actual, well, virtual tour. And he'll be with us in a few minutes.

"I'm really glad there's such a good turn out. First I'll answer a question you haven't yet asked, but are probably considering: 'What's a virtual tour? Is it like virtual reality? Will we be wearing gloves and visors? Having visions? Traveling through pumps and turbines?' Well, it's a bit like that, but as the rental car ad says: 'Not exactly.'

"We're using virtual in two ways here. First of all, ZYX is becoming a virtual company; that is, we work within a model that calls for us to

1. Form product-focused partnerships and alliances with anyone who has a competency we need -- or we can provide

2. Develop a rich set of virtual operations to accomplish our work: business and teaming processes, communications, and a learning system, all supported by a networked electronic information infrastructure.

"We also use virtual today to emphasize that although today's tour will show you what goes on in our world, past and future, here in La Jolla as well as in other places. You really won't be leaving this room...or those comfortable chairs. You will 'virtually' experience ZYX Corporation.

"Another question you may have is 'Why the seminar? Why go to all this trouble?' The best answer I can give you is that as we've been transitioning to virtual work we've learned a lot about learning. For one thing, we've learned that the best way to stay ahead of rapid change is to keep a lot of learning channels open. We know a bit about all you folks and your organizations: you have been risk takers, pioneers, innovators -- some going up the same virtual path as we are. While there may be a bit of self-celebration in this morning's program, mainly it's about learning: your learning about us today, and in the future, our learning about each other.

"Any questions? OK.

"Seriously, there can be questions. Your personal workstation there next to you will be your communications agent during this meeting. Already you've seen slides displayed and printed. That's automatic. Now you'll see a Question Mark Icon appearing in the menu bar. Click that, type your question in the box, click the Mailbox Icon....and you'll have a response by lunch time. By the way, everyone will get everyone's questions and responses, anonymously, unless you request a personal response.

"Now the Agenda:

1. Getting Together -- John Harris, ZYX

2. ZYX Today -- A Virtual Organization (more John Harris)

3. Going Virtual: A Preview -- CEO Nigel "Harry" Harrison

4. Visioning: Beginning the Virtual Transition -- Ann Bardini, VP of Operations

5. Visioning: Setting the Context - Ann Bardini

6. Going Virtual with Eastern States Hydraulic -- Kate Sampson and Dileep Prahad

7. Designing Our Virtual Operations

8. What We've Learned about Virtual Operations

9. Trip's Over, for Now

"I'd say we were already through Item 1, so let's take a quick look at ZYX today as a virtual company. Then my colleagues will conduct you on a virtual tour of how we got where we are. I think you'll find some valuable lessons here."

ZYX Today -- A Virtual Organization

"ZYX is $1B international company with about 3,000 employees. Our products, once limited to valves and turbines, now include a growing roster of high-tech controls, displays, servo mechanisms, and even training packages in fluid dynamics, powerplant operation, and petrochemical processes. At any one time we have about 100 alliances or partnerships in place; some for six months, some for three years, some for longer. Our partnerships enable us to access best-in-world competencies for design, marketing, distribution; at times even manufacturing. Our core of highly competent people not only are world-class experts in their disciplines, but are committed to and highly skilled in building relationships, working in teams, using electronic information and communications processes, and learning continuously. Working with virtual partners gives us the flexibility, speed, and consistent quality of product we need to stay atop our markets.

"Increasingly we work with our customers and partners electronically. For example, we run a 24 hour a day, continuous TQM/QFD program over our global network. We ALWAYS know our customer's desires and priorities, and our partner's competencies and capabilities. We work in virtual teams, from the top of the corporation down...and across to other stakeholders.

"So this is where we are. In a moment you'll find out how, and why, we got here. But first....."

Now the lights dimmed and a gigantic star shape appeared on the projection screen. Each of the star points was labeled with a word starting with C: competency, communications, commitment, concurrency, collaboration. And above the star the title: ZYX: OUR GUIDING STAR."

Competency

Communications   Commitment

Concurrency   Collaboration

Figure 2.1   ZYX—Our Guiding Star

After giving us a few moments to digest what we were looking at, John picked up the narrative again.

"I was tempted to do some real multi-media here; you know, Willie Nelson in the background singing 'Stardust,' but Jan Lee, my ah, mentor, advised me to rein in my PR perspective a bit. Anyway, this star is what's important. It captures our company's shared understandings of the forces that need to be kept ever in mind to sustain our business vision: sort of our collective mental model. The points of the star guide our every business decision. From designing a process, figuring out training requirements, undertaking an alliance, to hiring a new employee. And the star itself represents an information and communications network, linking all the stakeholders in whatever the current activity.

"This simple visual instantly reminds every employee, every supplier, every partner, every customer of our work priorities; our code, if you will. Being visual, it's international. Our partners in the People's Republic of China use it with their own characters, no loss in translation. You'll notice an icon of the star is on your programs as well...just labeled with C's.   Finally, we hope that during the course of this tour you'll see the attributes signaled in the star played out not only in what we say about virtual operations, but what we do."

Going Virtual: A Preview

At that moment the large video monitor came to life and the face of a well groomed man filled the screen. "Hello. I'm Harry Harrison, the CEO here at ZYX." His voice bellowed out across the hall; John discreetly cranked down the volume. "I've been watching John's presentation from here in our St. Louis office. Actually, we don't have a St. Louis office; I'm in Jeanne Gray's office here at Graycorp." The camera panned to a smiling woman, evidently Jeanne Gray. "We're here discussing a joint project we'll be partnering on - are partnering on - as of about ten minutes ago. Funny, a couple years ago the only way we'd be in the same room (neutral territory at that) would have been with lawyers in between us. Fair competitors we were. Still are; but now we see a common market opportunity - can't tell you about it yet - and we're going after it together, as a virtual organization."

The image on the screen changed, as Harry directed us to a wall chart in the Graycorp room: The star. "Yes. We've even decided to share the star...for the length of this project anyway." He turned to Jeanne, "Will I need my lawyers to get it back?" Jeanne just smiled, and Harry continued.[2]

"I thought this would be a good way to demonstrate how far we've come on the virtual path in just a couple years. We still keep our lawyers busy on old business, but in this project we work together, no go betweens, no walls: one virtual organization.

"Let me tell you something about what you'll see this morning. This is not a sound and light show designed to show off a lot of whizbang technology. In fact, the less you notice the technology, the better. We do want to give you insight into the situations and events that triggered our decision to become a virtual organization and ultimately transition to virtual operations. We want to show you what that transition looked like in our case....and will continue to look like. In hindsight, with the machete work done, our path looks pretty clear. On the way up this hill it was trees, brush, wasps, and snakes. But it was worth it.

"By the way, we'll use a little multimedia, but remember, all this support technology is off-the-shelf and competitively priced, and we don't sell any of it! The performance, the achievements you see here are equally within your reach: just follow the star."

At this point the star expanded right of the screen, and was replaced by a series of black and white stills of a factory between shifts: lots of commotion, laughing jostling workers, smoke stacks, and steam and machin-

---

[2]We do not minimize the role of legal stakeholders in virtual organizations. There are many legal implications to the shift to virtual relationships. For example, traditional contractual processes cannot meet the need for rapid, flexible, formal relationships, and the added emphasis on trust severely stresses current legal models. The legal stakeholders in the virtual world must learn how to meet the emerging needs of virtual organizations, not hold back the transition by applying outmoded contractual standards to new situations.

ery. In a minute or so the montage changed, now the film became grainier and emptier as the same factory, now appeared empty: No noise, no smoke, no steam. Then, suddenly, color video graphics took over, zooming in on modern open office spaces, with designers at work at computer workstations: then a switch to state-of-the-art, lights-out robotic factories; again computers, people in video conferences, zooms into CAD drawings.

Harry's voice returned. "You've just seen a visual history of ZYX over the past decade. We all look at it a couple times a year. New employees see it as part of their orientation. It's a short, but powerful reminder of what happens when you get too complacent...and what can happen if you face up to the challenge of change. Ann Bardini, our VP of Ops is somewhere in this virtual presentation and she'll tell you more about these pictures and how they represent our particular transition. I'll check back with you later. Jeanne and I need to switch over to a virtual conference scheduled with some bankers, who we assume have some virtual bucks to throw in the game (the numbers will do; we don't particularly need the paper)."

Visioning: Beginning the Virtual Transition

A still of Ann appeared in a corner of the large screen as she began a voice over of the camera panning through the empty yards of the manufacturing plant. She began. "In the 1980's we sold standard products, nothing fancy, tubing, pipes, valves up to a certain size. In about '85 -'86 our sales began to drop off. There were plenty of scapegoats around to explain the downturn: the bad economy, bureaucratic government, lazy workers, subsidized competition from abroad, fluoride in the water. But blame didn't fix the problem. It wasn't until 1991 that we all realized we weren't looking for answers, we were just laying blame. And it took a customer to show us what we should have seen ourselves.

"Joe Gideon, purchasing manager for Eastern States Hydraulic was a longtime customer and personal friend of Harry's. Business from Joe had dropped off dramatically over a three year period. Well, dramatically when you looked at the three years, not so much was visible month by month. We were like the lobster dropped in a pot of cool water. The burners were on, but we didn't notice the little changes in temperature until the pot was almost boiling.

"We'd gone through some rapid turnover with account managers for Eastern States, so no one was paying a lot of attention to what was going on. Then one day one of our salespeople mentioned casually to Harry over lunch that the account was going sour. After blowing off a little steam about 'why didn't anyone tell me this,' Harry took some action and went out to see Joe Gideon.

"During their conversation Harry demanded to know what the problem was: 'What's wrong with our products?' 'Joe replied that there was nothing wrong with the products, but times had changed and his company didn't particularly need them anymore. Quality was great, price was competitive; but, sorry, wrong product!

"Eastern States was actually diversifying into more high-tech applications that made better use of their core competencies, more sophisticated systems building -- like hydraulics systems for new aircraft -- and our product line didn't fit in. And Joe was more than a little puzzled. 'You know, ' he said, 'you folks have all the hydraulics componentry design talent in the world. Why aren't you getting into these new markets. I'd give my right arm to be able to tap your design experts when I'm trying to configure a system to an airframe.'

Now Ann's relaxed image filled the screen, as she spoke to us one-on-one.

"Well, Harry catches on quick. He intuitively saw a whole new future - a ZYX for our company. Before that day was over, by means of a real handshake, he had engaged us in a virtual relationship with Eastern States...although no one called it that. All that Harry had to do was come back and sell it to the rest of the company, then figure out how to do it.

"So Harry got us all - about three layers of management - together in a small lunchroom and announced that we had to stop discussing our "problem" and begin doing something about it. He suggested two tracks of activity. The first track would be a management task-force chartered to develop a vision for ZYX. In parallel, each of us, alone or as part of a team, was chartered to come up with some initiative that recognized the nature of the current situation and respected the spirit of the vision. This initiative would be a real project, involving real stakeholder teams within and outside the company. That was the bottom line condition. This project - not research, not study, not review, not philosophy - would attempt to lead us out of the stagnation of the present situation. There would be no penalties for bad ideas, for failures, for duplication of another company's tactics. The goal was to do something, accomplish something, and to learn from what we did.

"Then he looked at us all sitting there and said, 'I'm told there are three layers of management here. Next time we meet I want two. Go up; go down. Whatever's best for the company. You'll keep your salaries; but let's focus on producing value for our customers, not on administering organizations.' Surprisingly, Harry's technique worked so well that he's made a habit of starting meetings with, 'I'm told there are three layers of management here....' He leaves the rest unsaid. We get it."

Visioning: Setting the Context

Ann went on. "The first thing we did was convene a plenary management meeting. Every manager -- of anything -- could come and participate. The prime movers in the meeting were Harry, Andrea Rowans in IS, and Gary Goldman in Human Resources/Training/OD. We had decided that in the meeting we would spend half of the time understanding the issues, half the time seeking solutions, and none of the time blaming people or inanimate things for our current situation. In fact, we spent very little time on the current state of affairs and what consultants like to call our 'As-Is' processes. We preferred to focus on the possibilities for the future, not present reasons why we couldn't get there from here.

"Andrea suggested that if we really wanted to focus the meeting, we should use a technique her own group had found effective when beginning to design a product. She proposed we use our E-mail systems to not only announce the meeting, its topics and ground rules, but help clarify questions people might have about what to expect. We made the announcements, and surprisingly got immediate feedback...more than we could handle. After about a week Gary noticed the information overload problem. He suggested that instead of E-mail, we try his Bulletin Board system, the one that he used to post internal job openings and for employee support discussions. On these bulletin boards we could post any guidelines, agendas or pre-reading materials we wanted to. And so we did, and after a few false starts ended up with a pretty good way of handling the discussions about the upcoming meeting.

"It did not escape us that we had learned something important: we had some pretty good technology and processes around to support important tasks. With some lateral thinking, we could find new applications based on existing investments in technology. We learned that we could learn from ourselves. And that felt good.

"Well, we had our first meeting, and a second, and a third. Each time the crowd got smaller and the issues got tighter. By the third meeting, in fact, much of the dialog had shifted into the bulletin board, where between meetings issues were hashed out. For example, one topic to be dealt with was the scope of the company's vision: what did we want to be in five years, ten years, twenty years?

Early discussions focused inwardly: 'ZYX will be the most innovative company in the industry'; 'ZYX will be a learning organization'; 'ZYX will be a virtual organization.' Finally, at one group meeting, someone said; 'Hey, who besides us cares about the ZYX organization? Shouldn't our first concern be to satisfy, to delight our customers? They care about our products, not how we organize. Let our vision include their perspectives, not just our philosophy. Let's have the vision say what we do for customers!'

'Better still,' offered Andrea. 'Let's make them part of the visioning process itself! They all have E-mail and can get to Internet. It would be no big deal to give them accounts on our E-mail/bulletin board server.'

"The reaction to this ranged from shock to horror. First of all, for an IS person to suggest opening up the corporate system to the outside was unthinkable. Furthermore, who else's business was it but ZYX's what ZYX's vision was to be. But fortunately, since Andrea herself had made the proposal, and enough of those present had been through QFD exercises requiring the participation of customers in the formulation of product specifications, the opposition relented and customers, not to mention suppliers and industry experts entered the dialog.

"Bringing customers in operationally into our work system, instead of treating them as occasional remote consultants, was a watershed decision for us. For that was our first step toward designing the virtual operations that would support our goals as a virtual organization. Next we would look to bring in partners, suppliers, yes, even competitors like Graycorp...from whom we learned a lot about the potential of virtual operations.

"Over the next few days Harry spoke with all of us in upper management, both about the visioning and about the concept of the first project -- his contribution. We did engage in virtual project, a prototype, with Eastern States, but the work turned out to be much more difficult than we expected. Each company had different technology infrastructures, different work philosophies and cultures, different business motives, and different everything it seemed. So while no collaborative product emerged, when the project was ended, both stakeholders realized that they had learned a tremendous amount of what it took to 'work together apart': what essential agreements needed to be in place or developed, what the barriers were, what the technology requirements were. Indeed, several weeks later a second virtual alliance with Eastern States, proposed by senior design engineers in both companies, had excellent results."

Intermission

The screen went blank. The ZYX Star appeared again, with Ann's voice over. "Now we'll take a 30 minute break. There's a phone behind everyone's monitor, with several more scattered around the lobby area if you need privacy. Also, you'll notice now the icon of a flying lightening bolt on your screens...That's your E-mail gateway to Internet. You can Telnet to your own account, or send mail from here (address= yourlastname@vops.zyx.com).

"When we return Kate Sampson, and Dileep Prahad will bring us to Item 4 on the agenda, zooming into the virtual operations involved in the second ZYX/Eastern States Virtual Initiative."

Going Virtual with Eastern States Hydraulic

After the break the presentation continued. It was really a conversational discussion that included ZYX's Dileep Prahad, Manager of Strategic Products, Kate Sampson, the Senior Design Engineer at Eastern States and co-proposer of the IGR, the Inert Gas Recapture project, and, because of the large screen and the peculiar intimacy of the setting, us.

At this point Kate picked up the discussion. As she spoke, she illustrated her points from logs of the project's on-line activities: public E-mail folders, computer conferences, audioconference "dialog-bites," product design iterations, real-time management visualizations, and so forth.

She spoke of her initial meeting with Don Janseki of XYZ and the idea for a new product which sprung from their mutual understandings of each company's competencies -- and each other's problems -- all learned in the first prototype project.

"After Don and I had talked for a while," Kate began, "it became clear that not only did we have complementary competencies for this new product, but we also had complementary business problems. Whereas ZYX was off the mark in the products they produced, we were having severe pains in meeting aggressive time-to-real-revenue schedules.

"Our usual product cycle went something like this:

- 1 year of Research and advanced development
- 1 year of prototyping
- 6 months for corporate approval to continue
- 6 months of specification and review
- 1 year of development and testing
- 2 years until customer feedback evidenced in next product version.

"That's 6 years to get the customer perspective in the product -- and to begin a solid revenue stream." She illustrated her point with a flow chart showing sure linear progress, but with a lot of feedback loops, including ones for customer response, and yes, six years elapsed time. For different reasons, Eastern States had reached very much the same conclusions as ZYX. Something had to change. The old, familiar processes were not going to keep either of them competitive.

Kate continued. "So we were a natural. XYZ was fast and Eastern knew how to build the right products.

"Dileep and I had clear instructions from top management: design a product that exceeds the "best-in-class" benchmarks in our industry. Get input from the best people we have or can get our hands on. If we could deliver a plan that looked good, we knew we would get total commitment from management to get the job done.

"Identifying the key stakeholders was the critical step. The key stakeholders are the individuals that have responsibility, authority, and resources. Our challenge was to make sure that we identified the full range of stakeholders that needed to be involved in the design and delivery of a world class product. We saved time by following a project/team design process that works for us. Our experience is that by using this approach we cover all the most important factors. Notice that we don't make a distinction between project and team design; we have learned that these are essentially the same thing. Our plans and design focused on sustaining virtual operations by making sure that our processes, communications protocols, learning initiatives, and teaming activities were supported. Once we have these designs we have what we need to ensure management support.

"We found that we became the channel between management and the team. The team has the knowledge needed to do the work; our job is to ensure that they are free to concentrate on their tasks. We deal with the barriers that might prevent information from flowing between team members, other stakeholders and management. We make sure that everyone keeps focused on their tasks, but at the same time we look for good ideas that constantly pop up as people power up and get engaged. Communications is the key, between us, the team, and management -- as long as the information flows, we get results.

"Borrowing an idea from the visioning crew, we started a private bulletin board for interested stakeholders in both companies. The bulletin board was secure in terms of need to know, rather than organizationally limited. Don went one step further by bringing in a colleague who happened to have expertise in audioconferencing. With facilitation from experienced 'virtual communicators,' our stakeholders designed communications protocols: methods, purpose, structure, frequency, behavior—all the attributes of communication that become barriers if not explicitly agreed to.

"Between the bulletin boards and well designed and executed audioconferences, time and space suddenly became irrelevant. It didn't matter what organization you were in, where you worked or lived or traveled, you could constantly be part of the product defining dialog.

"The next step was designing new, virtual work processes: simultaneous, electronic, collaborative."

Designing Our Virtual Operations

Dileep's image appeared in a new window, live, and he elaborated. "The big job was to start THINKING virtual. Not only did we have to build the knowledge and skills to work together, in parallel, electronically, but we had to believe it was the only way we could succeed. In other words, we realized that the competencies we needed were as much cultural as they were substantive. It doesn't matter how much each of us knows about the coriolus effect, if we can't trust each other over the wire to make the best decisions for the team. Furthermore, we had to learn how to use the new electronic tools together. Groupware, as much of it is called, doesn't solve any problems; what matters is that collaborative procedures run smoothly and predictably.

"Briefly, what we did was take our high-level specification from management, convene the stakeholder team, and begin the virtual process of defining product and processes. We put a lot of care in choosing stakeholders. And we made it clear that a condition of being a stakeholder was full commitment to accomplishing project goals -- as part of a virtual team. The stakeholders did not have to know everything, but they needed to be willing to learn.

"To show you the variety of our team, I'll introduce you to some of our stakeholders now."

At that point a series of snapshots of individuals began filling the screen. I thought, "This is like my college composite!" Indeed, after their names, titles, and roles had filled the screen, a banner scrolled across the bottom: The IGR Virtual Team. The pride on the faces of the team members showed clearly in the photos; this was a winning team.

Dileep picked up the narrative again. "We didn't re-invent everything: we used standard systems design approaches to describe what we were building and to specify the ideal system for building it–a system that assumed simultaneous, electronic, collaborative work. We studied what had happened in prototype 1, integrated what worked and avoided what didn't. Our philosophy was 'steal this idea,' rather than 'not invented here.'

As he finished speaking, Kate's image slowly faded in. She keyed up another chart, a complex network of interrelated, simultaneous activities. Here, instead of a linear duration for each step, numbers appeared– calculations of the probability of a step being finished at a particular time: probabilities dependent on the status of other parallel, dependent processes. And all processes, including customer input, began on Day 1. As complex as it looked, the bottom line was clear: Best Case: 24 months; Average Case 30 months; Worst Cases 40 months. "This is the process model we developed and used the second time we teamed with ZYX. A radical departure from what we previously used, but look at the numbers. It works!"

Kate's image receded and Dileep reappeared: She had passed the "virtual chalk" back to him!

What We've Learned about Virtual Operations

"Perhaps the greatest lessons we learned working through the first stages of this project is that neither Eastern States or ZYX has any choice but to work as if there are no walls or space between the people who know how to get the job done. This includes the people who design and build products, support customers and, in most cases, even includes customers teaming with us. We simply don't have the time or resources to waste on anything less than the simultaneous work design we use now."

Dileep then made a quick move at his workstation and one of the photographs suddenly blinked, expanded, and became a large size live image of Jan Harding. Dileep explained that Jan was a design engineer with experience in both the old and the new work systems. Before the transition she contributed designs based on specifications provided through organizational channels. She completed her work and passed her designs indirectly to the manufacturing engineers. Under the new system she is part of a cross functional team that normally includes marketing, manufacturing, support people from personnel, training and documentation, sales, and frequently people from key suppliers and even customer representatives.

Jan began. "I never worked so hard in my life. Everyone expects a lot from this team, but I know we will deliver the goods and our work will be appreciated. We take the time to design our work to optimize our virtual potential, and it shows in our results."

A second and third image appeared, pictures of two young men Jan introduced as George Karnov and Bill Parker. Jan explained that they were using a video conferencing application that allowed them to link most of their team members into a multi-media conference net. Jan asked Bill to display a copy of the design he was working on, and within a few seconds the remainder of her screen filled with a new schematic. She demonstrated how she could select different parts of the drawing, zoom in, make changes and, using audio capabilities, discuss the design. "This looks easy now, but it's taken a long time for us to understand not only the technologies for doing this, but the work protocols involved. Not to mention how to manage the stress Bill feels when he sees me hacking around with his design from a thousand miles away."

Jan then called up a file that had several pre-formatted forms she explained were used to process change orders, and the built in distribution lists make certain that everyone who needed to know and approve of changes received this information in real-time.

After a few more demonstrations Jan signed off and Dileep took back the screen. "Before we wind up this tour I want to introduce you to another key stakeholder in our -- in anyone's -- virtual teaming effort. Here's John Adams, our training manager. Training used to be the last process we thought about, but now training -- or rather learning -- plans must be part of each project's initial design. This puts us in a position to learn what new skills will be needed internally and by our customers from the beginning; learning will happen just-in-time, not months before or after it's needed. One interesting outcome of our new relationship with John's group is that we have been able to cut out many training programs that in hindsight were only needed to correct situations that should not have existed. Indeed, we have realized that the same electronic network that supports our design and communications activities plugs us into a worldwide learning network that helps accelerate our competence building. Our virtual learning system is getting a lot of attention these days—we're even using the network to sell our knowledge competency to other companies. Like Graycorp!"

Trip's Over, For Now

Just then a new voice broke into the conversation. It was Harry Harrison re-joining us using the mobile telephone in his car.

"See, training isn't last! I just wanted to make sure that I could be here for the wind up (OK, OK. To have the last word.)

"I want to make a final point: we have not reached the end state of becoming a virtual company. And that's the way it should be. Virtual capabilities depend on skills, knowledge, and processes that never stop evolving. The only constant in this game is change; and we will continue to transition to higher and higher levels of virtual capability.

"I know we're on the right track. Our results are improving tremendously, of course. But I see other signs as well: pride, less stress and frustration, lots of smiles, and more and more visits by people like you that are interested in learning what is happening here.

"Kate and Dileep, take over and I'll stay on line to see if I can help with any final questions. Thank you all for coming and please keep in touch."

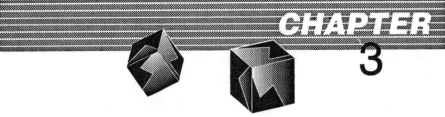

CHAPTER 3

THE AMERITECH STORY

Ameritech will be the world's premier provider of full-service communications for people at work, at home, or on the move. Our goal will be to improve the quality of life for individuals and to increase the competitive effectiveness of the businesses we serve. As we move and manage information for our customers, we will set standards for value and quality.
Ameritech's competence will reach worldwide, building on our strength in America's vibrant midwest. Customers can be assured that we assume no task we cannot do exceedingly well.
The Ameritech Vision, Ameritech Corporation
1993 Annual Report

This extract from the Ameritech Corporation's vision statement expresses both the business philosophy and the operational strategy of a major company moving toward the virtual future. In this chapter we, the authors, draw on our experience with one of the flagship virtual projects being undertaken by Ameritech. In this initiative, the Ameritech Cellular Services Division is moving quickly to capture a major part of the emerging wireless cellular data market, using a team of virtual partners who contribute key competencies to the project. We'll focus on that project here, but first, to provide context, we'll present a portrait of Ameritech itself.

Ameritech Profile

In 1984 AT&T spun off its local operating subsidiaries as part of its antitrust settlement. Ameritech, which began operations that same year, received five of AT&T's twenty-two telephone subsidiaries, Ameritech Mobile Communications (cellular service provider), and a share in Bell Communications Research (Bellcore, the R&D arm shared by the Bell companies).

In 1993, in order to improve its ability to respond more rapidly to the needs of a dispersed customer base, Ameritech restructured the regional companies into customer-specific business units. Ameritech has a reputation for being progressive and clear about the future, as their vision indicates. They know that success depends on understanding and responding to the changing needs of customers. Today, Ameritech is engaged in an ongoing program to reinvent the company and change its culture to meet current and future demands.

Ameritech has focused its market development opportunities in three broad areas where it perceives excellent growth potential:

• Education—driven by the need to support innovative, interactive, networked techniques that will create new experiences for students and teachers through the use of information technology

• Economic Vitality—to provide businesses with the improved access to information solutions that will help them strengthen the national economy and compete in the global information marketplace

• Quality of Life—to enjoy the individual benefits associated with information applications that make possible more affordable health care, the additional personal control that electronic transactions provide, and the safety and security that result from better, more mobile communications.

As the vision indicates, growth and expansion require that Ameritech move beyond its current business portfolio. For example, the company believes that customers will want to make extensive use of video-based information services to meet their information needs. Ameritech acknowledges that to succeed in video access it needs to enlist partners and new competencies from outside the organization. Again, from the vision:

> Such alliances will create a powerful combination of technology, customer services, creativity, programming skills, and marketing expertise. And they'll open broad new opportunities for Ameritech in tomorrow's interactive video marketplace.....The future, as we see it, is in helping both consumers and businesses move up on the value chain of electronic services.

Ameritech's strategic vision also reflects a determination to become a global business and to invest outside their defined region. They intend to stay focused and concentrated on what they feel are their core competencies; partnering to augment those competencies. They already have a global position with investment in New Zealand, Poland, and Norway, and have joined with Deutsche Bundespost Telekom in an equal partnership to hold 30% of MATAV, the Hungarian telephone company.

Ameritech Cellular Services

The new Ameritech is reorganized into twelve business units, one to run the company's local phone service operations and the remaining eleven to provide services to specific customer groups. Their portfolio of products and services reflects core competencies in traditional telephone operations, data transmission, and information access. One of the units is the Cellular Services business unit. Cellular Services provides cellular and other wireless communications services to nearly 1 million cellular telephone subscribers and over 500,000 paging units in eight midwestern states and Hawaii. Cellular Services also identifies and pursues new wireless services such as data transmission and the personal communications services and applications that have become critical to the emerging mobile office market.

Cellular Services has become one of the high visibility investment areas for Ameritech. Since divestiture, Ameritech's cellular and wireless operations have experienced rapid growth, and have consistently taken technology leadership positions within the industry. In partnership with Bell Canada and Telenet, Ameritech started iNet (1987), an electronic mail and information services company. In 1988 the company invested in two companies to gain a presence in voice messaging and audiotext services. Two years after Ameritech joined Bell Atlantic, GTE, NYNEX, and Contel to develop a nationwide mobile telephone network. Later that year Ameritech and Singapore Telecom acquired a 49.9% interest in Net-Com GSM to construct a cellular system in Norway.

The Cellular Data Challenge

A small but very aggressive segment of Ameritech Cellular Services is focused on the rapidly emerging cellular data market. Cellular, or wireless data technologies and applications provide information users with the mobility and flexibility to support newly reengineered, distributed work practices -- certainly the mobility and flexibility features associated with and essential for virtual operations. These cellular-based data technologies effectively eliminate the need to design work processes around the local physical information infrastructure; with some of the satellite based services that have recently become available, the wireless reach is being extended worldwide.

While cellular voice usage has skyrocketed, cellular data applications have been slower to develop, primarily because of the more complex and costly technologies involved. Another inhibitor of cellular data use is the difficulty in getting unfamiliar and dissimilar systems to plug into the traditional information infrastructure. However, over the last few years there have been significant breakthroughs in technologies and process design that are making cellular data a viable solution. By the year 2000, data communications are expected to account for half of cellular traffic -- a market projection that is financially promising enough for Ameritech Cellular Services to launch an initiative that will assure an early and significant presence in this market.

The Ameritech Cellular Services Virtual Project

The focus of our interest is the initiative launched by Ameritech's Cellular Services division to establish a leadership market position in the wireless data business. Their specific business goals are to

1. Generate new revenues from products and services

2. Stimulate and capture new traffic volume (line time) generated by data applications that use their cellular network as a transport medium.

Ameritech managers did not set out to design a virtual organization as they developed the business plan for this new business. They did realize that "under-one-roof," business as usual would not work. One reason was that the unit did not have, nor could it quickly develop all the competencies needed to bring the product to market; another was risk. Going it alone on such a major project did not make investment sense. A few innovative managers considered alternative approaches that ultimately led to embracing the virtual organization model. Not that they named what they were doing "virtual"; they were close to their first public product announcements before they were formally introduced to the concept of virtual operations.

But a virtual endeavor it was, and it was our good fortune to become virtual partners in this effort, offering suggestions to support the virtual operations and in turn learning a great deal about, well, virtual reality in the workplace. Our contact in the project was Greg Oslan, who was then the leader of the initiative, and has since become Vice President for Business Development of CNET, Inc. What follows will be an account of what we observed in the project and what struck Greg as his most significant learning experience. Keep in mind that Greg was the spokesman, not the whole virtual team. He makes it quite clear that his observations are based on team learning; the successes were team successes. He allows that he was the leader, even the champion of the virtual effort, but he was not the hero.

Greg is by formal training an engineer and started out with Ameritech working on the technical side of telephone operations. He's aggressive, ambitious, and competent -- he knows his engineering, his marketing, his industry, his product, and the company. He speaks with passion about his work and has a powerful intuition about how the telecommunications business is changing. He is creative and open to new ideas from any and all sources. And he is a leader.

The Business Plan

Greg was placed in charge of the new business from the start. With his team he developed the original business plan and nurtured it through the management approval process. The original plan indicated that of the 600,000 cellular users Ameritech was serving, only 2% were using their cellular phones to transmit data. The initial estimations were that a user friendly product package would add between 10,000 to 15,000 new data users very quickly. Market research indicated that potential customers were inhibited from investing in cellular data solutions because the state of the market required them to pick and choose from several vendors and to integrate the various parts of the required cellular and peripheral technologies into their enterprise systems themselves. Also, potential customers were scared off by uncertainty about training, cost, coverage, reliability, and other factors, including the availability of customized software applications. The opportunity for Ameritech Cellular Services was to provide customers with "one-stop-shopping."

As an established supplier of cellular telephone services, the Ameritech group would have the advantage of credibility. The challenge was to make it easy for businesses to buy complete solutions that would provide them with capabilities they would value, make sure that everything worked properly, and to supply the support services that would neutralize their concerns and accelerate acceptance. The belief was that once customers began to experiment with wireless telecommunications, they would discover new and creative ways to reengineer their operations to use even more of these capabilities.

The details of the original business plan are not relevant here, but it is important to remember that Ameritech Cellular Services is, like their parent, a regulated utility. Many of the business considerations are unique in regulated industries. Most have to be approved by regulatory agencies, and all are constantly under review and controlled by rules and regulations that change frequently. But even regulated industries are conventional in the way they internally process new business proposals and plans. What is significant is that this plan opened the door for "virtual operations" as a viable alternative to business as usual. To quote from Greg's original mission statement, "To meet customer needs by using strategic partnerships to develop complete wireless data solutions using Ameritech Cellular's Cellular, Advanced Paging and Packet networks."

"Complete wireless data solutions" implies that users have the ability to access the data they need wherever, whenever, and however they need it; "access" meaning the ability to send or receive data. One-stop-shopping for a cellular data solution meant integrating several disparate technologies into one package: voice, E-mail, fax, file transfer, data base inquiry, and imaging. The networking and the voice segments were Ameritech's strong suites, but effective data handling and processing required competencies that exceeded Cellular Services' internal resources.

The business plan proposed a series of alliances with vendors who had products and services that could fill these competency gaps. Initially, off-the-shelf products were used; over time, as the collective knowledge of market needs and trends matured, customized components would be developed.

Greg recalls that in their initial planning meetings the team focused on identifying strengths held by various partnering candidates. "We proposed to the component suppliers that we create wireless data solution packages. Those packages would include all the components necessary to deliver a wireless data solution, and we would differentiate ourselves by ensuring that our solutions included components, systems, and services that were all compatible." The solutions would have to meet four criteria:

• The customer's investment cost would have to be affordable -- the target for the initial offering was $1000.00 for a package that included a cellular phone, a modem, and a wireless interface that would transform a notebook computer into a mobile office.

• The cost of the "airtime" (the connect time for the cellular network) could not be prohibitive.

• The products would have to be accessible -- easy to buy. This required that special attention be given to creating an innovative, effective distribution system.

• The products would need to be fully tested, certified, and supported.

In addition to the hardware and software package, Ameritech needed to ensure that the cellular connection would effectively link their users with the information that resided on their "home" systems. To mediate the protocol differences between the mobile and fixed segments, Ameritech designed and installed a "modem pool" at selected cellular switch sites. Greg explained, "The modem pools handle any protocol translations and make sure signals received from a cellular data transmission are sent to a landline switch in language that the switch's computer can understand. Customers won't have to change their host modems. The modem pools concept allows the service to cover better than 90% of the modems is use today. If customers can dial in from their notebook computers today, they can do cellular data communications." The modem pools also serve as a monitoring point for detailed billing services, providing customers with the information they need to track expenses.

The compatibility issue prompted Ameritech Cellular to launch a comprehensive testing program. This project started in 1992 and continues to this day as new and more complex configurations become available. "Our focus was that these products had to work under real-life, user conditions. We tested modems and connecting devices with 600-milliwatt portable phones, three-watt mobile phones, in moving and stationary environments, fixed environments, in buildings, and away from the office."

Greg noted that the testing activities had other benefits. "We learned a great deal more than technical performance characteristics from our tests. We started to learn which manufacturers truly shared our market vision. Those who simply saw our interest as a chance to sell more product were not nearly as cooperative as the ones who heard the same music we did. We were committed to solutions not compromises. It didn't take us long to value those relationships that shared this perspective."

The Virtual Organization Forms

As the project matured, identifying and building relationships with partners and collaborators became a central issue in Greg's agenda. Bringing the first offering to market required interactions with several companies. Some of them eager and accessible, some more reluctant and less willing to fully commit. Among the first outside stakeholders were

- AT&T Paradyne, AT&T's modem unit which has developed a PCMCIA Type 2 card modem product, the standard peripheral configuration format used in notebook computers

• Anderson Consulting, a leading provider of business process design and information system integration services

• NEC, developers and manufacturers of the Versa notebook computer.

Several smaller suppliers were also included to provide specialized expertise in several components needed for one-stop-shopping. These included

• AST Research, portable computers including PalmPad, a pen-based PC

• Business Partner Solutions, which provided the ASD/Messenger systems integration software that transmits pages to IBM's AS/400 computers

• Evtek, developers of touch-screen device for paging systems, and pen-based software for sending messages to alphanumeric pagers

• Sphere Systems, a publisher of pen-based computer software including PenSales, Pen Script and Pen Stock

• Tech Data, a major distributor of computers from Apple, AST and Compaq

• Verifone, the developer of point-of-sales equipment for wireless applications in retail sales environments.

Announcing the Products

Extensive market research indicated that the early adopters for this kind of information access were likely to be found in sales organizations and field service groups. To address these market opportunities, the team focused on three fully integrated products. These products, and all marketing, development, and support capabilities emerged from the matrix of virtual partner relationships negotiated and sustained by Greg and his team. The products included the following:

• The Wireless Field Messenger Data Solutions. This offering utilizes Ameritech's paging networks, providing enhanced messaging capabilities with personal computing software and newly available sophisticated paging units known as palm-sized data terminals. The system delivers numeric and/or word messages equal to the size of a typed page. Applications for this service include messages for

• conveying detailed instructions

• describing locations to field technicians

• giving product service histories

• providing special time scheduling information and other time-critical instructions.

The objective of this product is to deliver critical information to field workers instantly.

• The Wireless Field Partner Data Solutions. This product combines wireless communications and network services with software applications, providing mobile workers with the same level of access to information as they enjoy in their offices. This product creates the mobile, or virtual office; it consists of

• a notebook or pen-based computer, and the choice of operating systems including DOS, Windows, and Macintosh

• a cellular modem, tested and certified for cellular operations and designed to compensate for anomalies common in cellular transmission modes. The modems are equipped with communications software for file transfer and electronic faxing

• an intelligent interface that supports the requirements of cellular telephones and provides a seamless link between the computer and the cellular network

• a digital pager that notifies users that information awaits retrieval in private mailboxes within a store-and-forward service. Voicemail can be added to give the pager more functionality.

The objective of the Wireless Field Partner is to provide the user with total access to required information without the constraints of physical connection.

• The Wireless Field Merchant Data Solutions. This specialized retail business product brings together equipment and software to perform credit card verification in the field. This empowers retailers to operate in non-traditional purchasing venues by accepting and verifying credit purchases on-the-spot. In addition, the system can be used to access product pricing and availability information. The package consists of a credit card verification unit with a card swipe reader and a key pad for entering purchase amounts, and LED readout for displaying approval or denial codes. Through a cellular transmission unit, the reader connects to the cellular network. Accessories include a padded shoulder case and a printer that provides receipts and, for further protection, can be used to collect signatures.

The objective of the Wireless Field Merchant is to provide retail merchants the mobility they need to become more accessible to their customers and to reduce their exposure to credit risks.

As of this writing, the business has moved through marketing and product development, and is now focused on delivering the results committed to in the business plan. There have been a few major and encouraging successes, some disappointments and frustrations, some luck, and a great deal of hard work. Above all there has been a tremendous amount of learning by the team, by Greg, and by us. Although Greg has since left Ameritech for an executive position with a company that is exploring new concepts for wireless communications and solutions, we've attempted to categorize the learning involved in this project often in Greg's own words.

Virtual Partnerships

Ameritech did not start out to build a virtual organization, even though it was clear from the beginning that success depended on the collaboration and commitment of several key collaborators. When Greg's group began to form these relationships, their expectations were based on the traditional prime contractor/sub-contractor model. As it became obvious that the partnering relationships required much more than the exchange of specifications for product components, more and more time and energy went into building productive relationships.

A good insight into the difference between traditional and virtual relationships emerged from this experience. Traditionally, business relationships have been viewed as a means to an end. Suppliers are chosen, largely on a low-cost basis, to provide a necessary product component. Expectations are set, a contract is signed, and all that remains is fulfillment of the terms of that contract.

Virtual relationships are not only a means to an end, they are ends in themselves. Building and maintaining the relationship, not just the contract, is the focus. One reason is that complexity and change make static contractual relationships stifling, rather than just binding. When integrating a complex product, along with its marketing and distribution plan, partners must constantly interact. This requires commitment, and wherever possible, the use of virtual processes and virtual technologies. Relationships, therefore, are much richer and demand much more nurturing than they do in the spec-for-component model.

Cellular Services also found that some organizations had products or services that could have added significant value to the business, but were unwilling or unable to become productive virtual partners. The reluctant organizations gave several reasons, but the common issues seemed to be that

- They found it difficult to trust some of the partners, so the prospect of sharing key information with the rest of the virtual team was threatening

- Their contact person for the relationship was not senior or inspired enough to negotiate full support and commitment from their organization's senior executives

- The organization had an agenda that did not appear to benefit from the relationship; this unfortunately applied to some potential stakeholder organizations within Ameritech itself.

Virtual relationships demand that both leaders and virtual team members invest a great deal of time in sustaining relationships over the project life cycle. Indeed, Greg saw this activity as an ongoing juggling act, and referred to himself as a full-time juggler; he had to keep a lot of plates spinning in the air, knowing that if a plate fell it was his fault, not the plate's!

The key to maintaining these relationships was, of course, continuous communication. But Greg knew that he and the team were in that stressful situation of trying to support a virtual organization with little support from virtual operations. They used all the traditional techniques: meetings, telephone calls, faxes, letters, and even experimented with the publication of a newsletter designed to keep the partners informed on what was going on. But as is often the case, the pace of the project was faster than expected, and communication became reactive and crisis driven. There was simply not enough time or budget to sustain full communication with all the stakeholders.

According to Greg, "Today's business environment requires that we choose our virtual partners very carefully. Things are changing so rapidly that today's partner is tomorrow's competitor, your owner, or an acquisition of another company. This makes what we are doing very challenging because we simply cannot place all our eggs in one relationship -- we don't know where they will be tomorrow. In hindsight I can say that I would be very uncomfortable focusing on a single stakeholder providing a critical competency, but for certain, I would avoid dealing with several candidates and having more balls in the air that I can effectively manage. I would pick a couple of players who would invest and commit in our shared vision.

"In all of our partnering relationships I had an individual, a leader, a single point of contact, a champion that I could depend on to get things done. These relationships were based on mutual trust and respect for each other's expertise, and as the project went on this trust grew as we shared information, did favors, and came to relate to each other as friends.

"One of the most important things we found in working as a virtual organization with our partners was the importance of not losing our identities. The trick is to have each partner working as part of a virtual team, but to make sure that each can find its own name on the final product as it comes out the chute.

"I would say that we had about six or seven partners that shared our vision and saw themselves as part of a virtual organization with us, and with these core partners I was certain that we would get where we wanted to go. The rest of our partners didn't share the same vision, but it probably didn't matter, and we would simply reach our goals in a different way with these organizations. It's the difference between a pure academic definition of a virtual organization and reality. It doesn't matter what we call it. What does matter is that on a daily basis we work together, do business together, and make money together.

"If I had to do it all over again I would do more to make my stakeholders understand the virtual process. I would bring in a third party to calibrate everyone on the concept of virtual operations and the steps that each stakeholder should take in their own organization to make sure that we started with the full measure of commitment to the goals and objectives. The second investment I would make is in a communications protocol that we could use from the start–something structured that would force us to see ourselves as a virtual team.

"Our reality was that we had very few fully dedicated resources within our stakeholders. At best we had 20% commitment, and this means that in any given week we could easily lose them completely to some higher priority. A continuous communications protocol could help us maintain our connection with these resources and keep them in the loop more effectively."

Marketing

"Our marketing strategy depended on the success of our relationships with our new distribution channels. I saw this as another virtual operation, and we put this together based on our learnings from our ongoing experience with our original team. Some of the key activities involved training and incentives. We began recruiting distributors by working with our partners to identify who were potential distributors and listing the attributes we all agreed were essential competencies for representing our products and services. Once we made our selections, we asked for their commitment, and that commitment included their willingness to invest time to train their people.

"We also introduced a creative incentive and compensation program. Normally, distributors do not get much residual revenues from their sales except for maintenance contracts. In our case we brought them an ongoing revenue stream and a way to maintain contact with their customers. When they sell a cellular based solution they get a piece of the air time, based on volume and other factors. They are also provided with collateral sales materials and access to all the component manufacturers, so that in effect they are able to fully participate in the virtual organization.

"Our thinking was that if we treat the channels well, we could take advantage of their long term relationships with their customers. Many of the new partners realized the value of this synergistic relationship very quickly. Some of the benefits include several excellent case studies of sales situations that we made available to the entire distributor network. Another was a competency matrix that showed the special competencies each distributor brought to the network. Some, for example, had deep vertical experience within industry segments. With this information the team could link together to address opportunities that an individual distributor might have passed on because of limited experience or resources. Even Ameritech's direct sales force could tap into expertise from the matrix to enhance their own position with potential customers."

Virtual Operations

"Virtual Operations is like any other management philosophy: you don't just read about it or hear about it, then just jump in and do it. First you think about virtual operations in the context of your own work, how the new techniques and technologies would fit into your ongoing operations. It's easy to buy into the virtual concept because its so logical, but you still have to find a problem that appears to match your understanding of the new process. If there is a match, you try it.

"The communications infrastructure for the distributor channels is being built as we speak. We decided to use Lotus Notes to link each distributor into an information exchange network. They will have E-mail, a technical bulletin board and an idea board. In the future they will have computer conferences, and the plan is to use the electronic infrastructure extensively to keep this team connected. They expect to have everything available online: sales materials, manuals -- everything that is needed to respond to and support a sales opportunity or a customer."

Virtual Teams

"The best example of how we organized virtual teams is in the modem area. Because of our focused interest in wireless data communications, we teamed with most of the companies who are interested in this technology. We set up a testing facility where we collaborate with each other trying to determine what would be best for the industry. We saw some very positive results in this area and this work has clearly influenced the quality of the products that are coming into the market today.

'Every day I saw examples of how our teams benefited from being linked together through our communications infrastructure. For example, I recall a note on the computer bulletin board used by our sales team. Someone announced a lead with an insurance company and asked if anyone had experience with the type of application the client was interested in. The questioner was also looking for the name of a distributor who had experience in the insurance industry and with whom they could partner to make a proposal. Within minutes, comments began appearing, including several specific responses that exactly met the salesperson's needs."

Leadership of a Virtual Project

"My experience is that leadership is a function of two things: trust and time. Building trust is clearly the most important and it's something that we have to work on all the time. I found it relatively easy to go to a potential partner with what we knew was a red hot idea. Almost everyone signed up, and most were enthusiastic during the early design and planning stages. But time had a tendency to erode some of the foundation work we did at the beginning. Primarily because over time we had to shift from the theoretical aspects of building a virtual organization and face the reality of virtual operations. People change, situations change, and early expectations fall short. For us, the passage of time was a challenge of shifting from planning a business to running one -- putting results on the bottom line.

"The leader is the evangelist, the cheerleader. You have to constantly hype the crowd. Your partners have to think that you're the one who can think out of the box, that you always have the vision in mind, and that you will consistently do what is right for the team and the industry. Communications is essential. What's important is not just the fact that you communicate, but that communication sustains the consistency of the collaborative process.

"As the leader, you have a great personal stake in the outcome of the project. And you can't do it alone. Of course there's the team. But there's also the need for support from the top. And no question, within the corporation we received great support for this project. We were fully empowered to act where and when we needed to."

Virtual Competencies

"Ameritech's fundamental core competency has always been and continues to be the delivery of network services. In this virtual situation, in addition to their competencies in network services, the real added value was in marketing and program management. What they created is essentially a new channel for component and application suppliers: the pagers, the PCs, the modems, the automated sales applications, the mobile faxes, and all the other components and services we and our virtual partners have integrated to provide the end user with a complete solution. And that is what customers want, need, and buy."

Virtual Knowledge Workers

"The further down you go in the organization, the less inhibited are the workers. The workers we recruited for this project seem to welcome new ideas. The people who are doing the work will die to make this happen, to succeed. They respect each other's expertise and don't appear to mind sharing information. I was often more concerned about them sharing too much rather then not at all."

Executive Management's Role

"Besides the key players, there are executives that can influence, pro or con, how the project works even though they are not directly involved. Because of the way things are structured at Ameritech, we did not have the benefit of a single top-level champion. If we did, two things would have happened that would have made our jobs easier. One, it would have helped me to keep focused on the tactical activities needed to build and sustain the virtual relationships that moved the project along. As it was, I spent a great deal of time just trying to keep management informed about what was happening. Two, the champion would have been directly involved in the relationship building process. When we approached virtual partners outside the company, my contacts needed to go to their top management for instructions or decisions. If we had had an executive champion, there could have been direct peer-to-peer dialogue; the results might have been the same, but a lot of time and energy would have been saved."

Stakeholder Roles

"I know now that I should have taken the time to bring all my key stakeholders together at the very start. I would have encouraged them to bring their stakeholders in turn, and we would have used the opportunity to make sure that we had a common strategic vision, and buy-in on the major goals and objectives at the very start. With this kind of top level commitment, the mid level managers we dealt with on a day-to-day details would have been more confident in the project.

"We couldn't have moved as fast and as far as we did without the participation of effective, committed stakeholders, internally and within our partner organizations. Sometimes we had 'influencers' rather than decision makers in the room; but generally they were willing and able to get the decision when needed. We discovered that with a few potential partners that did not work out, the willingness was there in that they shared our vision, but the ability to commit resources was not."

Final Comments

In wrapping up his recollections, Greg Oslan had some final comments to make about what he learned from Ameritech's wireless data project:

"When we started this project, the majority of my time was committed to building and maintaining our virtual relationships. As the program matured, I found that most of my time was spent working operational details: product management, marketing, advertising, promoting, and an endless list of things that needed to be done yesterday. At the end of my association with the project, I estimate that only 15% of my time was available for sustaining virtual relationships. I was not happy with this, and neither was my boss because we both learned how important the nurturing of virtual relationships is.

"We underestimated the impact of several areas that were not directly in the main development stream. For example, when we reached the point where we had a product in the market, ownership became a major factor. Who owns the product? We had questions about issues concerning royalties for completed work essential to the integration of the components into a system. We might have been able to anticipate some of these issues, but in hindsight we would have been well advised to have included the legal and procurement departments as stakeholders from the beginning."

Through Greg we have seen what it's like to be immersed in the realities of virtual work, without the benefits of planned virtual operations. It's important to keep this sense of reality in mind as context for what we'll be discussing for most of the remainder of this book: the up front design of key aspects of virtual operations. From recent conversations with the new VP at CNET, we know someone who believes in the value of lessons learned.

VIRTUAL OPERATIONS: COMPETENCIES AND ROLES

The ZYX and Ameritech dramas reveal a lot about the nature of virtual operations. While the engine of virtual operations is clearly information and communications technology, and the fuel is that wonderful blend of information and knowledge, the soul of this machine is the convergence of key individual and team competencies, supported by a set of new organizational roles.

In Part II we take a look at the needs of people working in virtual environments. A virtual worker, in any speciality or role, faces the challenges of complex, simultaneous work, teammates outside the organization, rapidly evolving specialized knowledge, continuous change, and the need to learn, manage, lead, and work using new technologies. Those who work in virtual environments must be highly competent in all these dimensions. These are highly trained, high performance people, not replaceable parts.

So must people be willing to learn and adapt to the new competencies and roles, the behaviors that move virtual work forward. For example, consider the role of manager. We've mentioned that *organization*, really isn't the point any more. What counts is collaborative operations across all sorts of boundaries. Bill Johnson, General Manager of Network Hardware at IBM puts it this way: "Today *organizations* are mainly concerned with administrative issues: who's here and who gets paid what. *Management* needs to get beyond the four walls of the organization to create and manage the processes, the operations that get the job done."[1]

With all this in mind, these chapters will examine virtual operations first in terms of the individual and team competencies that must be developed to implement and reap the benefits of virtual business, then from the perspective of emerging virtual roles for executives and stakeholders, operational leaders, and knowledge workers.

[1]Bill Johnson, conversations with the authors, November 1994.

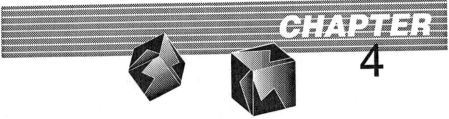

CHAPTER 4

THE VIRTUAL ETHOS: BELIEFS, KNOWLEDGE, SKILLS, EXPERIENCE

The fox knows many things, but the hedgehog knows one big thing.
Archilochus[1]

I see what I believe.
Anonymous

A virtual project is essentially a system of complementary competencies in people, designed to carry out complex, collaborative, simultaneous, electronic work. Just like other systems, a competency system is effective because it possesses capabilities beyond the sum of its component parts, and it meets all the demands of the system (i.e., the virtual environment) within which it works. This phenomenon is known variously as *gestalt*, the *team factor*, and in some instances (as we will see later) the *phantom reviewer*. Eastern and ZYX had world class competencies within their organizations. So did Ameritech and its partners. They agreed to combine those competencies in more of an act of multiplication than addition: The virtual partners did not go off and do their own thing, then combine the parts. They built the result through the continuous and simultaneous interactions of their competencies.

[1]Archilogus, quoted by Isaiah Berlin, in *The Hedgehog and the Fox: An Essay on Tolstoy's View of History* (New York: Simon & Schuster, 1953) p.1. This book was recommended (actually handed) to us by Dick Davies, an international business consultant working out of Malmesbury, U.K. It is about multiple perspectives and how they can co-exist in a single system. In Berlin's book the system is Tolstoy's mind, which could simultaneously carry the perspectives of the large picture (history) and the detailed portrait (fiction). The system we focus on is any organizational network.

However, a virtual operations system also has its limitations: for example, care must be taken to optimize the overall system, not particular components. As the visionary Russ Ackoff has pointed out, you can pick from across the auto industry the best transmission, the best engine, the best clutch...the best of everything that constitutes an automobile, and end up with component excellence, but no car that runs.[2] It's the same with a system of virtual competencies. As Ameritech discovered, the value of a virtual competency is a function of more than just knowledge or skill or technology. Unless these attributes are accessible through virtual operations, they remain hidden under the bushel of traditional work methods. We call this "The Myth of the World Class Competency"; well, maybe not a myth, but at least a misinterpretation. The "world-class" quality of a specialized competency is of no use unless the person possessing that knowledge can integrate into the collaborative work at hand.

Virtual Competencies: An Introduction

There's no simple way to sort out the complexity of people's competencies. But for convenience sake we'll segment the whole issue of virtual competencies into four approachable sub-categories, or perspectives: beliefs, knowledge, skill, and experience.

Consider a person working in a virtual team that is collaboratively producing the designs and specifications for a suite of office furniture, a college curriculum, or an advertising campaign. The virtual worker is physically remote from fellow workers, in a mutual dependency situation, with electronic tools at hand for communication, as well as for creation and revision of product designs. Furthermore, the worker is "empowered" with the expectation that she or he will make decisions and solve problems with little or no immediate supervision. The competencies that such a worker factors into the initiative are emotionally, intellectually, and physically grounded and include the following:

• A belief system that places trust over suspicion, knowledge sharing over secrecy, and commitment to the end product over just "doing my job"

• Deep and evolving "domain" knowledge that will meet the expectations that the rest of the team has on this particular person and role

---

[2]Russell L. Ackoff, *Creating the Corporate Future: Plan or be Planned For* (New York: John Wiley & Sons, 1981), p.18.

• Skill in working with the electronic tools of the trade and with virtual operations

• Experience with similar situations, from which the beliefs, knowledge, and skills have developed.

What follows in this chapter is more of a suggestive starter list than an exhaustive survey of virtual competencies. The competencies mentioned here will be further developed and augmented in later chapters dealing with specific aspects of virtual operations. Perhaps this chapter will raise questions rather than provide answers; but then once issues are visible, work can start on approaches. First, some general definitions:

• Beliefs—These are the lenses through which, in this case, virtual workers see their purpose and responsibilities, set expectations for success and reward, and generally make sense of their place in the environment--what Peter Checkland might call their *weltanschauung*, or world view.[3]

For example, in a virtual environment a manager should believe that, as IBM's Bill Johnson has pointed out, his or her job isn't to know everything, or balance budgets or write historical reports, but to do everything possible to sustain the virtual team doing the work: provide resources, mentor, teach, and deflect disturbances from upper management. Consciously practicing such behavior is admirable, but wholehearted belief in the rightness of the role is essential in times of crises and rapidly changing circumstances. These are the stresses that cause the uncommitted to backslide into traditional management occupations.

• Knowledge—Within the framework of beliefs, of attitudes toward what makes sense and has value and what doesn't, people alone and collaboratively build knowledge. This knowledge can involve learning a science, craft, role, technology, or anything. The virtual paradigm demands many traditional forms of knowledge, but also knowledge particular to working in the electronic, cross-cultural setting.

• Skill—Belief and knowledge contribute to the virtual work at hand through various skills: using communications, modeling, design and testing technologies, working sensitively but effectively with people from other cultures -- from companies to countries, or writing and drawing in accordance with team developed templates.

• Experience—Having a track record in putting together the beliefs, knowledge, and skills of virtual operations is invaluable to an organi-

---

[3]Peter Checkland, *Systems Thinking, Systems Practice* (New York: John Wiley & Sons, 1981), p. 319.

zation undertaking a virtual project. Nothing fixes and validates belief, knowledge, and skill like experience. Indeed, more and more learning experts argue today for situated learning as being the most useful kind of learning. The pragmatic insights of the experienced hand are as invaluable to the virtual initiative as is the trained guide on the hike up the Matterhorn: few would try that trip on the basis of commitment, books read, and a few days rappelling down a health club wall.

Of course, life would be a lot easier if these were really discrete elements of a stable model; sadly they are not. They are just four of many perspectives, and far from being discrete they share properties, interact, and intertwine. The relationship between these four perspectives on virtual competencies looks more like, well, a quadruple helix, than a simple table.

Figure 4.1   Interrelationships Between Competecy Elements

Finally, the perspectives and the examples that accompany them are not randomly chosen. They are particularly important not only as key competencies in performing virtual operations, but as change agents. Recall that virtual operations is a continuous transition; we can take snapshots of the state of the system at any time. But virtual operations never stop evolving; and the key points of leverage in the ongoing transitions are competencies relating to information and knowledge, process, communications, and learning. A full discussion on how to capture the power of these change agents will be the subject of Parts IV and VI.

We'll begin with "Beliefs," because within the belief system (or culture) rests the foundations of any new work paradigm.

Beliefs–Essential Virtual Mental Models

In the introduction to this Part we noted the challenge of moving people to the new set of mental models that defines the virtual operations culture. What follows is a brief description of some of the mental models that need to be operative to create a virtual operating environment. First we'll look at some key beliefs about information and knowledge that need to be ingrained in the culture for virtual operations to be a success. Then in turn, we'll look at attitudes toward work process, teaming, communications, and learning.[4]

1. Beliefs about working with networked information

OK, the information age is here; in this information society, value will be generated by information workers. No argument. But, so what? This was always the case. Stone age cave drawings were produced by information workers; information societies have existed ever since commerce began. And the Renaissance was certainly an information age -- multimedia at that. What distinguishes today's situation from the past? Shouldn't any twentieth-century person recognize and believe in the dominant role of information in human society?

The same holds true for networks and networking (though not electronic). Captain Ahab in Melville's *Moby Dick* used the international network of whaling ships at sea and the protocols of "carrying the news" to help him (unfortunately) find his great white whale. Tenement mothers as

---

[4]Peter Senge is rightly credited for bringing the importance of mental models and the learning organization into the organizational dialog. Our use of prototyping parallels his use of scenarios in bringing work teams face-to-face with possible futures. *The Fifth Discipline: The Art and Practice of the Learning Organization* (New York: Doubleday/Currency, 1990).

early as the nineteenth century in New York City used dumbwaiters and hallways as their infrastructure to carry voice messages up, down, and across to their small children. Protocol and process was primarily a function of loudness of voice.[5]

What's different today is the amount of information we need to continuously process, the complexity of information and the rate at which we must process it to create value; for example, save a life, build a product, ring up a sale, learn a profession. Virtual workers must shape their attitudes and perspectives toward information for this new context. As with other transitions, old perspectives on information inhibit development of the new.

What follows is a quick look at some of the key beliefs about information that mark successful virtual operations:

• Hello, electronic information; good-bye paper documents.

Well, almost. Paper as a medium for information has many roles that will ensure that books will never disappear But for text, graphic, image, and animated information that is flexible, changing, or reusable, it make sense to keep it in electronic form as long as possible. The value of information acts as more than a historical record; information supports the basic "acts" in a virtual environment: influencing decision making, and designing products and processes. Paper unnecessarily binds information to its medium and to the mental model of the paper page, making it impossible to keep relevant in content and form. Electronic information can be augmented, subdivided, transformed (e.g., spreadsheet to graph to animation), accessed and communicated with much more ease and accuracy, thereby increasing its value to information suppliers and consumers.

• Work in the electronic network, not the office.

The network must be considered the place of work, of value creation, communication, management, and, to some extent, social intercourse. Logging on is not just another activity, but a signal of your arrival in the virtual workplace. Today some people "live" in the Internet, or Information Superhighway, feeding their own computers on the vast fare now globally accessible, interacting with scholars, researchers and other professionals worldwide, and conducting their social lives in what Howard Rheingold calls the "virtual community." Networking is not an adjunct to the work-at-hand; it is the basic virtual work process.[6]

[5]Jan Morris, *Manhattan '45* (London: Penguin Books, 1969), pp. 159-160.
[6]Howard Rheingold, *The Virtual Community: Homesteading on the Electronic Frontier* (Reading, MA: Addison-Wesley, 1993).

• Seek needed information and knowledge, don't wait for it to come to you.

The watchword of the 1990s is information access, not just "flow," or "distribution." The advantage of the virtual environment is that it provides you with independent access to information. The information superhighway is always open, and it goes almost everywhere, and you can take it to the information you need.

The information explosion of a few years ago led to people being swamped with information they didn't want, and overwhelmed by the prospect of trying to look for what they needed. Artificial Intelligence promised filters to handle the former and agents the latter. But the advent of well indexed, navigable public and private online libraries, topic-oriented computer conferences, and E-mail access to a world of experts has removed many barriers to finding just the information and knowledge you want.

In many ways, information networks have brought new ways to ask questions rather than seeking or waiting for (or wading through) vast amounts of information in search of answers. Issue based computer conferences are specifically designed for "posting" of questions to a wide interest group which can provide the answers (not always right, but answers nevertheless). Increasingly, electronic information systems or information bases include files called FAQs (Frequently Asked Questions). There, a networker can peruse a collection of most-asked user questions, with the probability of finding his or her own solution.

• When in doubt, share: Hoarding information and knowledge does not give you power, it only delays results.

Information and knowledge in the virtual environment do not diminish by being shared. That's because, unlike a pile of gold or a jug of your favorite single-malt, information and knowledge have no intrinsic value in the context of accomplishing virtual work; value is realized by sharing information with others who need to know what's going on in order to collaboratively achieve results. Being blindsided in the fast paced, simultaneous, collaborative work environment is particularly devastating. Everyone depends on being fully informed all the time. "I didn't know you were doing that," is an unacceptable excuse in an open access, fully informed environment.

• Get the information you need to act, but don't wait for all the information.

As complexity increases, the temptation to withhold decisions and other actions until all the facts are in becomes more powerful. After all, it reduces risk. But as complexity increases, particularly in environments where the rate of change is high, it becomes increasingly unlikely that all the facts will ever be in. First of all, the more you know the more you know you don't know. Second, when all aspects of the environment are rapidly changing, total knowledge would be little more than a highly focused historical snapshot, not a picture of today's, let alone tomorrow's, reality.

Don't wait for perfection. Progress is driven by iteration of unfinished information work; think in terms of what will be just enough information and knowledge for you to meet your goals in the present iteration and satisfy your virtual partner or internal information customer. From the other perspective, don't demand perfection from your neighboring links in the value network. Negotiate acceptable completeness standards, go with what you negotiate, then iterate. Think in terms of the 80/20 rule: that 80% of the information that can be provided in 20% of the time it takes to reach perfection.

2. Beliefs about work processes

Virtual work, or task processes need to be designed within a context of beliefs that enable the designers to seize the potential of virtual operations. For example, the logic of traditional work process design considers constraints such as where resources are located, transportation, and ramp times for hiring and training. In designing virtual work processes, these constraints should be replaced by options: Who has the required competencies and what will it take to link them in? Here are a couple of assumptions that can support the logic of virtual work process design:

• Think "While," not "After"; "During," not "When."

Significant time is saved in virtual work processes because they are simultaneous, not serial. However, designing parallelism into complex work, even with today's modeling tools, takes a great deal of thought, skill, and practice. Old ideas about what "has to come first" may be hard to dismiss. Of course, concurrent engineering brought a lot of breakthroughs into this activity. Virtual operations extends the concurrency model by

• covering all business, work, and learning processes, not just engineering or development

• assuming the networked, electronic, not physical environment (face-to-face communication, paper documents)

• accepting virtual alliances as a primary source of competencies

For example, the traditional method of producing a textbook
(like this one) follows a sequence of writing, editing, illustrating/
designing, producing, and distribution. Virtual writing efforts have
produced books in which authors from different organizations first
agreed to templates of form and content with designers, illustrators,
and producers. Then, in parallel and electronically, the writing,
editing, design, and illustration were iteratively accomplished and
networked to the producer for on-demand publication.

What enabled this all to happen was first a belief that it could
be done, then a willingness to negotiate the mutual expectations of
the continuous work process: How much text, in what condition,
would an author release at once? What were the editor's responsibilities? How much iteration could the producer tolerate before taking an unacceptable cost hit? Also, process was decided: How much
time between author-editor-illustrator exchanges? What was the
communications model: What was sent E-mail? What was accessed
in a computer conference? How?

• When you plan work, think competencies, not geographies, not
organizations.

Conventional wisdom into the 1980s (even in organizations
that developed networking technologies!) was own and control. A
manager's power, status, and very likely his or her salary was
directly proportional to the number of people in the organization.
Usually the motivation was the fear of dependency: "I'm doing
Project X and I need to have authority over everyone connected
with it." But often organizations grew because growth was generally considered a good thing. In this same networking technology
group, technical writing, user interface development, facilities management, and several other functions were gathered in a group
called "Services," whereas the name should have been, "Not network software development."

During this period, strategic planning usually involved a high
level product decision, followed by a search for the appropriate
organization to carry out development. "We want to build a new
four-wheel drive lawn tractor. Let's see, Nancy's group does lawn
and Bill's has some four-wheel drive experience from the forklift
pilot...and they're both at the Hartford site. Bill's working on the

XDivot Golf cart now....so let's give the tractor to Nancy and she can pick up the people she needs from Bill."

Nancy of course loved the deal, Bill hated it, and both organizations and the parent company suffered the consequences of the decision:

• The lawn tractor group needed to train and assimilate new members into their workteam.

• The new product would be developed exclusively by an organization grounded in traditional product thinking.

• The four-wheel drive organization would need to backfill the slots left empty by the personnel going to lawn.

• Everyone would take a significant time, cost and probably quality hit.

In the virtual context you would not be constrained by

• where people were located

• who in the company might be available

• retraining and acclimating people from one organizational home to another.

Virtual project planning would be concerned with what competencies were needed to start the new project, and what processes would be followed to gain access to those competencies as well as new ones as further needs were discovered. Access to competency is what counts, not location or organizational affiliation.

3. Beliefs about teaming (We get a little recursive here, so watch out.)

One of the first things a virtual team has to do is build a common set of beliefs to guide its activities. Any team should do this, but it is in the nature of electronic, cross-organizational work that unexamined assumptions can cause havoc downstream in a virtual effort.

One specific belief that all individuals need to bring to the ah network is that they will contribute to this constructed, shared belief system and not insist on clinging to or trying to impose their own personal and organizational beliefs on the team.

For example, a virtual team designing a claims handling procedure might include some customers, forms suppliers, process designers, technologists, as well as insurance adjusters, and supervisors. Some of team beliefs might be performance determiners, amount of work that can be done on-line rather than on paper, acceptable time-to-completion of a claim, decision powers, what stakeholders are involved in which decisions, processes for group decision making, and so forth. Each stakeholder will have a personal perspective on all these, and unless the team explicitly negotiates common ground in these and other areas, the effort may not succeed.[7]

• Trust the other stakeholders; they want the same results you do.

A partner to the "own the resources" mental model is "don't trust anyone outside the organization." In virtual teaming you probably need to trust your extra-organizational, stakeholder teammates more that your cost-center colleagues. For you communicate with and depend on these stakeholders far more than you do with your administrative cohort. In fact, you may be wary of letting everyone in your organization in under the tent because you will be doing things differently from the others. And change always draws suspicion.[8]

But there are important reasons for not alienating your own group; a free flow of information between you and those on other teams will accelerate everyone's learning about innovation, and keep you on the organization's competency track.

• You are finished only when everyone's work is done.

You are not finished when you toss a spec, plan, or design over the wall to the next step in the value chain. You are part of a network of competencies whose work is complete when the team's product is complete.

• Recognition and rewards are based on the value the team creates, not the activity level of any individual in the team.

Results count. And in a collaborative environment everyone contributes to those results. Instead of blame, give help. Instead of censure, provide training. If all else fails, change personnel. Every piece of the system must work for the system to succeed.

[7]D. Lawrence Kincaid, "The Convergence Theory and Intercultural Communication," *Theories in Intercultural Communication* ed. Young Yun Kim & William B. Gudykunst (Newbury Park: Sage, 1988). pp. 280-298. See also Mary O'Hara-Devereaux & Robert Johansen, *GlobalWork--Bridging Distance Culture & Time* (San Francisco: Jossey-Bass, 1994), for an excellent investigation of what the authors call "third way," which must replace "our way" or "their way" as the cultural context for global business teams.

[8]Dr. John Gundry, of *Knowledge Ability, Ltd.*, Malmesbury, Wiltshire, U.K. Gundry has been a long-time proponent of using electronic communications. especially computer conferencing, to build the common ground for communicating. In his work of integrating electronic communities, he interprets trust as meaning "mutual understanding," as well as the more value-laden "dependable."

4. Beliefs about communications

Beliefs about communications may be the most critical to virtual operations. Communication is the life force of the virtual initiatives; work and learning depend on communication. With good communications, you can develop or find most of the competencies you need; without a strong virtual communication infrastructure, little will be accomplished.

The communications we speak about here is not just equipment and wires and switches. We mean the process of continuous and effective communications: text, graphics, images, and voice, as well as the agreed to policies for using them to link the virtual team.

- When in doubt, communicate.

Don't wait till you have all the news or results; don't worry if you have nothing particular to say. Communication builds the ability to communicate. So an informal call or E-mail to a person out there on the team serves the purpose of strengthening the network for when you do have really important news or problems, questions or issues to settle.

It has become clear that communication builds trust which in turn builds better communication. So this is a positive feedback loop that you want to feed, not constrain.

- This meeting's not over, it's just gone to another medium.

Think of a project as a carefully designed continuous meeting, a process by which collaborative work is accomplished primarily through electronic communications. The conducting medium changes according to the need: face-to-face, audio conference, video conference, computer conferencing, and so forth. But only the medium changes; the meeting is always there, holding the virtual team together in a value producing network. Meetings are no longer events for reviewing the past, casting blame, and wasting everyone's time, but rather the conceptual basis of the work process.

- Out of sight, but never out of mind.

So what if the Chief Designer is across the Atlantic this week. She's still in the virtual network. She's still working with you in the virtual meeting, continuing the value adding process. Think of the face, not the place. Imagine the face if you've never seen it. Remember, the office may be empty but the network never is.

5. Beliefs about learning

In a virtual situation there is a tremendous need for learning, but not for classrooms. Classrooms are useful, but like offices they have a physical location that constrains access. Therefore, they are secondary to the network as learning venues. The emergence of the networked learning model makes it possible to meet the demands for flexibility, timeliness, effectiveness, speed, and cost in virtual learning situations through designed use of the network and networking communications. But, this requires a shift in belief from four-walls and a lecturer, to a networked community of stakeholders in a learning situation. Here, everyone is a student, and everyone is a teacher. We'll take a much closer look at this paradigm in Chapter 18.

- Learn from everyone, everywhere.

As Abbie Hoffman put it, "Steal this Book." Creativity is wonderful, but it takes time to re-invent wheels. Banish not-invented-here barriers. Beg and borrow whatever knowledge, skills, or processes you need to fill out your competency card. The goal is the completed product, not in your developing and exercising a full complement of skills.

Yes, learn from teachers, but don't expect them to be sole sources; look to experts everywhere in the network. You yourself should teach as well as learn.

- Failure is learning.

Don't use the word "failure." Designed virtual teaming brings with it a certain amount of checks and balances for risk control. Let people take chances, the worst they can do is learn. "There is no progress without failure."[9]

- Learning is systemic, not episodic.

Some competencies are acquired through teaming with other virtual organizations; some are core competencies within a lead virtual organization. But none are static, bubble-wrapped, off-the-shelf, and ready for consumption, at least not for long. Competencies, whether in-house or acquired, need to continuously evolve to address changes in environment, mission, technology, society, and process innovation. Top level competencies are sustained through continuous learning.

[9]Henry Petroski, *To Engineer is Human: The Role of Failure in Successful Design* (New York: Vintage, 1982). This book provides an excellent perspective on the nature of design. No virtual work here, but the problems described pertain to and are aggravated in the electronic environments. See especially Chapter 6.

The Knowledge Perspective

Given a comprehensive mental model that supports virtual operations, an organization, or team, can address the specific kinds of knowledge competencies it needs to fuel its system. Somewhat arbitrarily, knowledge for virtual operations can be categorized as 1) personal and social knowledge, 2) virtual process knowledge, and 3) domain specific knowledge. An overview of each type follows.

1. Personal and social knowledge

• Knowledge of Self

Much is said today about personal mastery. With virtual teaming comes additional responsibilities for the individual. To support the team, each person participating in virtual operations must have a good sense of her or his own capacities and capabilities: Overcommitting doesn't make an individual look good, it only hurts the team effort.

Virtual work, because of the number of relationships continuously supported, the pressures of time, and the complexity of the work and the products produced, is extremely stressful: There is always more work to be done, there are few boundaries but lots of communications, there never is enough time, and there's always a need for more learning. So people need built-in governors; they need to know when to ask for help, when to ease-off on communicating (but not stop), and when to engage in the networked learning system.

Another critical area of self-awareness in the virtual work is one's own learning style. Some people learn by doing, some through class lectures. Some are receptive to visual information or sound or writing. Some learn sequentially or analytically; others learn by tackling whole concepts. While it is good in the general sense to understand one's own learning style, in virtual situations it is imperative. Virtual learning is learner centered: You are responsible for accessing information and knowledge suited to your situation in the form that suits your learning style. Yes, learning is accelerated, brought to the workplace, learner determined. But with that empowerment comes the responsibility for knowing both what you need to know and how best you can learn.

• Interpersonal Knowledge

In an environment supported by relationships, knowledge of others is as important as knowledge of self. People must take it upon themselves to learn and keep current with the beliefs, knowledge, skills, and experiences of others with whom they work. They must understand other's expectations of them in work related situations, in communication styles, and in social interaction. In many ways, they must know the mental models of people with whom they work most closely.

• Role Knowledge

Virtual roles create so many unique demands on people that we devote an entire chapter of this book to them. Mangers, leaders, mentors, stakeholders, designers -- all have new knowledge expectations placed on them. It is essential that you know your role, and know everyone else's, especially in the border areas, where you have mutual expectations of each other

2. Knowledge of virtual processes

Processes reengineered for virtual operations reflect many of the core virtual beliefs: simultaneity, open information access, cross-organizational communication. A body of lore is developing about designing such processes, including ways of conceptualizing how best to design a process, modelling the probabilities of success in various environments, providing management windows into the process to monitor its actual effectiveness. Not everyone needs to develop this competency to a high degree, but certainly the organization's innovators need to stay on the leading edge.

• Communicating Electronically

In five years everyone will know a more or less standard set of protocols that will enable them to communicate electronically with any other partner in any other organization. Now there's the Internet; in the future there will be many Internets, more transparent than today's long distance phone systems. Today that is not the case. Everyone uses phone and fax, most have used audio-conferencing, some video conferencing, fewer electronic mail and computer conferencing. While a certain etiquette, or protocol has evolved for phone calls (people usually offer a greeting, identify themselves and their organization, and ultimately say good-bye), the other electronic media are still used randomly and idiosyncratically.

An organization that understands how to effectively use virtual media is a prime candidate for virtual partnering. The competency of virtual process knowledge (and of course, skill) is as valuable as is any specialized competency because it helps make all those specialized competencies available to the virtual team.

- Soft Prototyping

Many industries today, in parallel with investigating the virtual organization paradigm are looking at a specific kind of virtual process: soft prototyping. This process keeps the product in electronic form as long as possible in the development process: through design, through active modeling, through testing, through redesign. Products of all kinds are candidates for soft, rather than hard prototyping: Aircraft, automobiles, boilers, baseball bats, and computer chips all are being prototyped electronically in order to increase quality, maintain flexibility, and postpone the investment in hard tooling.

Knowledge of soft prototyping is still relatively rare; a manager at a leading aerospace corporation pointed out the irony that at this point in the evolution of that competency, "The people who know how to design and prototype are older, and are skilled at hard prototyping. Those who understand soft prototyping and are skilled at CAD and modeling are younger and don't know aircraft design." The value of having both kinds of competency - aircraft design and soft prototyping—is quite clear.

- Virtual Operations Design

Processes range in nature from high-level strategic guidelines, as might appear in the first few pages of the annual report, through business processes such as "order fulfillment" or "remote customer service," down to tasks like "welding the X joint," "rolling the carpet," or "calculating the load." In all cases designing the processes for the virtual environment requires extensive real world knowledge of how you can get from resources to goals through the process. So you need to involve experienced process users every step of the way in process design.

3. Domain, or specialized knowledge

This kind of knowledge is what most people think of as "core" competency. Here, an organization's competitive advantage usually resides. If you had the best financial analysts, you put together the best budgets or funds; if you owned the two best minds in the world on nuclear hardening, you owned the bomb-proof boiler market. While it's still a good idea to have a lot of the "bests" around, today's products are so complex that you're unlikely to have all you'll need, nor will you have the time and money to build those competencies in your organization.

So, along with people who have excellent knowledge of the field, your organization must have certain access competencies: knowing how to recognize the competency needed, knowing where it resides, and knowing how to get it into the value stream.

* Knowledge: in Product, in People

An organization can seek external competencies in a variety of forms. When the folks in Florida were putting together the first IBM PC, they looked for the best off-the-shelf components for their product: The competencies they sought were already captured in products and components. Many organizations today are creating virtual alliances with external research or design. Everyone reaches beyond the organizational walls for advertising competencies. Here the competency resides not in an existing product, but in people. As often is the case, there are hybrids: In the computer industry alliances are formed on the basis of a current product, with the real intent being to have access to the knowledge that will build the next generation product.

* Boundary Knowledge

Simultaneous electronic work, the basis of virtual operations, requires near-seamless collaboration across disciplines, perspectives, organizations. It's important that knowledge workers understand the perspectives of those with whom they work. A key to the success of the electronic documentation process mentioned earlier in this chapter was that up-front time was spent so that all team members could learn the perspectives of the other functions and the reasons for those perspectives.

Any person who has this boundary knowledge for particular virtual work settings has far more value than one who brings only specific domain knowledge to the network. And an organization that commits to helping people develop boundary knowledge greatly increases its own potential as a virtual partner.

Skills

The various kinds of belief and knowledge discussed above are manifest in the skills with which people operate in virtual environments. Like knowledge competencies, these skills generally fall into three categories: personal and social skills, process skills, and domain specific skills. In all cases these skills are manifest in behavior: how a person works in the virtual situation.

1. Personal and social skills

Taking a holistic view, we must include observations on emotional and social aspects of virtual work. We will not go into psychology here, but focus on the behaviors that relate to individuals' psychological and social circumstances in virtual operations.

• Personal Skills

The virtual work environment is extremely stressful. The operative mental models include maintaining a high tolerance for ambiguity, constant communication, continuous redesign, complexity and time compression. Working under these conditions for too long a time can consume a person. Some of the survival skills in this environment include the following tactics:

• Be a squeaky wheel when you're overloaded (after all, management has empowered you, so use the power to tell them what's really going on).

• Don't do back to back virtual projects.

• Develop your own sense of "appropriate reaction times"; don't accept other's sense of urgency unless norms have been negotiated.

• Don't hesitate to ask the team for help.

• Get issues on the table, or rather the network; in virtual situations there isn't much room in your head, or overhead, for accumulated grievances.

• Social Skills

There are indeed virtual social skills that are important to sustaining the work pace. In many organizations engaged in virtual operations, an electronic social network is encouraged, with bulletin boards and computer conferences, and occasionally video conferences dedicated to creating and maintaining the social fabric that sustains teamwork. On a personal level people should use these facilities to

• build and sustain teamwide relationships

• develop skills in using virtual tools

• maintain cross-cultural dialog.

Specific in-work social skills revolve around communications: learning how to negotiate creatively, mediating online disputes, making new members of the networked community feel included, using the network to transform the team's ethos from position authority to knowledge authority.

2. Virtual process skills

There is set of skills, or behaviors that enable a person to fully utilize the potential of virtual processes. We recall back at ZYX how Kate and Dileep "passed the virtual chalk" during a networked presentation -- a virtual process. In all virtual processes there are skills related to the networked nature of the process: In an active modeling session being conducted over the network, modelers, interviewers and clients need to have the skills to communicate and represent their information in ways that meet each other's needs. They need to follow turn taking procedures and follow cues from the work in the system, since face-to-face interactions are limited.

3. Specialized Skills

Here again, specialized, or domain skills in the virtual environment are different from the traditional ones. Doing a collaborative 3D model of a bridge to understand aerodynamic behavior is a lot different from going off, building a model, and setting it up in a wind tunnel. The new skills embody the core knowledge of bridges and aerodynamics, but also adeptness of using specialized instrumentation and design tools.

Managing virtual work is another crucial skill. You don't own the people doing the work; influence, not position gets things to happen. This influence needs to be conveyed electronically; the physical presence managers have long used to get their way must be replaced by subtler communication skills.

Members of the documentation team mentioned earlier all had to develop new skills: word processing, online illustration, electronic typesetting, electronic communications. New skill needs emerged during the project: One member became the prototype of the "circuit rider," traveling from work site to work site, ensuring that all issues were getting aired, forming a human link between sites, disciplines, and cultures that augmented the electronic links. This "circuit rider" skill is becoming highly valued in virtual efforts of all kinds.

Experience

Douglas Levy has remarked of the great composer Vivaldi, "The joke has been made...that this Italian composer of some 500 concertos actually wrote one concerto and copied it 499 times." Of course, experience does not necessarily mean great capability. A person claiming ten years experience may have one year of experience repeated ten times. In the virtual environment, the experiences that have value involve having applied one's competencies many times in a variety of situations and having learned from those experiences to quickly assess new situations and act appropriately.

In a wider sense, experience is a team competency, with the key being accessibility both to the store of its members' experiences and, in real-time, the capability to preserve the experience of the current work scene for future use. Recall the lament of the aerospace manager, whose people had either traditional design experience and specialized knowledge, or electronic design experience and no specialized knowledge. As a team with a real electronic design problem before them, they could overcome their shortcomings and aggregate their experience, their competency, in addressing the project at hand.

Final Comments

The intention of this analysis was to make more visible the intricacies of the virtual ethos. While any one of the sub-areas mentioned can be addressed as a specific target for investigation or training, or as candidate for continuous learning, the real strength of the model is in the system, not the component. To use an analogy from the science of Artificial Intelligence, mastering these aspects of competency should be approached in a "breadth first," not "depth first" manner. Slowly bringing the team up in all these areas has far more payback than developing world-class ability in one or two, without attention to the rest.

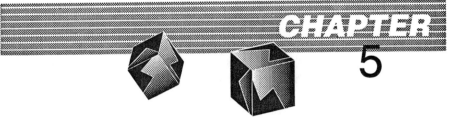

CHAPTER 5

EXECUTIVE
AND STAKEHOLDER
MANAGEMENT

We are beginning to invent the America of the information age....We don't know yet what, in effect, our intellectual constitution for the future is.
***From Virtuality to Reality*, Newt Gingrich**[1]

In this chapter we'll look at the organizational roles of executive and stakeholder management in the light of virtual operations. Being operational, the stakeholder role in virtual initiatives will be a recurring theme throughout this book. Therefore in this section the emphasis will be on executive management, with the understanding that many executive attributes are just as important in the stakeholder and leader roles, where the sphere of influence is at the project rather than the corporate or strategic management level.

Our approach will be to present composite "portraits" of successful executives and stakeholders who are currently operating in virtual situations. The intent is to convey what we feel are the competencies, behaviors, and attitudes that sustain these major figures in virtual endeavors. The success attributes, or indicators, can be useful in

- Understanding executive receptivity to change
- Assessing executive readiness for virtual operations
- Selecting and developing candidates for these key roles
- Guiding those executives who find themselves already immersed in virtual situations.

[1]Conference address at the Mayflower Hotel, Washington D.C., January 10th, 1995

Virtual competencies are evidenced in the ways that people perform specific organizational roles. By tradition, some of these roles coincide with position: A top executive is a top executive performing executive management duties. But other managers can find themselves in these positions as well; mid-level managers, empowered with executive authority for particular projects can also be considered executive management. Performance, not just position, is what's important.

Our performance criteria have been derived from both experience and research. We've been involved in and observed virtual projects. We've interviewed executives responsible for virtual initiatives. And we've studied the work of the Management Research Group (MRG), of Portland, Maine, a consultancy that is a leader in the development of techniques and instruments for identifying management potential in a variety of contexts. We used their Management Effectiveness Analysis Diagnostic Questionnaire (MEA) as one source for our analysis. This instrument, which is based on thousands of interviews with executives, measures twenty-one management practices that describe the management role in behavioral terms. The MEA has evolved over the past twenty-five years and now addresses attributes that support virtual as well as traditional behaviors and capabilities. We've validated these indicators through our first hand experiences with virtual projects and the people who led them, and while our sample is still too small to be statistically valid, there are strong indications for a short list of management attributes critical to the success of virtual operations.

Definitions

We define executive management as the group that has the responsibility and the authority to identify business objectives, determine strategy, provide political sanction, and assure a level of resources for a virtual initiative. This category includes top officers, as well as line and support managers who are empowered to make the executive level organizational commitments.

Stakeholders, on the other hand, are those people in each participating organization who have the responsibility and authority to commit and manage specific resources, agree to schedules, and participate in the detailed design of the virtual project.   Stakeholders have direct operational roles; they are engaged in the day-to-day support of the value adding work: designing and redesigning the virtual operations, providing the right mix of resource competencies as situations change, making schedule adjustments, keeping top management informed of status in near real-time, keeping the learning channels open, and constantly balancing work requirements to resources, design, and production. Within an organization some individuals may be engaged as both executives and stakeholders simultaneously, we distinguish roles here to keep the focus on the responsibilities, not the people.

Responsibilities of Executive and Stakeholder Management

With the power, influence, and sanction that top-management can bring comes the responsibility to provide clear and decisive leadership. At some point during every virtual project, crises of resources, partner satisfaction, threatening delays, and political squabbling will occur; these can be most quickly resolved through the intervention of an informed and motivated management.In virtual environments, executive management has particular responsibility for

1. Leading and sustaining continuous visioning

2. Building and sustaining relationships within and outside the organization

3. Providing resources

4. Leading the adoption of electronic information, virtual processes, and technologies

5. Leading by example: setting the tone for virtual operations through action

6. Championing the transition to virtual operations.

1. Visioning

Executive managers develop and articulate clear motivational visions that reflect what the future success of the organization will look like. To do this successfully and consistently, they acquire and practice the skills and techniques needed for continuous, collaborative visioning. Visioning is at once a mind-set and a process that results in clear, practical, and dynamic vision statements: statements that will provide everyone associated with the enterprise with a sense of who they are, what they do, and where they are going. Continuous visioning is essential to make sure that the strategic vision reflects the rapidly changing environment. Active participation in the process also ensures that executives can clearly and enthusiastically communicate the vision throughout the organization. Over time they become visioning "carriers" so that subordinates will be encouraged to engage in the visioning process as they design, launch, and execute tactical projects that support the strategic goals and objectives of the organization.

The vision itself can be introduced by the executive, or can emerge from the efforts of a virtual champion anywhere in the organization, at any level. The successful executive will be quick to hear the music, to support the champion, and provide the environment in which the virtual organizational vision can emerge. We saw Harry Harrison of ZYX do something like this: He articulated to his organization what he intuitively felt was the future of the company. He created an environment which encouraged collaborative visioning and he let the operational champions emerge.

2. Building and sustaining relationships within and outside the organization

Relationship building has always been a preoccupation of executives. Long before the recognition of virtual organizations, executives have been in a virtual situation, needing to maintain relationships with an extensive variety of internal and external counterparts: senior managers, bankers, the media, government, industry associates, key customers, and more. In the virtual environment, the relationship focus manifests in the areas of down-the-line empowerment and support of innovative efforts to achieve the vision, as well as in building virtual alliances and creating a virtual community.

• Empowerment and support for innovation–Executive management must exhibit the confidence and discipline to empower others to make decisions that they, in turn, can support. Executives understand the need to enlist the talents and skills of others to help meet objectives, to innovate, and to sustain the pace of virtual operations. Executives delegate because they understand that spreading responsibility throughout the virtual organization enables decisions to occur at the point closest to the actual work. They have confidence in the abilities of others and can give them the freedom to take risks and make mistakes; and they gain satisfaction from seeing others learn and grow.

Bill Johnson (BJ to his friends) is the Managing Director of IBM's Network Products Group. He is responsible for all engineering and product development that support IBM's extensive family of networking hardware products, overseeing the efforts of several thousand engineers and production people spread over the world. A couple years ago, being a newcomer to IBM, BJ sensed that there was a very well-entrenched culture that was not as tolerant of risk as he felt was required in today's virtual business environment. BJ tells of one way in which he demonstrated to his group the value of taking intelligent risks:

"The thing here is that people, in the past, have tended to go along, not take any big risks, maybe omit some things that could have been done because they were risky -- they would go along with the pack. I am trying to change the culture in this organization. I am trying to make everyone understand that I will reward them for failure as well as success, if they took a risky path and tried to move forward, failing by the sin of commission not the sin of omission.

"I had one fellow go off and launch a risky operation that would have resulted in a fantastic gain. It failed, and because the effort cost over a million bucks, everyone wanted his head. I gathered all the managers together at one of my regular open town meetings and called up my risk taker. Before all the assembled managers I presented him with a significant award, then I explained why."

• Building virtual alliances - Executives are a driving force in creating virtual relationships outside and inside the organizations. Like Harry Harrison and Greg Oslan they have the energy and charisma to build trust with their counterparts in potential virtual partners. These executives are effective advocates, they know how to get things done; they use language effectively to convince others of their commonality of vision. They get excited, sometimes even passionate, and they know how to energize others. They have the capacity to quickly establish free and easy interpersonal relationships, utilizing control systems designed into the support infrastructure and into the work practices to give feedback to the group in a straightforward manner, sharing perceptions on performance and expectations.

They let people know where they stand at all times; a critical element in building trusting relationships. They provide positive feedback whenever possible, re-enforcing desirable behavior; but they also address inadequate performance and provide the corrective support needed to resolve deficiencies. They have high levels of expectations, manifesting strong, bottom-line orientation, and don't hesitate to push themselves and others to achieve at the highest levels. They respect competency and are committed to using the best to achieve the results they envision.

Windmill International is a small business which has specialized in providing systems engineering and technical assistance to

Japan and thirteen NATO nations who are participating in the Airborne Early Warning and Control Program (AWACS). They are a group of AWACS professionals who have in-depth experience in all phases from acquisition procedures through testing and actual operations and maintenance support of this complex defense system.

Recently, the CEO, Richard Manganello, decided it was time for the enterprise to expand their scope of operations and position themselves to compete for new business opportunities, leveraging their core competencies in project management of government sponsored international initiatives.

Manganello chose a Request For Proposal (RFP) issued by the US Agency for International Aid as a springboard for "going virtual." Entitled "Technical Assistance in Support of Privatization and Economic Restructuring Program for Central and Eastern Europe and the Newly Independent States of the Former Soviet Union," the RFP described a program of twenty five or more awards with at least five set aside for small businesses. Windmill took the initiative to organize a consortium of small companies and individuals with demonstrated performance in Eastern Europe and named this venture Eastern European Privatization Group (EEPG).

This is a virtual organization that uses the bond of deep ethnic roots shared by most members of the network with the target countries (particularly the Baltic States and Hungary) to leverage what they believe is a significant opportunity. They have created a critical mass large enough to get and hold the attention of the customer, USAID, and broad enough to provide the group with the flexibility and confidence to compete with even the largest international consulting firms.

Richard Manganello makes it perfectly clear that Windmill's progress is a team effort; that he is not a "heroic" manager. The team at Windmill is rich in specialized competencies and empowered to seek out opportunities and to "do the right thing." They have a strong sense of themselves as a community -- soon to be a virtual community as external organizations come into the virtual fold. But it is the CEO's vision, network of competency based relationships, and virtual perspective that has provided the impetus for Windmill's virtual efforts.

• Establishing a virtual community - Each of the executives whose stories we describe here look upon their extended group as a virtual community, rather than a formal organization. This is, of course, by definition the virtual organization. But "community" implies more subtle attitudes about the nature of the collaborative work. The community perspective recognizes that the strength of the virtual group is in the relationships among the participants. It suggests that the social aspect of the group is as important as the work focus. The Windmill team periodically publishes a newsletter that communicates the news, gives people an outlet for their ideas, and provides a group identity for the participants. Bill Johnson mentioned the periodic town meetings he calls for his managers; in the true spirit of the New England town meeting, these are gathering for management to hear what the people think, rather than to tell them what management plans to do.

As teams move into using virtual technologies, the sense of community can be sustained electronically, through virtual town meetings and online social forums. New members of the virtual community, such as potential customers or competency partners, can be brought into the whole community immediately, rather than having to remain on the outskirts, perhaps interacting with only one or two point people from the lead organization.

3. Providing resources

While the assignment of specific resource competencies to a project is a stakeholder responsibility, creating the environment that makes those resources available falls to executive management. Ask any experienced project manager what takes up more time, generates major frustrations, is responsible for most changes, and is most likely to precipitate failure; the answer will probably be begging, borrowing, midnight requisitioning, and otherwise trying fill or work around resource shortfalls. This is equally true regardless of project size or complexity, and is independent of the special competencies, experience, enthusiasm, or wisdom that world class resources bring to the job. The most common explanation for why this situation occurs is that the resources that project managers assumed were locked securely into their project, weren't; people who had the competencies they needed, didn't; and the facilities they needed had conflicting priorities. None of this is unusual, these are common events in any project, and compounded where resources are widely distributed and involve relationships with outside collaborators. Successful project managers have traditionally anticipated these situations and have built extra time and budget into their project plans. But virtual operations do not offer that escape clause: time is too short, goals are too aggressive and too many organizations are involved.

A project design model optimized for virtual operations will significantly improve many of the resource management variables. The stakeholders who control the resources and the leaders and project managers go through a disciplined process that formalizes resource commitment. But even with the most committed and conscientious planners and stakeholders, there is still the risk that the unexpected will derail the best laid plans. The extra measure of insurance can be provided only by the sanction and oversight of executive management. This insurance is actualized by management's active participation in several key events associated with the planning process and continuing through the execution phases.

How far do executives need to go to support the resource requirements for virtual operations? In the recent movie that re-introduced us to Elliot Ness and the "Untouchables", Sean Connery appeared in the role of an experienced street cop who knew what the "project" needed to succeed. He pressed Ness, who was the executive manager of the initiative, to provide the commitment and resources, and to take the actions to achieve the goal: get the Capone Gang in jail. As Ness wavered with half-hearted measures, Connery repeatedly hammered at him: "What are you prepared to do?" Finally Elliot got the point, made the full level of resource and strategy commitments, and set a successful venture in motion. The rest, as they say, is history.

In support of their resources responsibilities, executives are expected to

• Provide project planners with clear specifications concerning the goal and objectives management expects from the effort. These specifications are the starting point for estimates of required resources based on the best inputs of knowledgeable stakeholders. These also provide the basis for justifying investments needed to fill any shortfalls that might compromise the results.

• Fully endorse the final project plan so that identified resources are clearly committed as specified in the plan. This provides project mangers and stakeholders with precise marching orders and puts in place a process to mediate any changes that influence resource allocations.

• Create and support a process to establish virtual relationships with outside suppliers. Project leaders are empowered to act decisively to negotiate, manage and dismantle relationships they feel are necessary to the success of their project.

• Play an active role in learning activities designed to enhance the competencies and effectiveness of all individuals committed to projects and related tasks.

• Ensure that a viable and valued reward and recognition process is in place.

Executives have a variety of alternatives for developing a resource pool. Bill Johnson gives us this example to show how his group managed a significant resource issue through organizational and technological innovation. IBM envisions huge opportunities in China for computers and communications technologies, and knows a presence in that country is extremely important. The problem is, where do the resources to do the work come from? BJ tells how his group handled that dilemma:

"We decided to put a networking executive over there, someone who was not a corporate officer, but someone at the VP or General Manager level. One of my people signed up to go, but we concluded that it would be impossible to deploy the technical staff he would need. So what we did was to provide him with a direct tie into each of the departments, about ten, that make up our network hardware and software group. With access to these technical competencies he has been able to move aggressively into new market opportunities. Even though the groups don't work for him directly, they are virtually his and they want to see him succeed because it means new revenues for their businesses.

"One of the tools he is using is an electronic bulletin board which has become the equivalent of the in-house conferences where people discuss what is happening and what they need. A lot of people have been watching the information flow in these conferences and are adjusting their product specifications to reflect the capabilities and features the emerging China market wants and needs. The concept of a person out there with a virtual team back here and a communications network that is open to everyone has made some significant changes in the way people look at their jobs, and enabled us to get better use of our resources."

4. Leading the adoption of electronic information, virtual processes and technologies

Executive managers of virtual efforts, like Bill Johnson, not only encourage the use of electronic information and information systems, but set the example for using these technologies. They are comfortable working electronically, using various communications media to maintain their management links with distributed teams and work groups. They have acquired a wide range of business perspectives and sensitivities so that they can assimilate, evaluate, and process the abstract information they extract from the electronic information infrastructure. They know how to use the infrastructure to support their strategic and tactical plans and processes. And they use the tools to maintain the tactical control they need to support day-to-day activities -- to virtually be there when their participation can add immediate value.

Hans Gyllstrom, Manager of the Enterprise Design and Development Group within AT&T's Global Information Solutions, exemplifies the executive as technology champion. ED&D is an international virtual group, spread across the US and Europe. They work with customers on a global scale, helping to design the processes and technologies that support enterprise and enterprises. Gyllstrom constantly encourages innovative exploration of technologies to address group needs, believing that his customers will ultimately encounter the same problems that his group does. When a person in the ED&D virtual community notes a problem and possible solution, Gyllstrom invites that person to "take the problem," offering support and autonomy to that person to demonstrate if not a solution, at least an approach to the problem.

What's remarkable about this approach is that through networking technologies, Gyllstrom extends this opportunity to ED&D's virtual community, not just the core group. When an ED&D manager along with Knowledge Ability, Ltd., a consultancy that is part of the ED&D virtual team, pointed out the need for better communication to support the ED&D worldwide dialog, Gyllstrom provided them the opportunity to "take the problem." The computer conferencing processes and infrastructure designed and implemented by Knowledge Ability and ED&D are now in place and being extended to bring in certain customers and virtual partners as well worldwide. And yes, the executive manager contributes to and is accessible through the group conferencing system.

5. Leading by example: Setting the tone for virtual operations through action

Implicit in the preceding accounts is the notion that successful executive managers lead by example, not by proclamation. They actively demonstrate the personal commitment and leadership styles necessary to inspire workers to overcome interpersonal communications and work-related barriers, and to know that their specified goals and objectives are realistic, necessary, and valued. These executive managers know that position authority is helpful, but not enough to motivate people to give that extra effort to pull off virtual work. They develop a reciprocal confidence with their subordinates and peers through non-authoritarian relationships. They gain the loyalty and commitment of independent-thinking and talented people as they move into leadership positions, yet they retain the flexibility to act as colleagues and peers with the virtual team membership.

Developing and exercising personal power outside the explicit authority given in a traditional hierarchical organization, or choosing not to use such authority overtly is a major challenge for executives and stakeholders who accept the leadership of virtual operations. It requires a great deal of energy and the capacity to keep others enthusiastic and emotionally involved to succeed. The goal is for workers to feel good about themselves and the activities of their team. When necessary, they must be able to respond positively to extreme time pressures, to situations in which the executive has confidential information that cannot be shared, or where there is an urgent reason to initiate significant change in goals or processes.

6. The executive as champion

Very few people rise to top management positions without a well-developed sense of commitment, but virtual operations require an additional measure of commitment from executives and stakeholders. By definition, virtual operations are complex, faster paced, and depend on very complex human behaviors and relationships. Someone, a champion, needs to provide anchors to hold everything together and keep everyone pointed in the same direction -- very much like the captain of a ship at sea. From conception through execution to final wrap-up, virtual operations rely on champions who are willing to make personal commitments to the success of the activity. In fact, most virtual projects will likely have several champions at different stages representing different functional areas.

These champions are the individuals who make things happen, break down the barriers, and come through with the right fix at the right time. They provide excellent project insurance. But the best situation develops when a champion also happens to be a senior executive who can act effectively as a channel between operational managers and top executives. When there is an executive champion, the project benefits from the intervention of someone who understands the importance of the project, its relationship to the strategic vision, the value expected from the investment of time and resources, can intercede when problems become political, can expedite the procurement of unplanned resources, and provides the project leaders with quick decisions when required. Commitment at this level is also essential for a credible reward and recognition program.

This degree of personal commitment is somewhere between the passive hands-off management style very common today where executives empower subordinates to act independently, and the opposite extreme: "I'm the only one who I can trust to get the job done." The level of commitment that seems to work best for virtual operations includes:

• Playing an active role in developing the instructions and specifications for work projects, making sure that planners know what is expected by formalizing executive commitment prior to the start of work

• Being actively engaged and interested in the virtual team's review process

• Being pro-active in problem solving when issues need top management involvement

• Looking for opportunities to praise, encourage, coach and/or provide constructive criticism

• Keeping the information flowing

• Contributing to and facilitating the continuous learning process

• Demanding results consistent with the commitments made by leaders and workers

• Looking for and promoting creative virtual initiatives and alliances

• Maintaining the quality and effectiveness of virtual relationships by providing top management visibility

The tactical responsibilities for executives and stakeholders in the virtual paradigm are more demanding. The reasons are again driven by the changes that now influence our environment. The faster we try to work, the more we need involved leadership. At the executive level this translates to commitment and support -- full time. Again this is mostly emphasis, but it also includes a high degree of personal involvement that is extremely demanding and sensitive.

For example, one of the most critical tasks for top executives is to select leaders for virtual projects, and then empower them with the authority and responsibility to act effectively as leaders. This relationship requires trust, and trust is not a virtue that is very common in today's work environment. Since trust is so essential, executives need to place the highest priority on activities and processes that create and nurture a trusting environment. Collaborative visioning providing clear specifications based on needs generated by the vision, the enthusiastic support of virtual initiatives, the selection and support of project leaders trained and personally committed to virtual operations, and pro-active participation in project reviews and other electronic information and learning forums are tactics that provide endless opportunities to create a trusting relationship between executives and the leaders and workers who they depend upon to create value.

Final Comments

Executives have great leverage in changing organizational behavior, and virtual operations require major shifts in beliefs and behaviors. What we've tried to do here is suggest the executive competencies and behaviors that can mean the difference between a successful and sustained virtual effort. We've offered these guidelines with the belief that executives and stakeholders don't intuitively know all the details of their roles and responsibilities in this new environment. And we are well aware of the reluctance of many executives to admit that they don't already know everything. So we've put these on the table for consideration, suggesting that executives wear the shoes that fit, and everyone else consider these insights as useful in helping them manage their virtual executive management.

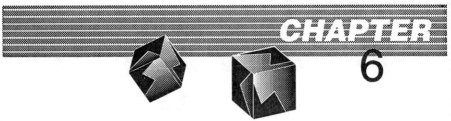

OPERATIONAL
LEADERSHIP

How hard it is to keep from being king,
When it's in you and in the situation.
In the Clearing, Robert Frost [1]

Libraries hold entire collections of novels, histories, business books, and memoirs that describe in great detail favored concepts of leadership. The arguments run the gamut from praises of Attila the Hun to treatises advocating the abolishment of leadership in favor of blanket empower. ment. Presenting yet another set of principles of leadership is not our intention; however, in every successful or failed virtual operation we have personally witnessed or researched, leadership has had a major influence on the outcome of the initiative. In most successful projects an effective leader was very much in evidence; someone who took charge, made things happen, generated enthusiasm, took risks, and believed that he or she, sanctioned or not, was doing the right thing. In failed virtual projects, leadership was generally absent or at best ineffective.

Our intention here is to examine the leadership role, but only in the context of virtual work. While leadership is operative at every level of the organization, the focus here is on the individuals who are given, or assume, the authority and responsibility to deal with the tactical agenda -- the planning, designing, negotiating, and real-time management of programs and projects that will move the organization toward its virtual vision. However, these tactical leaders do not operate in a vacuum; their management must

[1]Robert Frost, *In the Clearing*, "How Hard It is to Keep from Being King, when It's in You and in the Situation" (New York: Rinehart and Winston, 1955), p. 84.

also practice exceptional leadership in order to create an environment that supports them through all the turmoil and risk of transitioning to this new way of working.

In this chapter we'll present what we see are the qualities of virtual leadership and make some suggestions on how these qualities can be developed. We focus on qualities rather than a job description because leadership is not a position; rather it is a behavior that operates throughout an organization, whenever someone takes charge of resources or activities that generate action. Teams can have multiple leaders, depending on the situation, the competencies needed, and the particular strengths of individuals on the team. Leadership may be an art or a science, or both; but in the last analysis what matters is that good leadership yields strong team performance -- action -- and team performance is the true strength of any virtual organization.

Our bias toward leadership does not really conflict with current thinking about empowerment: that knowledge workers should be given freedom to construct their own processes, goals, and destinies. Here leadership is even more important, to set direction, to set boundaries within which empowerment operates, even loose boundaries. We should be wary not to fall in the "false dilemma" traps of command and control vs. influence, or hierarchy vs. network, or leadership vs. empowerment, or Attila vs. team consensus. The complexity of the virtual environment demands that all these forces, metaphors, mental models coexist at different times, even simultaneously: Indeed, it is the leader's responsibility to manage, if not resolve, conflicting practices to achieve the best ends for the team.

It has been said that in human affairs, the distance between leaders and the average worker is a constant. If leadership performance is high, the average performance will go up. The effective executive knows that it is easier to raise the performance of one leader than it is to raise the performance of the whole mass. There is tremendous leverage in identifying and turning loose good leaders. Here we will try to describe the qualities that make for exceptional leadership in virtual environments.

Virtual Leadership: The Realities

Leaders are the individuals who assume tactical responsibilities for virtual teams and make virtual operations work. Some project leaders are appointed, "commissioned" by top management; others emerge during the course of a project. Leaders are also responsible for maintaining a viable communications channel between themselves and the executives and to keep the executives sufficiently informed and able to effectively support the project. They are also responsible for the planning and designing activities needed to guide and fully engage workers and physical resources in the value creation process.

What follows are some basic observations that characterize and differentiate virtual leadership:

- Virtual projects do not succeed without good leadership.
- Leadership of virtual teams is more demanding than leadership for "four-walls" teams.
- Usually leaders have native talent, but in virtual settings, talent must be augmented with developed skills.
- Virtual leadership is performance, not a role. People in all role capacities are called upon at some point to lead.
- In virtual operations, value cannot be created without leadership.
- Good leadership brings out the best practices of followership.
- Good leadership is contagious.

Virtual Leadership: Qualities of Practitioners

Leaders of virtual projects often come from the ranks of middle management. It's the "middle" role that seems to be the qualifier here. Middle managers, by definition, learn how to survive and thrive on multi-dimensional relationships. Even in traditional organizations they deal with the workforce, executive management, customers, suppliers, regulators: They are in the middle. Good managers at this level develop the skills to get work done through relationships, the soul of virtual leadership. They know how to influence, cajole, ignore, praise and correct, obey and refuse as the situation demands. They don't normally have executive position clout, so they must learn to use other, more persuasive techniques and to develop sensitivities that help them recognize and understand what makes people tick to get their programs carried out.

What follows are short statements about some of the qualities of successful virtual leaders that seem to be particularly effective in virtual situations.

People Qualities.

Leaders take the responsibility for the effectiveness, productivity, development, and welfare of the people in their team, regardless of their organizational homes. They support and articulate the organization's vision and objectives, and facilitate the building of the teaming culture...the virtual community. Leaders, with stakeholders, identify and negotiate for the competencies, internal and external, needed for the project.

Leaders remain continuously involved in the team's activities, and tactfully intervene when the team gets into difficulties. Leaders are effective in balancing opposing views of a team; they maintain the creative tension of differing perspectives, yet bring enough resolution to keep the work moving. They facilitate negotiations among the team's participants, and support individual and the team's continuous learning efforts. They know how to delegate authority while maintaining responsibility. Leaders make decisions and are not afraid to change those decisions if they are ineffective or if the variables of the situation change.

Leaders are adept at alleviating the stresses that accompany simultaneous work and high rates of change. They are decisive in rewarding high levels of team performance and in rectifying performance problems. They provide public and private feedback to team members; they also are the primary feedback channels to other stakeholders in the extended project community, including executive management.

Virtual Process Qualities.

Good leaders stand out in the way they apply themselves to their jobs. They demonstrate a high degree of commitment to achieving organizational and personal goals and objectives, attention to detail, sensitivity to developing and maintaining productive interpersonal relationships, and adherence to the techniques that are particularly important in sustaining virtual operations. These leaders understand the necessity of a vision and value the process of visioning. They value the potential of virtual work processes and support technologies and encourage innovations that yield better ways of achieving team goals.

Leadership Styles.

Nothing is quite as painful as watching someone behave counter to his or her normal style in order to follow some kind of prescriptive norm. We've all had managers, who are easy going, accessible people who, upon returning from a management training exercise, start making table-pounding demands on the group with little or no effect or success. Likewise, tyrannical managers (whom we've learned how to manage) come back from sensitivity training and begin treating the most critical issues with smiles that ill-conceal their frustration.

Leadership styles vary too. While certain behaviors and results are hallmarks of good virtual leadership, a naturalness of interpersonal activity is very important. Some leaders believe in giving clear directions and constantly reminding "the troops" of that direction. Others give wider berth to how things get done, if not what things get done.

Successful leaders we have met come in all sizes and shapes. Some are well lettered, and have deep experience resources; some are on their first solo flights. Most are very self-confident, thrive on challenge and change, and are personally committed to success. They are hands-on types and do not hesitate to get involved with the actual work. They are good at interpersonal relationships: They listen, get excited, even passionate, about their projects and the people they work with. They have leadership attributes that we might call "natural," admit that they have to work hard, are constantly looking for new ideas, and want to keep learning how to do their jobs better.

Ideally, leaders use their exceptional skills in influencing team efforts through consensus building dialog. But with virtual operations often there isn't time for such ongoing, personal interaction. There is constant demand for speed and global reach to engage the best possible competencies and satisfy customers. Everything has top priority and the project seems on the brink of chaos. Management sends strong hints that failure won't be tolerated. Leaders work enthusiastically to keep the team's eye on the ball, while neutralizing the destablilizing effects of management sniping, poaching, and criticism.

At times like these, effective leaders bypass the extended dialog. They quickly and firmly define the goals and objectives for the team, articulate management's expectations, and manage the development of detailed action plans that keep things moving. They set the pace for endurance and energy, resolve conflicts, measure results, keep management informed, and give praise where it's due.

Perhaps above all else, leaders excel in communication skills and help the team become skilled in using the information and communications systems that support virtual work. They assure that learning occurs, that metrics are monitored, and that changes are processed effectively.

Not to put too fine a point on it, today there is a leadership vacuum. As more organizations move into the virtual operations paradigm, this shortfall will become critical. Projects will fail, not because of flaws in the basic process, but because of the leadership gap. The solution to this immanent problem is in finding the talent, applying the science through training, and nurturing the art of leadership through experience.

Leadership Development

Many of us can appreciate the total commitment the military services have to the concept of leadership. From the first day as a raw recruit reporting for basic training, through technical and professional officer and NCO schools, the military provides an individual with continuous leadership training. The training is formal or included as part of On-The-Job-Training (OJT). It is included as part of every in-processing and orientation for new assignments, and as part of de-briefings at the end of assignments or operations. Performance reviews focus on leadership, and recommendations for future assignments are based on demonstrated leadership, good or bad. For the military, leadership is the foundation, the keystone, the DNA of the military mission.

The military leadership model evolved as a response to the unique and demanding life and death situations associated with combat. In spite of the war-room hyperbole of today's market-driven and downsizing addicted corporate boardrooms ("shoot the messenger," "nuke the R&D program," "annihilate the competition") the civil sector is not the military. Influence, rather than command is the persuasive technique of the corporate virtual initiative On the other hand, we have seen many business opportunities flounder or turn into nonproductive chaos because either everybody or nobody assumed leadership.

What we can take from the military is the commitment to leadership training. There is ample proof that individuals can be trained in various techniques that enable them to lead effectively even under the most stressful and demanding circumstances. Leadership training is also a very effective process to build the quality and effectiveness of followers. Followership is covered in detail in the next chapter, but the fact is that nothing lightens the load of a leader more then good followers, and nothing encourages followers more than understanding and appreciating the basics of leadership. Leadership training, then, is not just for "anointed" leaders, but virtually for everyone that needs to understand the function in the context of virtual work.

But such training is not generally a top priority in industry, even though everyone agrees that leadership skills and techniques are critically important. The notion that some people will lead others may be less politically correct, or attractive than more fashionable notions such as self-directed teams, individual empowerment, and other concepts that avoid structured or hierarchical relationships. Also, leadership capability is assumed to be a de facto attribute of management: If the boss didn't know how to lead, then he/she wouldn't be a manager!

A formal leadership training program is essential for any organization transitioning to virtual operations. There are many outstanding programs available that focus on the basic art and science of leadership which can be augmented with the "virtual spin." Almost any course would be better than just assuming people knew how to lead. In conjunction with experiential projects, these courses could be constantly modified to reflect the learning acquired in actual projects. Not least of all, such a program would demonstrate the commitment top management has to the organization's transition. It will send an unambiguous message: "Pay attention everyone, we are changing our direction. We need to do what we do differently to make sure we succeed. One of our top priorities is to sharpen our leadership skills, and to make certain we have people in place who know how to get us moving in the right direction."

Final Comments

We'll close with suggestions for an agenda for virtual leadership development. Eliminate the word "virtual" and each of these topics seems fairly traditional. The suggestion here is to investigate these aspects of leadership in the virtual context, as a basis for providing a practical perspective and leadership training with relevance to your present business context. Virtual leadership topics include:

• Multiple leadership in virtual operations
• Leadership as managing a network of dependencies
• Leadership through decision and influence
• The leadership role in designing virtual operations
• Creating and sustaining virtual relationships
• Supporting virtual teams
• Stress management through communication
• Introducing virtual technologies in non-threatening ways
• Leading by example: teaming, communications, and continuous learning in virtual environments
• Keeping virtual teams focused.

Virtual leadership responsibilities and qualities are still at the discovery stage. The more the virtual paradigm is exercised, the more leadership demands will become evident. This is a starter list, not a fixed curriculum. But it is certainly enough to seed a living organizational program in developing virtual leadership for the future.

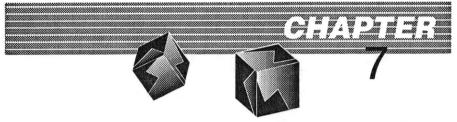

CHAPTER 7

VIRTUAL KNOWLEDGE WORKERS

Every knowledge worker in the modern organization is an "executive," if by virtue of his possession of knowledge, he is responsible for a contribution that materially affects the capacity of the organization to perform and to obtain results.
The Effective Executive, Peter F. Drucker [1]

The term "knowledge worker" has replaced "information worker" as the sobriquet of today's most valued members of the workforce. The new title rightly emphasizes the coin of the realm of virtual work: knowledge. Information is now recognized as a raw or intermediate material resource in the organizational value chain. To have value, that information must be collaboratively built into knowledge, and that knowledge into products and services. Building this knowledge, through the use of networked, virtual operations, is the job of the virtual knowledge worker.

In virtual operations, knowledge workers exhibit both benchmark competencies in their areas of specialization and the "lateral" competencies required to sustain virtual operations. For example, it isn't enough just to be a highly competent architect. In virtual efforts architects, whose training may have included building three-dimensional cardboard models, suddenly are called upon to render their ideas and concepts using networked personal computer or workstation modeling applications. They use E-mail and shared-screen presentations, remote databases, structural design applications as well as collaborative free-hand sketching facilities. Virtual knowledge workers have competencies in their specialties and in the design and teaming protocols needed to represent, communicate, and integrate that specialized competency in the virtual team effort.

[1]Peter Drucker, *The Effective Executive* (New York: Harper & Row, 1966), p. 5.

Responsibilities of Virtual Knowledge Workers

The principal responsibility of the virtual knowledge worker is to commit his or her knowledge, skills, experience, and energy to create organizational value. In the virtual environment this means using the information infrastructure to support the development of knowledge as value. This involves

1. Understanding the organization's commitment to virtual operations

2. Understanding the virtual team's goals

3. Developing specialized and virtual operations competencies

4. Using the network to access information and knowledge in the network, and to integrate that knowledge with the other knowledge/competencies in the team

5. Representing or embodying that knowledge in a product or a service.

We'll take a closer look at each of these areas to get a better idea of the scope of challenges that face the virtual knowledge worker.

1. Understanding the organization's commitment to virtual operations

Knowledge workers should know why their organizations have chosen the virtual path. They should understand and accept the business conditions and rationales that drive decisions to transition to the virtual paradigm. They should know what the organization believes are its core competencies and what principles guide its selection of virtual partners. To do this, virtual knowledge workers must know the organizational vision. They should know what it means, not just what it says.

They must know how far upper management will go in supporting them: what is management's commitment to providing resources to virtual teams; what are the success criteria; and what metrics will be used to monitor their progress.

Virtual knowledge workers enter unfamiliar territory on a daily basis. In order to deal with new challenges they must fully appreciate the context in which they work. History is not a guideline; understanding organizational purpose is.

2. Understanding the virtual team's goals

Virtual teams are aggregations of competencies focused on one or two clear purposes. As organizations begin to transition to virtual operations, they formalize team activities into prototype projects. These projects have real operational value, and are carefully designed to ensure the greatest probability of success and to capture the learnings about virtual work in real-time. Upper management's business goals for the project should be explicit. In the best situation, team participants would be part of the virtual operations design process. In any case, the knowledge workers should be given the opportunity -- and the time -- to build a belief in what they will be asked to do. Simply assigning them virtual tasks can be a prescription for failure.

It's important to recognize that not all workers, even established knowledge workers, care to be, or have the potential to be virtual knowledge workers. The stresses of virtual work such as distrust, technophobia, unwillingness to change, and intolerance of complexity are perfectly natural traits that make it impossible for certain people to function well in the virtual environment. Everyone should have the opportunity to join the organization's virtual venture, but those who can't or won't develop the competencies and behaviors required for the job should be directed elsewhere. In virtual operations there is no room for straphangers: In such webs of mutual dependency everyone adds value and supports the team. Each individual must make the personal decision and build the commitment to go virtual; no one can just drift along with the tide, expecting business as usual.

The implication is that organizational leadership needs to give workers the opportunity to understand the implications of choosing to become part of the virtual ethos, or choosing another path. Knowledge workers should have some idea of what the future looks like in their organization for people who take the new road, and for those who decide that virtual operations are inconsistent with their personal goals and preferences.

3. Developing specialized and virtual operations competencies

No one needs to be told that we are in an age of specialization. This is especially true in the world of virtual organizations, where the ethos is to bring together world class competencies. Virtual knowledge workers must understand the nature and rationale of the competency-based teaming model; they should be receptive to the high-pressure, short-term virtual project as a new and viable alternative for organizations trying to stay on top. They should appreciate the opportunities inherent in virtual technologies that support well designed virtual operations: networks, information systems, communications applications.

While not much has changed in the demand for specialists, the nature of the competencies in demand has changed. First of all, the freedom organizations have in accessing the competencies they need has made it dangerous for anyone to become complacent about a competency. The drafting department down the hall used to get by with its "put it in the queue and we'll get to it when someone frees up" approach. This internal sole source was the only game in town; there were no alternatives. Now the team can go out through the network to access the drafting competencies that suit best them in quality, capability, and timeliness. The in-house group can either upgrade its competencies or wither away.

This need to continuously learn and develop one's competencies is true also in the dimension of those lateral, or virtual competencies. Having information, knowledge, and skill in a specialty is only part of the game. A market research specialist who dwells in the world of the printed page can learn a lot about the demographics of foreign markets; but if the consumer of that knowledge is a virtual team that works through shared information data bases and E-mail, the specialist had better become part of the team's electronic work processes and supporting infrastructure. Otherwise the researcher's information, even if scanned into the system, cannot be integrated into the value adding process of the team.

4. Using the network to access information and knowledge in the network, and to integrate that knowledge with the other knowledge/competencies in the team

Virtual knowledge workers are pushing the envelope in their use of the so-called Information Highway. Indeed, to them the Internet and other networks have become more of a "Knowledge Airway"; the medium for the acquisition and sharing of knowledge. In many ways virtual work signals the end of the individual contributor paradigm. The work that virtual teams undertake is too complex and too fast-paced to be accomplished by single workers, interacting with their favorite personal computer applications. Knowledge hoarded in one's skull or a private personal computer file is of no use to the virtual product. Instead, globally available information and knowledge must be quickly pulled together from some specialized perspective, than shared within the team's wider perspective.

So part of the virtual worker's tool kit is a set of skills for using such readily available resources as the Internet's Worldwide Web facilities for finding information, E-mail gateways, and Telnet connectivity to interact with teammates around the world. Other skills involve the use of audio-, computer-, and videoconferencing facilities: not just the technologies, but the processes and protocols specifically designed by the virtual team.

With this ability to communicate, share, exchange information, and build knowledge comes the obligation to reset one's individual contributor thinking to a sharing model in which the individual

- Is willing to share and receive unfinished work or incomplete information without frustration

• Knows that communications capabilities enable the team to work simultaneously; a practice which saves project time, but creates stress as one's own efforts are always subject to being made irrelevant by other work in the system

• Accepts the reality that in a virtual team, one's own, comfortable work culture will be replaced by a culture built by the team itself; a converged culture that will provide the stable ground of assumptions and expectations that make communications and information sharing possible

• Makes the effort to learn the boundary skills of one's teammates; to understand their expectations, intentions and success criteria as well as one's own.

5. Representing or embodying that knowledge in a product or a service

The ultimate goal of the knowledge worker is to help embody the team's knowledge in the product or service that represents value to the project. If the team has been working well, this will not be a project-end task; rather, from Day 1 that product or service will have been the team's focus. For example, consider a team that is developing a new fabric that will meet the needs of airline seat makers worldwide. The evolution of the knowledge product goes something like this:

a) Seed Knowledge	Product concept: Fabric with standards of appearance, softness, durability, weight, and cost
b) 1st level integration	Knowledge input from potential customers and Virtual Development Partners: airlines, manufacturers, textile manufacturers
c) 2nd level integration	Preliminary designs: iterative building of product from all virtual team perspectives
d) Nth level integration	The collaborative knowledge-based product builds progressively, from all perspectives in parallel
e) Final Stage	Knowledge integrated in manufactured and tested product

The whole point here is that while work is fragmented into simultaneous, virtual tasks, that aggregation of knowledge that is the product is never fragmented. The knowledge is integrated in real-time throughout the effort, so that the ultimate product is a stage of evolving knowledge, not a last minute integration of separate parts. To make this happen, knowledge workers must always focus on sharing their knowledge to further the evolution of, in this case, the fabric. All other activities are means to getting to product. No organizational, administrative, personal, or technical agendas should draw the knowledge worker away from the product center of gravity.

Qualities of Virtual Knowledge Workers

In several successful virtual projects we've observed, knowledge workers have exhibited a common set of characteristics that have positively influenced the project's outcome. Here we've pulled these attributes together into a generalized portrait of the virtual knowledge worker:

Knowledge workers are comfortable wearing multiple hats (metaphorically speaking). Like workers in start-up ventures, they do what's necessary, not just what their job description says they should be doing. At the same time they are more concerned with accomplishing team goals than observing formal organizational structures or respecting turf.

1. Belief in the virtual model

Knowledge workers recognize the power of the competency model and respect others because of their competencies and willingness to be contributors to the team effort. Virtual knowledge workers exhibit the capacity to form trusting relationships with teaming partners. They are not "homers," believing they and their organizational chart-mates can do everything better than anyone else, because of tradition or divine blessing. They are proud that their organization is open to finding the best competencies wherever they exist. They see the virtual model as having infinite possibilities for new competencies, not a zero-sum competitive game.

They understand the necessity of knowledge sharing through electronic communications. They actively participate in audio and computer conferences and encourage more reserved teammates to do the same. They communicate continuously by phone, through E-mail, even when there's no crisis, no news, or no agenda. They communicate because communications build trust and that trust is needed when there is critical information to be shared and acted upon.

These knowledge workers are results oriented. Short, fast, project cycles are not a problem for them: more rapid cycles provide more opportunities for learning, for success and for celebration.

As participants in virtual teams, these knowledge workers respond positively to effective and committed leadership. Furthermore, they understand the concept of followership -- the attitude that permits them to support the objectives of the leader without themselves feeling like slaves. This may need to be a learned behavior in an age when individuals often expect to be self-directed and empowered to self-lead. In the virtual environment, followership is a reflection of the commitment workers make to the leader to deliver as the plan requires. Even within these boundaries there is room for individuality, but for the leader to lead effectively the workers must commit to follow.

2. On positive action

Even though they are good followers, knowledge workers tend to act proactively. They are used to going on incomplete information and are inclined to act when action is required, not sit and wait for more information to come in or for someone else to take the lead.

Working in an environment where the unknown is always around the corner and the unexpected expected, virtual knowledge workers actively seek out and nurture creativity. Ideas are likely to pop up anywhere but can become lost in the ambient noise of a busy project. Workers are best positioned to recognize the real value of creative ideas on improving tasks and processes. They are also able to add value by building on ideas with their own knowledge, fostering team creativity.

Accepting empowerment and followership, knowledge workers develop new sensitivities. For example, so much depends on continuous activity in virtual operations that workers are constantly alert for signs of gridlock. And being close to the action they can shake things loose or escalate roadblock issues to project leadership. Knowledge workers are sensitive to other potentially disruptive situations as well. They quickly spot indications that

- A team member may be experiencing excessive stress. Virtual teaming is extremely demanding and everyone has different comfort thresholds for working in this environment. Workers need to be sensitive to their own limits and look for signs of overreaching in others.

- A team member is having difficulties in using some or all electronic communications support systems. Since communication is so critical to the team's work, it's everyone's business to help the team maintain a level of communications that includes everyone, not just those who are natural communicators.

• A work process is not fitting in or delivering to expectations. Early warning of process failure is essential in virtual operations. Unlike the situation in most traditional organizations, the energy required to keep broken processes working is not available in the virtual environment.

• New sources of competencies have become available. Often workers are the first to learn of breakthroughs in their area of specialization and can help augment both the initial and mid-stream competency pool.

• New technologies that can help implement or improve the teams' virtual work are available.

• Project designs are flawed. Again, the earlier the detection, the more likely (and less costly) the resolution.

• Opportunities have arisen to celebrate success and to reward significant team or individual efforts.

3. On attitude

Successful knowledge workers are unique in two other ways. They work through change and they address change through continuous learning. They also know the roles of teacher and learner are flexible, even reversible. Title or role is not important in the continuous learning paradigm. What matters is that, heat flows to cold, knowledge and information flow from those who have to those who need. As with all aspects of virtual operations, workers embrace the technologies that support continuous learning.

On the emotional level, virtual knowledge workers are passionate about their work. Reading the electronic journals, the captured dialog of virtual projects, one can see the fire come through even through the cool medium. The excitement of virtual knowledge work is contagious, encouraging participation and sharing. While there certainly is room for reserve, passivity is not generally appreciated.

Knowledge workers are dominated by project goals, by action, not fear or excuses. They don't avoid action, retreat from confrontation, cast or avoid blame. The litany of traditional excuses has no place in the virtual worker's lexicon:

-- "I was never trained to do this."

-- "This isn't in my job description."

-- "I thought you meant.....So what did you mean?"

-- "It didn't happen on my shift..."

Virtual knowledge workers are always in a hurry, but they know the value of reflection. They take time to think out ideas and give others the same opportunity. They take the time to record their discussions, their decisions, their actions; they know the value of this learning record to the next generation virtual teams; and they also know how unlikely it is that any "post-project" review can capture what really happened.

4. On commitments

Very early knowledge workers come to grips with the necessity of making and meeting commitments. During various phases of the virtual process, they will be asked to contribute their expertise and to make commitments that will support the commitments made by leaders and stakeholders. This is also why virtual operations depend so much on utilizing the best competencies available; the best should be able to make commitments that are the most realistic and valid. The most sacred of all these is the commitment to immediately raise a flag when one can't meet a commitment. Nothing is worse that letting a problem slip by. Given the pace and complexity of virtual work, there will be no chance to catch up, no problem will go away, and no divine intervention will fix the chain of disasters that an undetected, missed commitment will cause. With the missed commitment made visible, the worst case scenario is this: Nothing can be done to fix the problem, a schedule will slip, a replacement will need to be found to replace a critical resource, or a new source will need to be identified to provide some service or product. But the project plan can be adjusted to deal with these; that's what management and leadership gets paid to do.

To increase the probability of meeting their commitments, virtual team members do the following up-front work. They

• Make sure they completely understand exactly what the commitment involves; unclear implications of a request are the major reason why commitments are not met.

• Learn what is dependent on meeting the commitment; learn what meeting the commitment is dependent on

• Become knowledgeable of and comfortable with the time factors, especially in multistage commitments

• Make certain the tools and processes to support meeting the commitment are in place, or soon will be

• Understand how performance is to be measured and reported, what denotes "completion," and how that notification will be made

• Make sure of the availability of virtual resources; resolving resource control issues.

As a final precaution, knowledge workers determine whether their commitments will be affected by changes in other parts of the project; and if so, they can adjust the commitment to meet the realities of the situation and satisfy the team's needs.

While on the subject of realities, knowledge workers are not naive; they know that virtual operations are not immune from political agendas. High visibility and high rewards attract individuals whose motives may be more self-serving than the perfect role models we tend to describe. By making team needs, intentions, and commitments explicit and open, knowledge workers can limit the risk of being blind-sided by hidden agendas or back-door deals. The cohesiveness of the team, supported by open communications, can go a long way to protect individual workers from being victimized by those who would undercut their contributions, competencies, or successes.

5. On stress

Although the effects of stress in virtual operations are discussed elsewhere, it is important to touch upon the specific stresses to which virtual knowledge workers are subject. Stress is endemic in virtual operations for the following reasons:

• Many of today's knowledge workers are in the midst of their organization's transition to virtual work. Many of these organizations don't know that they're transitioning. The knowledge workers are the first to feel the heat, asked to perform virtual work with traditional tools. Information barriers, organizational walls, communications systems that don't communicate, inter-organizational work processes that clash, competing goals, and pirating of resources make the job almost impossible.

• Time compression causes the most stress in the workplace. Virtual work is driven by time and the stress is multiplied by the need for knowledge workers to constantly share information, perform concurrent work, maintain constant communication, and continuously learn to keep up with complexity.

• Virtual knowledge workers, as has been suggested already, work in a converged culture. They need to let go of the familiar trees and go with the work norms that the team develops for itself, for the project. The team is cross-cultural from the aspect of disciplines, competencies, position, organization, and on occasion, language and nationality. While most celebrate multiculturalism, working closely in such heterogeneous groups, no matter how motivated the team, is stressful.

• The irony of virtual operations is that although people may be spread throughout geographies, they are, through networked communications, more visible and accessible than ever before. The work day crosses time zones; a worker is never out of reach, electronically. Not on a trip, not at home, not at the beach. This constant "knowing the phone, or E-mail box will ring," brings significant anxiety and stress to some. Some team members may be reluctant to keep up the level of communication, and visibility, the project requires. This puts stress both on the individual and on the rest of the team, which depends on full participation. Fortunately, some of the best ways to relieve these stresses are available in the nature of the paradigm itself.

The reluctance to communicate can usually be overcome early in the project. Normally simply briefing knowledge workers on the purpose of the communications plan designed for the virtual project will work for the majority, but for some, the leader will need to overcome individual barriers through special training. Once started, most discover benefits that improve their work situation, and will participate willingly. It is the leader's responsibility to replace the few who won't or can't sustain the level of participation required.

There is also relief from stress, solace perhaps, in the cohesiveness of the "virtual community." Even alone in a far out node, the knowledge worker is linked to the team, not only through the lines of electronic process, but through social connections: bulletin boards, E-mail chat, and occasional face-to-face meetings or visits from the "circuit rider." The typically short lengths of virtual projects also serves to relieve stress: more times to celebrate victory and take a break from the virtual whirlwind.

Final Comments

The participatory nature of virtual work gives knowledge workers a sense of ownership and some control of events. They participate in team design, they are privy to major decisions -- and their input is actively sought and honored. They share in the team's rewards, as well as receiving acknowledgments for their own extraordinary contributions.

As one seasoned virtual knowledge worker described her first project: "It sounded like a good idea; it was hell while it was going on. But wow, what a ride!"

TECHNOLOGY AND VIRTUAL OPERATIONS

The figure slowly climbed toward the summit of the mountain, hand over hand, pulling upwards toward the guru's cave. The climber reached the top, fingers raw and clothing tattered. He beheld the master: long white hair, wearing a flowing robe, indeterminate age. The master sat in the lotus position and seemed completely detached from worldly concerns.

The pilgrim knew he could ask only one question. A question for which there were no answers in the books, the journals, or the consultancies. He approached the master and asked: "Master, what is the secret of virtual operations?"

The Master was still for a long time, considering this question. At last she spoke: "You could have sent e-mail."

The Grenierian Chronicles

Not to put too fine a point on it, the appropriate use of information and communications technology is a necessary condition for virtual operations. But technology alone does not add value; witness the ballyhooed technologies that have ended up as expensive door stops over the years, the latest being the early versions of home multimedia systems. They sound great, but no one quite knows what use to put them to. We do not intend to knock the value of these systems for discovery and entertainment; our attention here, however, is using technology to get complex work done.

What's needed besides the technologies themselves is a clear sense of use; well designed processes based on the technologies, and personal and social acceptance by the people who must put the technology to work. This is especially important in collaborative, cross-organizational work in which common, accepted understandings and practices must be in place for work to go forward.

These chapters will approach the key virtual technologies from two perspectives:

•The attitudes and beliefs about technologies that need to be developed in virtual organizations (Chapter 8)
•Discussion of the specific technologies that have unique value in supporting virtual operations (Chapters 9 and 10). The technologies include:

-- Public and private networks/information systems
-- Communications
-- Workflow
-- Modeling
-- Design
-- Management.

Many of the technologies discussed fall under the category of "groupware," software in support of group work. Others, like audioconferencing, have been available for years and for this reason are undervalued as effective tools. We call them "virtual technologies" when they are used for virtual work in virtual environments. The distinction may be a fine one, but we need to place these technologies in the measurable, mainstream context of value-adding virtual operations, rather than the supportive, cost-incurring role of "supporting group work."

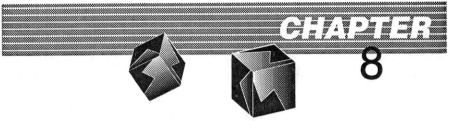

CHAPTER

8

ATTITUDES
TOWARD VIRTUAL
TECHNOLOGIES

Take away their pencils.
Larry Walker, General Manager of Network Products,
Digital Equipment Corporation

Many organizations have not invested in the kind of technology that enables them to collaborate electronically with outside or even inside resources. Early on in the Ameritech project, Greg Oslan realized that he needed more effective communications to maintain productive links with his widely distributed virtual team. Remember, we're talking about Ameritech, an organization whose business is communications technology -- the cobbler syndrome. For the first several months the best capabilities he had available were the telephone, fax, and audioconferencing. Continuous communications remained a dream. Finally, he was able to invest in Lotus Notes, a very flexible and adaptive groupware product that is beginning to meet this diverse group's needs.

In the ideal organization, especially a virtual organization, everyone from shop floor workers, to draftspeople, to upper management, to clerical staff constantly looks for and embraces technologies that make work more effective and simpler. However, in our less than perfect world, this idealistic relationship with technology usually remains a dream. In the typical organization, any of the following reasons for not investing in or not using technology might exist:

• Based on experience, management is unconvinced that investing in information technology produces acceptable returns; and replacing old technology that isn't used or doesn't work with new technology that will be equally non-contributing is bad business.

• Usable virtual systems demand seamless information access and communications capabilities. In many organizations IS protects its turf and telcom does the same. It's difficult for users to get integrated solutions.

• A significant percentage of managers and workers don't know or don't care about the potential of modern information and communications technologies -- they are satisfied to work and do business the way they always have. Even in the chaotic virtual environment.

At a more specific level, opinions and attitudes concerning technology often reflect people's positions and roles in the organization. It's important to appreciate these various perspectives because every constituency, or virtual cohort, must be enrolled in the quest to integrate and use appropriate virtual technologies in order to establish and sustain the information infrastructure.

Executives

There are several major reasons that are used to explain executive resistance to technology. Executives are responsible and accountable for the present and future financial position of the company, and technology investments and usage are more often than not viewed as a cost rather than a value generator. Reasons to avoid those costs are easy to come by:

• "Our business is sensitive to security. We can't have our propriety information accessible from all over the place."

• "We've built a successful company the old fashioned way; our methods were good in the past and they are good enough for me."

• "I have nothing against our people using technology when I am convinced it will significantly improve our business. But we're not going to spend a lot of time and money re-inventing wheels -- or processes".

• "These are tough times. We can't afford the time or the expense to hire trainers to teach people how to use a lot of new systems."

• "It's all about risk. Virtual operations sound interesting, but we don't have the experience to know how to measure results. We are very conservative and don't leap into things we can't measure."

And it's true, technical managers have difficulty representing their technology investments in terms and metrics that are meaningful to business executives. Distinctions like state-of-the-art, MIPs, user friendly, bandwidth, functionality, and other criteria used by technical staffs simply don't play well in the board room.

In recent years, however, progress has been made in developing quantitative metrics that relate technology investments to organizational value in ways that are consistent with financial management expectations. The *Cost of Network Ownership* model developed by Dr. Mike Treacy in 1990, for example, consistently, effectively, and persuasively represents the relationships between life cycle costs and provides a benchmark to support the value of networking investments. Such an instrument can be applied to other technologies as well.[1]

As far as actually using technologies, executives can be the most recalcitrant constituency. Some espoused reasons for not joining the world of virtual work include statements such as

- "I don't type; my secretary types."

- "I like to use the phone, E-mail is too impersonal."

- "Unless I can look people in the eye, I'm not comfortable. I need the feedback I get from seeing how they look, move, and act. This is how I know what's behind their words and whether or not I can trust them."

- "When I need information, or to reach out to someone in ways that involve technology, my staff does it. My job isn't to mess with a lot of systems stuff, but to make quick decisions and communicate on a personal basis with people."

What's interesting about most of these defenses is that they're based on the fact that most people are far more interested in preserving the way they like to work than they are in reaching new goals.[2] Executives are the only people in a corporation who can do things the way they like for the simple reason that, well, they like to. Virtual operations, however, are about collaboration and negotiation to develop common processes and joint goals. Executives are not out of the network of virtual operations -- they are

---

[1]Michael E. Treacy, *The Costs of Network Ownership* (Cambridge, MA: Index Group, Inc., 1989).

[2]Organizational Development professionals know this phenomenon very well: the natural attachment to work methods rather than results spawned the need for "change management." We know of one instance in which workers in a nuclear power facility would not adapt to command-line computerized controls, but quickly accepted iconic controls that looked like traditional dials and valves. Earlier testimony to "tree-hugging" can be found in the classical Russian novel, *Anna Karenina*. Peasants, totally unimpressed with the increased grain yields promised through new plowing tools and methods, choose rather to break the new tools in order to keep working the way they've always worked. Leo Tolstoy, *Anna Karenina* (Moscow: Progress Publishers, 1978), pp. 436-56.

in it. In fact they are best positioned to set the example for others: in the ability to change to virtual forms of work, to communicate through the system, and to effectively use the new tools of the trade.

To be fair, more than habit and ego are behind executive resistance to technology. Embarrassment and fear are also leading causes of executive resistance to learning and using even the simplest applications, such as E-mail, computer conferencing, or even spreadsheets. It's not hard to understand why videoconferencing is the favored virtual technology of upper management. Someone else, a technician, interfaces to the technology while the executives get to look each other in the eye. And there's no need to type. But videoconferencing has its limitations and its dangers; we'll look at some of those in Chapter 9.

Recently, a few clever training companies have begun addressing this cultural phenomenon. They appear at an executive's office, or home in a van identified as being from someplace like "Alpha-Omega Mangement Fitness Center," or, "Global Management Strategies Group," Then they spirit executives off to what are really plain-brown-wrapper applications training centers, where executives can, in privacy, be tutored in such trying exercises as using spreadsheets, sending mail across the Internet, and computer conferencing. They learn in a protected environment, away from those who might laugh at them, who (they believe) think they're off getting to know the leadership jungle survival techniques or the innards of NAFTA or GATT.

Another "real" reason why executives eschew technologies that, among other things, can significantly reduce travel, is that executives like to travel. They aren't the typical road warriors, hauling their sample cases, their documents, and their laptops from airport to airport; executives travel to nice resorts to meet with colleagues and discuss business at a strategic level. They don't need to spend their evenings calling up forms, collating documents, searching for the hotel's printer, or trying to get their modems to work. Travel is fun, why reduce it?

Change is on the horizon, however. In a very visible virtual alliance between Lotus Developments Corporation, Novell, and AT&T the CEOs are electronically linked through a videoconferencing infrastructure (of course) that keeps them continually in touch. These execs still travel, but they have recognized the importance of an instantly available virtual connection to bring them together as issues in their developing alliance arise. In other circumstances executives are discovering ways in which technology -- again, primarily visual technologies -- can help them keep track of what is going on in their increasingly complex virtual enterprises. One concept is the "situation room, "or "war room," model. Here, each participating partner, or site, has a room set aside that provides electronic windows into the enterprise and the products. An executive can sit in this virtual admiral's bridge, see computerized models of what's going on in the entire complex enterprise system, and simultaneously videoconference with counterparts in similar rooms across the world.[3] At this point we could ask the "So what?" question. Or as a mentor of ours used to ask after hearing some piece of interesting information "And? What are you going to do about it?" In this case, how do we help executives change their mental models about technology? At the application level there is the kind of surreptitious training we mentioned earlier, but the best appoach to systemic executive mind change is through visioning exercises involving peers at various points on the technology advocate spectrum. In visioning the virtual future the role of technology becomes quite clear, and with the supportive experiences of the veterans, understanding the value of investing in and utilizing technology naturally emerges; slowly, but eventually.

We can see the results of a proactive executive stance on virtual technologies in the performance of the Network Products Group (NPG) of the Digital Equipment Corporation. The General Manager of the group is Dr. Laurence Walker, a Vice President at Digital and by training, intuition, and experience a strong supporter of virtual operations. NPG designs, manufactures, distributes, sells, and supports a large portfolio of networking equipment. Indeed, the group has seen the emergence of the virtual operations phenomenon from the investment patterns of their own customers.

NPG has worldwide distributed resources. Many organizations, disciplines, and nationalities are represented on their collaborative teams. The group has implemented many of the virtual operations discussed throughout this book. What's of particular interest here is how the group, with the full support (and instigation) of the general manager, uses technologies to make a virtue of their geographically dispersed and culturally diverse enterprise.

For Walker, the virtual paradigm has arrived. Going virtual is not an option, it is a necessity. The epiphany came early to this group because their line of business is selling information support and communications (read "virtual") technologies. The cobbler's children don't always have shoes, and many businesses don't practice what they sell, but Walker's group is an exception.

For example, one ongoing program is dedicated to microcoding the networking chips that the organization designs and manufactures. Dr. Walker tells it this way

[3]We are beginning to see examples of such situation rooms, both virtual and physical. They range in scope from distributed, networked visual active modelling systems used to coordinate major product development efforts, to Tom Van Sant's Earth Situation Room™, Phase Four of the well-known Geosphere™ project, where the span of interest is the Cosmos.

> Our chip design and manufacturing unit is outstanding -- a best in world competency. Likewise our microcoding team. What could be a problem is that the design team is in Israel, and the coding folks are here in Massachusetts. I say 'could be a problem' because it isn't, thanks to how we've designed our work and the technologies that support it. There's really only one team, all on the same network. Everyone has full data connectivity, and they conduct their work as if they were all in one building. Better, in fact. Here's an example. Code writers at our plant here spend a day writing code. At the end of the workday they ship the code over the network to the designers in Israel, where it's about seven hours later. The designers spend their next workday testing the new codes, and they get the results back here just as our next workday starts. I'd say that's pretty good time management![4]

NPG lives by the wire, due in no small part to the reengineering of the organization that Walker led when he became manager. The reengineering established virtual principles for the group and they took up the challenge immediately. Dr. Walker continues:

> We invented a new type of sales agent and labeled them "Network Warriors." Their job was to team with our product resellers in their areas and provide them with the information they needed to sell solutions and support their customers. This would mean working electronically, both in communicating and providing access to information. You might ask how we got them to change from pad and pencil salespeople? Simple. We took away their pencils. Ok, it was a symbolic act but it got the message across that the old ways were gone...including pencil hugging.

Executives need to develop sound, high level competencies in virtual technologies if they are to lead their organizations' transitions to virtual operations. Aspects of these competencies include

• Belief in and commitment to the reengineering and development of work processes using information and communications technologies. This commitment should be reflected in the organization's vision, specifications for prototype virtual projects, goaling of managers, and their own management and work practices.

• Understanding how these technologies sustain virtual teaming, communications, and learning. This does not mean becoming technology specialists, but managers should understand the information

[4]Conversation with the authors, Littleton, MA, Winter 1994

architecture, and the degree to which this architecture delivers connectivity, interoperability, flexibility, and manageability essential for virtual operations. In addition, executive management should insist that every request for investment, change, or other modification address the impact the change will have on networking and information processing capabilities.

• Experiential skill in using the technologies in their day to day work. Executives are part of the virtual operations scene and their interactions with the operating groups should be designed into the system. The communications design, for example, can define processes and activities that enable executives to tap into the information flow, keep themselves informed, receive signals that indicate proactive intervention opportunities, and otherwise keep up with the work flow.

While building their own competencies, executives should lead the development of the virtual technology infrastructure. First, they should ensure that the organizational vision they articulate highlights the role that information technology will play in future operations. Since most organizations are already awash in technology, the emphasis should be on how this new commitment will change the status quo and enhance the ability to meet the demands and opportunities of the virtual environment. For example, an effective vision statement could set the following goal:

"In the future this company will form and sustain our relationships with partners and customers by linking our information infrastructure with theirs in ways that will protect proprietary interests, yet support collaborative efforts to meet business objectives."

Simultaneously they should work to overcome their own resistance and become believers. Executives, perhaps because most of them have been responsible for the decisions that created the current work culture, are often very protective of the status quo. But few could have predicted the massive changes in today's environment:

• Trends toward global business

• Breakthroughs in technologies that have empowered users to be able to work physically independent of organization based facilities

• Changes in personal lifestyles that make non-traditional work processes more acceptable

• Sophisticated and demanding customers

• Pressures of increasing complexity and decreasing time

• Capabilities to access and use widely distributed competencies effectively.

At any rate, they continue to hug the trees of past decisions out of conviction, inertia, or ego. To free the grip of the past, they should give themselves blanket amnesty; consider all past decisions to have been right for their time, given the situation and level of knowledge. Now that the situation has changed, executives should use their wisdom to seize new opportunities and to reap the benefits of all those past investments in technology. As someone once said, "every great change requires a funeral"; executives are good choices for delivering the eulogy and articulating the future.

Many of these reflections on executives and technology hold for other players in the virtual community as well. Keeping that in mind, we'll turn next to a discussion of the technology attitudes of virtual teaming stakeholders.

Stakeholders

Greg Oslan is convinced that he cannot succeed in his new business without a committed group of well informed stakeholders. One of the most difficult aspects of his job is to communicate with stakeholders to track their commitments and prevent problems from turning into crises. Impossible situation? Not at all, it just consumes a huge amount of time and energy; items in short supply given the size and complexity of the project.

Stakeholders make virtual operations run. They are the folks in the involved organizations that can make resource, scheduling, and financial commitments:

• "Yes you can have these individuals as part of your team, full time for two months."

• "The plan calls for manufacturing of these sub-assemblies starting in June. The facilities will be available at that time."

• "We're in for $4.2M; we'll track this real-time"

• "Our department will develop a training program to get all team members familiar with the FirstClass Conferencing and E-Mail system by the first of next month. We will deliver training online."

In most industries, individuals who are in stakeholder positions are already engaged pretty heavily in technology. They are the primary information consumers in the value chain and often champion new investments that will make it easier for them to access and add value to information.

Generally this is good, but there is a downside -- information overload. In one virtually operating company we recently visited, stakeholders had, out of desperation, appointed staff to filter the information that came to them electronically. One VP of manufacturing had his secretary read his electronic mail and "highlight the important stuff." Another stakeholder deleted, un-read, everything except messages from a very short list of colleagues. Both informed us that they often received over one hundred E-mail messages a day in addition to fax and phone communications. Reading them all was unlikely; responding impossible.

Stakeholders need to take the lead in making technology work for them. They need to learn how to specify what their operational needs are so that technology specialists can design effective solutions. Stakeholders cannot let themselves get into information overload, so this means that they have to take an active role in the design phase of virtual operations. The design phase is the opportunity to establish communication protocols that ensure that the information that reaches them is what they need not what someone else thinks they need.

Leaders

While executives and stakeholders work with information, virtual project leaders work in the information stream. One of the highest priorities for the leader of a virtual project is to help executives, managers, and workers understand the potential and value of technologies to the project: networks, communications, workflow, design, and management technologies all support essential virtual processes and must be considered in the project design.

Leaders need a number of skills, they must

• Understand the relationship between the use of information and the enabling technology. This includes obvious areas such as data processing and information networking, but it also includes technology intensive activities such as computer aided work process simulation; audio-, video- and computer conferencing; distance learning; and other techniques and applications that are now available.

• Become expert in technologies and techniques that are central to establishing and maintaining the flow of information during virtual operations: E-mail, electronic conferencing, accessing private and public database networks, for example. This expertise helps them design operations, gauge the performance of teams and workers during virtual operations, make the case for additional technology and training investments, and lead by example.

• Know how and when to replace traditional work processes with virtual ones. Technologists will provide the detailed designs, but leaders should visualize electronic rather than manual processes. These skills can come from experience, supplemented through directed exercises and simulations.

• Know how to calculate the value of electronic support systems and to identify and validate metrics that are meaningful to management, technologists, and the workers who compile them.

• Recognize and encourage creativity and technological innovation. Virtual operations generate good ideas about possible applications of technology. Leaders need to be constantly alert to these and be willing to experiment with ideas that appear to have merit.

• Be technology teachers, coaches, and motivators. They must insist that all players adapt to the protocols that are designed into the project. People under stress tend to return to older and more comfortable behaviors and practices, therefore the leaders must support continuous learning and be willing and assure its availability throughout the project, especially during fever-pitch rush periods.

Virtual Knowledge Workers

Knowledge workers are the center of this value creation process. In many ways the transition to virtual operations is most difficult for this group. Very often technology provides their only link into a virtual team or operation. Increasingly, their competencies are so dependent on technology as to make it impossible to separate the individual from the support system. Today, engineers are as good as their ability to manipulate their workstations and the various applications that they use. They cannot work at all, without some level of expertise in virtual technologies. At a fundamental level these workers need to

• Know how to use basic virtual technologies

• Have access to the networking technologies that link virtual teams.

• Believe in, understand, and observe the communications protocols that will structure their operating environment

- Visualize themselves in the virtual community: The network becomes the workplace, and communications and learning are as much a part of work as design and production are.

- Know that their inputs regarding the information infrastructure will be valued. In fact, the best ideas will be generated by the people closest to the action. Where communications are electronic, leadership should make the worker's insights and suggestions visible to the whole virtual community.

Final Comments

The virtual operations successes we have witnessed all demonstrated a commitment to using technology to hold the team together and to further the work at hand. However, the leaders of these efforts recognized that technology was not a silver bullet, not a total replacement for face-to-face work. They used direct personal contact between participating team members whenever necessary, although the day-to-day business became increasingly electronic. When they concluded their post project evaluations they reported how completely they had integrated their technologies into their work activities.

In all but a few cases, this technology/process integration was not accidental, it was designed. Perhaps not all up front, but at least along the way. Managers intuitively knew that communications were too important and complex to leave to chance. They worked at managing the risks associated with the introduction of new tools and ideas, making sure that they and their teams received the training they needed. Throughout the project they found ways to build confidence in the use of electronic support systems and reward creativity. And they learned a valuable lesson from the guru: there is no secret to virtual operations, there's just learning.

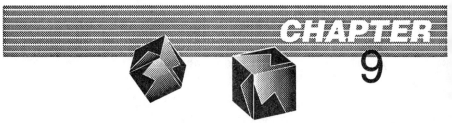

CHAPTER 9

VIRTUAL TECHNOLOGIES: NETWORKS AND COMMUNICATIONS

For me personally, messaging is my most important application. Over the last month I looked at how much time I spend in spreadsheets, in word processors versus electronic mail, and I found that I spend over five times as much time in electronic mail as in anything else. It's probably the most mission-critical application for Microsoft in terms of running its company. If we had to pick one application that would keep running no matter what, that would absolutely be it.

Bill Gates [1]

Throughout this book we have referred to certain technologies as being of particular relevance to virtual operations: we've even called them "virtual technologies." The technologies are available today; they're not even particularly new. In the next two chapters we'll take a look at those technologies from the perspective of how they contribute to and support virtual operations.

Most of the technologies we'll look at can be thought of as communications technologies -- "groupware" has been the term most often used to describe them. Since these technologies are so important in guiding the design of virtual operations and then supporting those operations, we'll first discuss them, then offer some scenarios that illustrate their use in virtual situations.

[1]Bill Gates, Keynote Address to the Electronic Mail Association, Anaheim, CA., April 19, 1994.

In this chapter we'll specifically discuss

• Public and private networks/information systems
• Interpersonal Communications:
  - E-mail
  - Audioconferencing
  - Computer Conferencing
  - Videoconferencing

Again, we emphasize that this part of *Going Virtual* is not about the intricacies of technologies, how they work, or which is best. We focus instead on their generic capabilities in supporting virtual operations.

Networks: Public and Private

Not too many years ago networks and information systems were considered to be separate infrastructures, fiefdoms of the IS or telcom managers, respectively. Little exchange of information passed between these camps and the clamor, of users for integrated systems generally fell on deaf ears. Networks were relegated to transport, whereas IS systems did the industrial strength computer work. Today, as computers are used more and more as communication rather than computing devices, information systems are increasingly dominated by major telcom vendors as opposed to the old guard computer crowd. The deals are being done with AT&T, with MCI, with Sprint, and with counterparts around the world. We see Lotus teaming with AT&T and Novell to deliver groupware services. We see E-mail coming from every communications vendor including the US Mail. The Digitals, IBMs, and Apples now find themselves pushed into the low margin hardware niches, while the telcoms are reaping profits on high margin global services. Networks, indeed, have become the byword for work, education, entertainment, shopping, law enforcement, health, even government. On a sunny afternoon in Los Angeles you're lucky to find anyone who isn't "into networking."

Ulf Fagerquist, a consultant at AT&T Global Information Solutions is not in the least surprised at the blossoming of the network age. He sees the evolution to global networks as a manifest destiny for the information age. "In the 1970s computer companies built proprietary information systems for local markets and unique buyers; complexity was fairly low," observes Fagerquist. "The '80s saw them expand into wider areas and markets. Open Systems, standards and interconnect between proprietary systems became the watchwords. In the early 1990s the communications companies lead the integration of computers and communications...and, as computer giants struggle, the communications providers are emerging as the new information/knowledge industry. Now forward thinking virtual organizations -- like the World Design Forum (see Chapter 18) -- are exploring the next step, and the step beyond: the Global Scale. The entire world is the only real market, not the limited segments defined by today's information systems providers."[2]

Obviously, networks have particular relevance to virtual operations: networks are about communications and communications makes virtual operations succeed. Although networks abound and are growing exponentially, the most visible network today is Internet. Every few days a new book sets out to explain it as our Information Highway. Let it suffice to say that the Internet has become the public network that interconnects virtually (no pun) the whole world of people and information. It is a network of networks, bringing to the desktop a variety of information access, navigation, and communications facilities.

The value of Internet to virtual operations is as a transparent connecting link for people who need to communicate electronically around the world. This connectivity comes in many flavors: bulletin boards, E-mail, information locators, hypertext information access, and electronic publishing (that is, no paper; we don't dwell on desktop publishing in virtual operations because the longer paper can be avoided, the more virtual the process). Internet as an E-mail carrier supports most E-mail systems; nowadays business cards carry a person's Internet E-mail address, as well as phone and FAX numbers.

Many companies, large and small, are taking advantage of Internet facilities to bring themselves closer to their customers. They create "Pages" on the network's Worldwide Web facility, a system that allows users anywhere in the world to follow information "links" to learn more and more about some subject. The user needn't know where the information resides physically, although that's no secret. Graphical user interfaces like Mosaic and Netscape make the information quest an easy one, empowering a worldwide generation of infonauts. Digital, for example, has used the Internet to make available product information, software updates...even letting prospective customers test drive their powerful new Alpha workstations across the Internet, from the customers' home facilities.

While Internet does not directly support the world of virtual operations, it connects the thousands of public and private networks in which most organizations work. The essential service provided by these organizational networks hasn't changed with the advent of the virtual environment,

[2]Conversations with the authors, Rockland, MA., August 1995.

it's just that the environment now demands what networks offer virtual organizations: the connectivity and interoperability that enables communication, as well as sharing of information and knowledge, collaborative work, and real-time management.

This new central role for networks places new demands on their care and feeding. So the first order of discussion here is to look at the key attributes of networks in this new light -- as essentially a "virtual workplace" that is replacing the friendly confines of the gang at the office, the lab, or the shop floor.

Connectivity

The networking infrastructure must be able to provide users with access to the systems that gather, hold, and transport the information needed to do the work. Information must be available to the workers wherever they work, whenever they need it, and be in a form that will enable them to turn it to value.

Today, public and private network facilities can connect people anytime, anywhere, anyplace. For example, a recent Board of Directors meeting was convened by networking the directors using an audioconference bridge service over the public telephone network. One director participated using a cellular connection from a wilderness camp site, another joined using the telephone built into his airline seat, a third, recovering from a surgical procedure in a hospital room, was connected through the hospital switchboard, and two used a satellite link from a European hotel conference room.

This kind of exceptional event has become commonplace in virtual organization. Especially with the advent of wireless access to communications networks, the cornerstone of virtual operations is in place: ubiquitous connectivity.

Interoperability

Once connections are made, information must flow to all stakeholders to whom that information is relevant. Within a single network architecture, interoperability is generally assumed. However, virtual operations frequently link stakeholders who are connected to different networks or services. Standards are in place to provide interoperability guidance, but this is no guarantee that when a distributed team links up, a seamless information exchange will result. Today it is possible to integrate most existing network environments, but often this requires investments and technical competencies that may not be available within the organization. The options available to virtual organizations include: investing in integrated systems, integrating existing systems, or engaging in virtual relationships with integrated system providers who not only provide the networks, but information services (e.g. access to public and private databases, Internet), training, support and maintenance. This model is the basis for the AT&T/Lotus alliance that will offer AT&T Notes services, and is becoming a highly effective solution in terms of both cost and level of service. It is the telecommunications industry, not the computer industry that is taking the lead.

Flexibility

The virtual operations model is by definition dynamic. One of the most significant network/information system expense items is the cost of maintaining facilities that are no longer required, but are so entangled into the infrastructure that they cannot be terminated. A graphic example can be seen by lifting the raised floor panels in any computer center that has been in operation for a year or so. What you will find is a rat's nest of wires and cables that have been left in place as they were replaced by new cables needed to support the constantly changing requirements of users. Newer network architectures and technologies, such as LAN's, Client-Server Middleware, Routers, Hubs, Fiber Optic network switches, wireless interfaces, cellular networks, and microwave links provide the kind of flexibility options we have in mind. These options, and dozens of others, deliver the two most important elements of virtual networking: access where and when needed, and easy disconnect when the job is finished.

Manageability

In the virtual environment the information infrastructure MUST work; there are no fall backs. And there is no alternative to effective management. This places a new and critical requirement on network and information support. For this reason, network and information specialists must be part of the key stakeholder team and participate in the virtual operations design process. Where the information infrastructure is less effective or reliable than required, informed, pro-active technical specialists can suggest alternatives. Specialists can compute investment requirements and calculate the value received. They can lead the technology learning process, helping users become familiar and comfortable with the systems they will rely on in their work. Most important, a well managed infrastructure provides project and team leaders with information that enables them to anticipate and measure the interaction of their teams.

The process of defining the specifications for the network/information infrastructure helps build teamwork among the various constituencies. Hammering out the goals and solutions provides a common ground for discussion among workers, managers, technologists, and executives, all of whom take a different perspective on networks.

Interpersonal Communications

Now we'll look at the key "virtual" interpersonal communications applications, or facilities. Commonly gathered into the category of groupware, these communications capabilities have long supported distributed work and casual communication. Here we address these technologies and the protocols involved in using them from the single perspective of how they can be designed into value producing virtual operations.

E-mail

In virtual operations E-mail can provide teams and stakeholders with the links needed to overcome time and distance barriers. Most communications do not require real-time interactions; the fact that we survive telephone tag suggests that instant access isn't always required. The store and forward protocols used with E-mail complement real-time technologies such as the telephone and audio and videoconferencing. Many E-mail systems enable users to create and use formatted forms and distribution lists, further streamlining communications processes. Calling up an online trouble reporting form is a way of encouraging workers to communicate important information quickly. Using distribution lists automates the task of making sure that people who need certain information get it, and helps those who suffer from information overload.

But here, as with all technologies and applications, communications doesn't happen automatically: a protocol for usage should be agreed upon by your team. Without being overly controlled, agree to use E-mail for specific kinds of communication: announcement of meetings, casual remarks, changes in schedule. More importantly, design E-mail communications into your work. For example, have all version levels of documents be announced to an updated distribution list by E-mail. The documents themselves needn't be sent around, they can be accessed in shared information bases, or in computer conferences.

E-mail is particularly sensitive to overuse. Some managers receive dozens, even hundreds of messages a day, multi-page epistles that they simply do not have the time or interest to read. Too much information is no information at all.

Some guidelines for using E-mail in virtual operations follow:

- Keep messages short. One question, one answer. One request, one response. One announcement.
- Avoid multiple addressees unless it is absolutely necessary.
- Generally avoid FYIs. If there's no action involved most people won't have the time to read the message. For information, place the message in the appropriate computer conference.
- Don't agonize over spelling or sentence structure -- everyone knows you are busy and haven't proofed the message.
- Don't request a reply unless it is necessary.
- Set the norm for short, clear, direct, timely messages.
- Create forms for repeatedly used message types: meeting announcements, schedule changes, travel notices.
- Learn the capabilities of the system. Share your learning with the rest of your network.
- Explore and be creative; find new ways to simplify your work using E-mail. Again, share the learning.
- If you have a problem with the system, someone else will probably have that same problem. Let the support staff know.

Audioconferencing

Audioconferencing has been around nearly as long as the telephone has. But as a practical tool for virtual operations it is being rediscovered by managers who need to "meet" with their virtual teams in real time. The audioconference has obvious benefits: it works, it is extremely easy to use, extremely cost effective, and available worldwide. Audioconferencing comes in two flavors: do-it-yourself, or have someone do it for you.

The do-it-yourself variety involves using the bridging capabilities found in most private telephone switches. The in-house conference coordinator simply calls the conferees and, using commands based on telephone touch tone signals, adds the conferees to the conferences. At the end of the conference everyone simply hangs up and the conference is ended. This service is also available from the major public telecommunications carriers.

The second variety involves scheduling a conference through a conference call, or bridging service. These companies offer basic and enhanced services for a fee. These services help structure, monitor, record, and facilitate the conference.

The decision on which option to use should be based on the expectations one has for the conference. For routine, frequently repeated conferences, like weekly status meetings where conferees are known to each other, the do-it-yourself conference will be less costly and require less preparation. For conferences that are more complex, have conferees who may not know each other, where the setting and outcomes are more formal, a bridging service is often a prudent expense. The service providers are expert at creating an atmosphere that reduces some of the barriers to non-visual communication. They monitor technical quality and know how to restore service without interrupting the exchange of information. One consideration that argues in favor of service providers is that they can become virtual communications partners in the team, bringing the competencies to help design communications and to provide specialized training for the team.

Communications Development Corporation is a world class audioconferencing service provider. Patti Bisano, its president, has witnessed the maturing of audioconferencing from a simple alternative for face-to-face business meetings into a powerful, interactive information exchange medium that supports worldwide business operations. She is constantly surprised by the innovative uses which she and her customers design with this tried and true technology. Consider the following examples:

- Training

    -- introducing new, sophisticated medical procedures and drug therapies to practicing physicians -- at hospital cafeterias during lunch

    -- enabling widely distributed insurance professionals to learn of changes in the laws and regulations that affect their certifications

    -- delivery of special programs sponsored by professional associations to provide special support to their members.

-- teaching extracurricular foreign languages to Connecticut school children.

• Polling and opinion research

-- Pollsters in search of rapid results, convene audioconferences, augmented by special voting technologies that enable participants to signal their preferences using the keys on their telephones.

• Marketing and sales

-- Want to learn how a new product, pricing strategy, or support program is being received by your customers? Conduct a series of audioconference focus groups that minimize personal inconvenience to participants. Some companies use this technique within days of the introduction of a new product or advertising campaign. They find that making small incremental changes in response to early feedback is easier, more cost-effective and less traumatic than dealing with negative customer reactions after opinions have solidified over time.

• As a support system for virtual operations. (Remember the Guru's wisdom, "You should have e-mailed.")

--The design team for a new product is located at facilities spread throughout a city. Design has progressed to the prototype stage, and the manufacturing team is ready to begin. Manufacturing is located in another city, and does volume manufacturing off-shore. The project is on schedule, but the schedule is short. To make sure that the transition from design to manufacturing is smooth, the project leader schedules a daily audioconference with the design team and the prototype team. Once a week they include stakeholders from the volume producers. These meetings are focused on schedules and problem resolution. They effectively keep the teams "together apart."

-- A sales manager decides to automate the sales force. A pilot team is identified to help the manager determine what process reengineering, system design, and training will be required. Each morning the manager convenes an audioconference using a service provider. Each member of the distributed pilot team knows the conference access number and they can connect wherever they happen to be -- as often as possible these conferences are scheduled early in the morning before the salespeople leave home.

-- A leading producer of computer chips needs to improve the return on the huge investments it must make to maintain its leadership position. A study indicates that it is possible to identify a small sample of customers who consistently discover innovative ways to use older generation chips in established products and services, effectively creating new markets for chips that have been replaced in their original role. A senior manager launches a series of audioconference brainstorming sessions with the innovating designers to generate ideas and position the chip manufacturer as a contributing partner in the process. These sessions not only result in revenue generating ideas, but help build a stronger sense of teamwork between the chip manufacturer and its customers.

Consider the advantages of audioconferencing:

- Very low cost. Even when using service providers, cost averages $20 per hour per participating location.
- Ubiquitous connectivity. With today's wireless services, it's very hard to imagine someplace that can't be connected.
- With preparation, there are no limits to the material that can be communicated over the medium. If visuals are essential, FAX and express mail still keep the costs far below those of traditional face-to-face meetings.
- The technologies and processes are tried and true and there is a considerable knowledge base of experienced audioconferencing users and designers.

But there are barriers associated with audioconferencing. Audioconferencing, by its very nature, eliminates eye contact and body language. Many find this communication bandwidth too constraining. As an example, a prominent think-tank decided to open up the distribution of their research reports to its members. The first step was the publication of a monthly newsletter that highlighted studies completed during the month. To further reach out to subscribers, they decided to host a monthly series of audioconferences in which lead researchers would answer questions from the members concerning their work. For the first conference they contracted with a service provider to ensure that they had the best possible technical quality. They hired a media consultant familiar with the audio medium to facilitate the session and coach the experts.

The experts in this case were experienced researchers and had, until then, always presented their findings in face-to-face presentations to clients. Because they knew their material and had learned through experience how to "work the audience," they felt they didn't need any coaching and took none.

The conference started as the service provider conducted a role call to make sure the technology was functioning properly. The facilitator introduced the experts and opened the forum to questions. As a voice materialized from the speaker in the center of the conference table, the expert experienced severe mike fright. After some fancy footwork by a well prepared facilitator and the fortunate intervention of an executive who had dropped in to see how the experiment worked, the session was gracefully guided back on track. Prior to the next event, experts received a few tips on how to communicate when "you can't see the whites of their eyes."

Audioconferencing should be a scheduled, designed-in aspect of virtual operations. But it can't do everything. It is after all, synchronous: Everyone needs to be on the phone at the same time. In virtual situations people are usually scattered across the globe, and the impact of different time zones affects the inclusiveness of these meetings. We now turn to computer conferencing, an asynchronous medium that enables people to conduct extended written dialogue across the network, at their own time, place, and pace.

Computer Conferencing

Computer conferencing is one of the most effective virtual operations support tools. The term "conferencing," although accurate in describing one function of this technology, can be misleading. The facility is really a communications application that enables an online community to conduct a structured, ongoing dialog through the computer network. The conference itself is hosted on one or many machines in the network. Each user has access to the conference through the network or phone dial-up. Members of the community -- project teammates, teachers, students, doctors, whatever group is linked in an electronic network—communicates with the conference, not between individuals. And each person that is part of the conference can access it at any time to see what others have written into the dialog or to enter their own notes. While whole documents can be "posted" in computer conferences, notes usually involve a page or two of text and graphic illustrations: This is a conversational rather than a publishing medium.

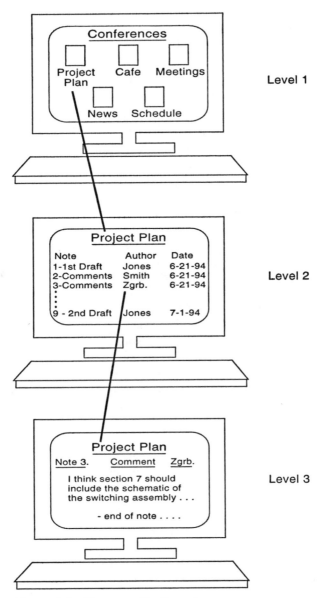

Figure 9.1   Computer Conferencing

There are several reasons why computer conferences and electronic bulletin boards are so popular and successful. Conferences

- Save time and travel
- Enable ad hoc participation by experts wherever in the world they happen to be
- Are easy to use
- Provide users with the time to reflect before responding
- Provide a record, or audit trail of dialog leading up to a decision.

Computer conferences run the gamut of complexity from simple bulletin boards to robust support systems for virtual processes. Indeed, computer conferencing can be instrumental in supporting all aspects of virtual operations: work processes, teaming, communications and learning. We'll look at some of these uses of computer conferencing now, beginning with the simplest form, the bulletin board.

Today electronic bulletin boards have proliferated, within both proprietary and public networks. Some are socially oriented, providing an electronic meeting place for groups with common interests. Members or curious guests simply dial up the number of a specific bulletin board or group of bulletin boards, or access them through the Internet or other networks, then join in the discussion. In these bulletin boards members share information about new restaurants, top TV shows, foreign travel. Some are in the public interest, such as bulletin boards where people can discuss town policies, or anonymously seek help for addictions.

Our interest is in the organizational uses of bulletin boards: Some, like those discussed, help support the social fabric of distributed teams. Others are more specifically used as part of the virtual work process: for example, an engineer in a virtual design team has a notion that a component technology he needs already exists, but he doesn't know where or in what form. The engineer can post a query in a bulletin board, asking if anyone knows of the existence of such a component. If the request is sensitive, he can request that the query be kept confidential within the project group or organization. If there is no harm in revealing the need for the component publicly, the query can be exported to other bulletin boards, even across the Internet. In any case, the technology has enabled him to ask the question to a wide community... he doesn't need to know who might have the answer. In all likelihood someone will come back with the information he needs. In reality, probably a dozen responses will be posted, followed by at least as many responses to the responses, debating the merits of each. It then becomes the engineer's task to decide which of the responses is best.

Computer conferences also are used for straightforward asynchronous communications support: electronic conferences. Instead of, or in addition to face-to-face meetings, dialog among a geographically distributed group can continue without interruption over some period of time -- addressing issues electronically, with each participant accessing the conference from wherever he or she happens to be. But conferences needn't go on forever. Some organizations have been very successful in opening a computer conference for, say, a two week period before an important face-to-face meeting, then a two week period after the meeting. During the first conferencing period agendas, expectations, attendees lists, and pre-work are finalized. After the meeting the conference is used for clarification, re-capping of action items, minutes of the meeting, and any other post-meeting information that usually drops between the cracks.

The most important difference between a bulletin board and a computer conference is that a conference is led, or moderated, by a person skilled both in the technology and subject matter of the conference. This moderator helps transform what would normally be considered information, into group knowledge. This is accomplished by taking the following steps:

- Setting up conferences, with input from participants, in categories that make sense for the work at hand. Categorizing is an essential step in building collaborative knowledge; the common set of categories built are a manifestation of the team's "converged culture."
- Structuring the dialog within conferences; setting up links between related entries using whatever technique is provided by the system: topics-replies, pointers, hypertext links.
- Facilitating the dialog, prompting with questions and ideas, weaving together threads of dialog. Introducing new conferencing members.
- Training to get participants started and keep them involved.
- Opening off-shoot conferences where desirable to pursue important side-issues.
- Administrating and managing conference attendance and access.
- Solving technology issues.
- Circuit riding if necessary.
- Closing conferences.

The moderator performs an extremely important function in virtual operations, being the person who skillfully guides teams through managing their dialog, while they bring their knowledge to bear on virtual work and learning situations. It is in these areas that the most sophisticated uses of computer conferencing are found. Conferencing can be used in support of such diverse activities as proposal generation, document revision control, and product design, as well as formal and informal learning activities. For illustration, we'll look more closely at proposal generation and document revision control.

Proposal Generation.

A virtual team representing several organizations spread worldwide collaborates to bid on a major systems integration proposal for a company that is equally dispersed geographically. A set of computer conferences is established on a proprietary network in which relationship building, information gathering, and proposal generation will be conducted or managed. Conferences are dedicated to

- The schedule, expected slips, and changes
- Who in the proposal team is seeing whom in the client company and when
- Each section of the proposal, for integration into the final proposal
- Management issues
- Training and support for conferencing users.

The fact that the proposal team is constantly adding and changing members does not affect the work: new members read the conferences and quickly come up to speed. Key people in the client organization are invited into certain of the proposal conferences, to give real-time feedback on the proposal team's perception of the problem and on the appropriateness of their solution. This moves the proposal out of the confrontational, serial, "here's our best shot" mode to a more effective, proposer-client collaborative effort.

Document Revision Control.

In large-scale, systems development projects a major time consumer and cost-adder is "engineering change orders." We know that changing a small piece of a large, complex system can have serious impact in unexpected places. In recent years the icon for this phenomenon has been the "butterfly effect." The theory goes that the global weather system is so complex, with so many interrelationships, that the simple act of a butterfly moving its wings somewhere in China can affect next year's weather in Mexico. The same thing holds in the design of a computer or an automobile or a ball-point pen. Changes made with the best of intentions often have harmful results. Add a chip to improve performance and the heat level becomes unacceptable; move a gasoline tank for collision-safety reasons and the vehicle becomes unstable; use a better and cheaper ballpoint pen ink, but over time the ball corrodes.

While all impacts of a change cannot be predicted, it's good practice to identify all you can to minimize risk. All stakeholders affected by the potential change must join in the deliberation and approval process. The situation most often looks like this:

- The need for the change is urgent, driven by marketing or technical considerations (usually overstated as "people won't buy it unless....", or,"it won't work right unless....").
- The project is already late, so time is short.
- The implications of the change are not fully apparent.
- The stakeholders whose inputs are essential to the change process are spread all over the world: A face-to-face meeting is impossible.

The ad hoc, makeshift solution -- or even the standard change order process --involves extensive air travel, FAXing, phone calls, E-mail, and partially attended meetings that slowly and serially lead to a decision. More often than not, by the time a change is finally accepted something else in the system has come up to change the variables. Repeat the dreaded "loopback."

Alternatively, this process can be designed using computer conferencing (with E-mail) as the support system. As part of the project's work design, a change order process is set up based on computer conferences dedicated to

- Detecting the candidates for change
- Identifying affected components
- Deliberating on impacts
- Voting on the change.

Distribution lists and conference membership lists are set up ahead of time; automatic notification is given to all involved stakeholders at each stage of the process. A roster of specialists at universities, elsewhere in industry, in retirement, is maintained to get ad hoc expert opinions...either directly in the appropriate conference or by E-mail, then copied into the conference. Relatively quickly all sides of the issue are addressed. A full stakeholder constituency is assured, without travel and the associated costs. And, a full record of the change deliberations, the intent of the change, and perspectives on its effects are part of the record: for future reference, orientation of new project members, sharing with other parts of the organization, and post-project reviews.

Computer conferencing is also extremely valuable in support of organizational learning. As we'll see in Chapter 18, conferencing is ideal for many distance and "networked" learning situations. The proposal and change order processes described above are really unstructured learning environments. Instruction can be provided within their framework at any time: a professor of fluid dynamics is asked to share his knowledge with a team deliberating a change in a valve system; a financial expert in Hungary joins the deliberations on changes to the international credit policies of a leading energy corporation.

In the academic environment, conferencing is often used as an "electronic classroom." Here, the traditional interactive class session, reading and writing assignments, homework, and office hours are all conferencing-based and offered in the structured semester model. Indeed, entire "virtual universities" exist, such as America Online's "Electronic University Network (EUN)," BESTNET, and The World Design Forum. These organizations are virtual both in their organizational forms, involving a variety of learning sources, and in their delivery, using computer conferencing and other software media.

Videoconferencing

Let's recall a bit of history. The initial move to video as a conferencing medium involved building a studio at each conference location. Special lighting, sound systems and control rooms for the support technicians were part of the investment. A videoconference was a major and costly production event. With the first business downturn, video studios were right up there on the auction block with the corporate jet and the Caribbean sales meetings.

Now videoconferencing has come of age. What used to be a glamour event, reserved for the organizational "suits" has been democratized. There are several reasons for this new accessibility of the medium:

• The demand created first by distributed, then virtual organizations for more real-time, graphic connectivity

- New digital compression techniques deliver high quality, full motion images, yet require lower bandwidth
- New tariffs offered by public network providers, which provide convenient and cost effective digital connectivity worldwide
- Video on the desktop - the workstation or pc - brings the possibility of participation to everyone, everywhere.

Today's videoconferencing products are portable, easy to set up, and use dial-up digital lines easily available from telephone companies. Full production capabilities are no longer required: a geographically dispersed design and manufacturing team can convene a next-day videoconference by E-mail, use hand held video cameras to show a design defect in the way the new toaster pops bagels, share the image of the product design specs, and even revise them; all at their respective workstations, in real time.

For regularly scheduled conferences, rooms equipped with pcs, workstations, and large screen monitors provide economical platforms for larger numbers of people to conference electronically, face-to-face. The costs of videoconferencing is higher than other forms of conferencing, but video meetings are the best choice when

- "Presence" is necessary: executives need to "see the whites of their eyes" and pick up every nuance of body language
- Objects need to be viewed
- Motion, fit, color, or other visual perceptions are important.

And, of course, videoconferences save time and travel. Currently, using compressed video terminal equipment and dial-up lines, coast-to-coast video conferences cost about $50 per hour. The equipment is simple to use and is easily operated by the conferees themselves. There are peripherals that facilitate the use of printed pages, pictures of every kind, video input, and high resolution cameras for complex objects.

The downside of video is that the more formal meetings still need to be tightly produced, and the very visibility that participants value also can work against communication. Most of us are not natural TV personalities, and video is less forgiving than audio. Most videoconferences tend to feature talking heads -- and fixing on facial quirks can detract from listening. At your next face-to-face meeting take a look around the table and imagine how some of your colleagues would look if their postures, expressions, yawns, side conversations, and other mannerisms that tend to be overlooked in conventional interactions were featured on a 27 inch, living color monitor.

Videoconferencing is most effective when

• Participants know each other
• Presentations are well done and the dialog well structured
• The conference is focused on one or two issues
•Time is limited to about two hours.

Like computer conferencing, videoconferencing has been success-fully applied in all the key areas of virtual operations. We've already seen how the medium can be used in the "fixing defects" process. One team extended the use of the medium to accomplish a very important social task. Several team members were working out of their home countries on a six-months extended exchange program. On national holidays in their home countries, families were brought to the "design/build" videoconfer-ences and given the opportunity to see and talk with each. This virtual social event helped keep morale and commitment high, helping to keep a very stressful virtual effort on track.

Finally, videoconferencing has become a very powerful distance learning tool at all levels of education. Again, the investment in prepara-tion is essential: this is not a casual medium. But from a two hour mod-ule on "Investing in Brazil," to a semester long TV course in small engine repair, the medium has become a key learning channel. It behooves vir-tual organizations, as part of their learning design, to know what's out there and available to them as their needs arise.

Enhanced Audio/Video/Computer Conferencing

Both audio and videoconferencing can be enhanced by using a variety of supporting technologies and techniques. In most cases the enhancements are designed to provide the conferees with graphic aids or help in record-ing and preserving results. For example, faxing visual aids to individuals participating in an audioconference is a simple and effective way to add structure and help the meeting leader capture and hold the attention of the participants.

Uploading electronic documents and designs through the network is easily accomplished. Using an electronic white board, a device that captures and transmits whatever is written on one board to another at a distant location, is another increasingly popular way to link the confer-ees into a working team. Today we have software that enables us to link pcs so that each conferee sees the same presentation on his or her moni-tor, and everyone can be empowered to make specific changes to a draw-ing or document. Parallel discussion can be conducted on a companion audio channel. New information can be scanned into the meeting by anyone, through any medium, from any place.

Final Comments

As we write, great progress is being made in uniting electronic communication forms through multimedia technologies. As one observer put it, "If this drive to multimedia continues, soon we'll have everything we used to have in face-to-face meetings." But with a significant enhancement -- worldwide competencies can be synthesized through this medium to build value without needing to move people about. The network will be the workplace.

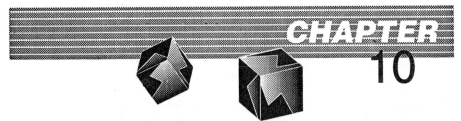

VIRTUAL TECHNOLOGIES: WORKFLOW, MODELING, DESIGN, MANAGEMENT

One theory about dreams is that they are the test programs, which we initiate during our sleep to test our responses.... our dreams are diagnostics that we create during sleep to make sure our processors stay sharp....Dreaming, then, is not like delirium, it is delirium. Dreaming is not a model *of a psychosis. It is a psychosis. It's just a healthy one.*
The Chemistry of Conscious States: How the Brain Changes Its Mind
J. Allan Hobson, M.D.[1]

Next we'll look briefly at a few of the more specialized virtual technologies. Each of these technologies relates to specific virtual work processes; the value added by using the technologies depends on how carefully those processes are designed and how well people are prepared to use them.

The technologies discussed here, when taken together, give a strong indication of where our focus is in virtual work. Since new virtual activities continuously emerge, we've focused on the core activities, the essentials of the virtual work model. To oversimplify, in virtual work competent, distributed contributors use electronic communications to build alliances, plan projects, design, deliver, and support products and services, and continuously develop their competencies and capabilities as a team. They do this work through networked applications that enable collaborative information work, design and redesign, and management.

---

[1]J. Allan Hobson, M.D., *The Chemistry of Conscious States: How the Brain Changes Its Mind* (New York: Little-Brown, 1994) p. 77.

There are other technologies that can be defined as virtual, for example, manufacturing tooling and production, facility management, and legal research. Virtual surgery, which we mentioned in Chapter 1 continues to evolve through technology, with the vision being the capability for 100% non-invasive surgery. But we feel that the few technologies we have chosen to focus on here, along with the dominant communications technologies, represent the 80% solution in virtual work.

Workflow

Workflow technologies have long been used to manage the flow of physical objects: manufacturing parts, supplies, document. Here we extend that definition to include, in fact to emphasize, managing electronic or information objects.

The notion of information objects is critical to understanding workflow, or any other virtual process. An information object is the electronic representation of a component, a product, a service package, or a document that is

• A precursor to a physical object, for instance, a CAD drawing of a wheel, representing an advanced state of the physical wheel itself; or an online report that will eventually be a printed report

• An object in itself, electronic, never to be rendered into a physical state: like an E-mail message, the contents of a computer conference, online magazine, or research database. Obviously, it should be the goal of virtual organizations to work through this kind of information object as much as possible.

Workflow moves information objects from station to station, person to person, through a network. This process can be as simple as electronically routing a travel reimbursement form through the required approval loop, to tracking where each component is at any given time in the manufacture of a space shuttle.

Behind the use of these technologies is a key belief in virtual work: Keep all output, including products and services, electronic for as long as possible in the life cycle. Electronic representations are more flexible, accessible, provide better multiple perspectives (rotating, transparent 3D drawings), and perhaps most important of all, increase validity and reduce overhead.

This last point needs some illumination. It has been our experience that bureaucracy springs up and errors occur at points in the value chain where information changes state: from voice to electronic, electronic to paper, from paper to plastic. We hear about the results of the "state-change-phenomenon" all the time: wrong account number charged, wrong fender painted, wrong kidney removed, wrong number dialed. Many organizations are now trying to achieve the same vision as the virtual surgeons: keep information electronic as long as possible - from brainstorming and research until the final part or paper emerges.

Workflow is commonly used as an automation technology that answers the questions, "How can we streamline the existing processes, which involve so much creating and moving about of paper?" A dramatic example of this occurred within the assembly plant of a major commercial aircraft manufacturer. Traditionally, with all the work done in-hangar, finding parts was a matter of a person riding around the stacks of parts on a bicycle, finally finding what was needed, decrementing the inventory list by one, and hauling the part back to where it was needed. As this company began partnering with other airframe manufacturers in risk sharing alliances, and throughput of products increased, this system was no longer viable. So they went to the next step. Inventory records were kept online, available for instant audit. Orders were placed through online forms. Instead of bicycle trips, electric carts made periodic deliveries from a central warehouse. Down the line the process was automated but not reengineered.

The same kind of automation is being done with document routing, such as travel approval and reimbursement. Instead of paper being physically sent from approval station to approval station, with the risk that someone in the chain is out-of-town, sick, or occupied with higher priorities, electronic forms are routed through the network. This too is automation, except that certain rules are coded into the system to automatically ship the document to an alternate if no one acts on it for, say, two days.

Both these responses to workflow issues are improvements rather than breakthroughs in that they automate existing processes instead of seeking to reengineer the processes to take fuller advantage of technology. Why continually order parts? Why not track the usage pattern and design a predictive process that enables just-in-time supply? In the case of the document routing, why move the document at all? Why not post in electronically in a special computer conference, where approvers can look in two or three times a day and handle the approvals. (The real question is, of course, why the need for all the approvals; or why travel. But those are cultural issues!)

Workflow is a kind of communication; knowing what the information value adding process is and tracking electronic information objects as they serially move from place to place. Or better, coordinating people's access to shared information objects in a work process. International consultancies use workflow technologies -- shared databases, conferencing systems, scheduling systems, document tracking systems -- to manage their extremely complex networks of people, engagements, knowledge, and technologies. Whatever the organizational mission, when designing the virtual work processes, workflow support should be considered.

Shared Modeling

Today there exists software that enables knowledgeable people to model, or simulate all kinds of complex systems: organizations, processes, and complex physical objects. We emphasize the role of people as modelers, because no software can build a model; the knowledge of the people must be built into the model by modeling experts, a new breed of specialists with technical, architectural, and process competencies, as well as extraordinary communications and people-skills.

Before a system is physically constructed, a model can be constructed electronically that will demonstrate, among other things

- How the parts of the system will interact
- The effects of various changes in the system (e.g., the butterfly effect)
- How the system appears from various stakeholder perspectives (remember, we see what we believe)
- What the system will weigh or cost, and so forth.

Models of existing systems help track the components, predict the need for maintenance, and link physical entity with a host of related objects: documentation, supplier history, and maintenance records. For example, a city transportation department would have an electronic model of every bus in its fleet, complete with pointers to associated design, maintenance, supplier history, and route history documents.

As an example of a complex, virtually developed system let us consider an offshore oil drilling rig. A virtual organization of designers, construction crews, geologists, oil company research divisions, drilling technologists, banks, and government regulatory groups all have a hand in this system. It's unlikely that a physical model of such complexity would be very helpful; however, an electronic model of the platform could include every part, every process, or method associated with building and integrating the part, every organization and its capabilities, every regulation, and so on. The model could be represented from a variety of perspectives: as a design, as a functioning engine for extracting oil, as a disturber of the environment, as a financial package, and so on. At any time, each stakeholder could examine the system from any perspective, gaining a better understanding of the expectations of other stakeholders, better appreciating trade-off situations and the impacts of change.

The virtual enterprise that builds or maintains the rig can be described within the same electronic model: people, processes, and technologies. With "active modeling," changes to organizations can be simulated to see the effects on the project or the structure. Cultural attributes can be modeled as well, showing where possible barriers of language, misfits in decision making processes, or situational mistrust may occur because of past experience. Competencies can be modeled as well, so that a needed competency can be found in *any* virtual partner, not just the ones that are expected to have that skill or knowledge.

As with Hobson's evaluation of dreaming, which introduced this chapter, models are not just representations of objects or processes, they are early versions of those entities. Modeling helps manage complexity and reduce risk. In virtual environments where there is so much that is unexpected, it pays to model as much of the situation, or the initiative as possible, so that the partners can at least know what they know and reduce the number of surprises. Finally, the processes of modeling is a team activity, in which perspectives are shared and new discoveries -- Ah Ha's -- are daily occurrences. In modeling sessions teamwork is built, learning and discovery thrive, and the quality of the final product is assured. Modeling is time well spent.

Shared Design

We all know about design tools: set up a form for E-mail, lay out the floor plan of your dream log cabin, use CAD tools to design an electrical circuit. These all are effective individual applications. Design tools that support virtual operations must be shared; they operate over the network as stakeholders collaboratively design a component, a process, a team. In effect, virtual design tools are combinations of a lot we've already been speaking about: networks, interpersonal communications, workflow, and modeling. Put these virtual capabilities together with software that supports shared screen graphics and participants anywhere in the network can draw and move lines, set angles, calculate geometries, establish relationships, and generate 3D models and animations—you have an excellent virtual design tool.

The key is to stop thinking of design as constrained to the products, prints, book covers or bridges. In the virtual environment every complex object, group, or process should be designed and redesigned as the inexorable impacts of change revise the environment. "Design everything, then do it again when things change," should be the motto: and it is in fact the motto of Part VI of this book. Don't expect packaged applications to design for you. Know what creative, structural, functional competencies you need to collaboratively design, know the capabilities of technologies, and maintain a dialog with your IS and telcom stakeholders to help fit the technologies to your design needs. Design is a whole team, not a "designer" effort.

Real-Time Management

We used to think it rather ominous that, over the past couple decades, one simple image has increasingly come to represent the richness of work, education, entertainment, commerce, government, finance, sport, publication, and management. That image is, of course, someone looking at a video terminal. We had a few laughs about this when, while working for a huge computer systems company with tens of thousands of products, we realized that marketing could do no better than advertise each application and each system with that same image: someone looking smilingly at a computer terminal.

The temptation to utter dark thoughts about life being reduced to "looking through windows" remains; many of us still won't give up the abacus and fire up the spreadsheet. But this gloom is tempered by the knowledge that this way of virtually engaging with almost everything has its advantages. We can do things never done before, we can reduce the consumption of physical resources, we can telecommute, we can......the list goes on. One of the greatest benefits of the "looking through windows" paradigm is that now we can manage huge and unwieldy virtual projects and examine extremely complex products, in real-time, by looking through windows.

These windows are produced through modeling and visualization software that graphically displays, even animates what could happen, what's probably going to happen, and what's happening now in a process, organization, or complex object. With the technologies mentioned in this and the previous chapters, as well as our knowledge of modeling and design, we are able to "instrument" virtual projects to provide management with the capability of seeing what is going on all the time. We've mentioned already that major organizations are using "situation rooms"(a semantic improvement on the "war room" label, which is somewhat out of step with the collaborative ethos of virtual work). In these rooms wall size displays, replicated at key stakeholder locations, visualize the current state of the model: what's happening in the organization, the processes, the resources, the finances. In keeping with the virtual pace, historical activities like monthly reporting or status meetings can be replaced by real-time interventions. Management sees what's going on NOW and can share and discuss that view with distant stakeholders-- on the spot, through the network -- to address and resolve issues; the lengthy reporting, contemplating and reacting (late) cycle is eliminated.

Executives can simulate the effects of changes to the models: "What happens to the Malaysian design competencies if we use the Irish designers for this first version of the widget? What are the probabilities of a six week delay in starting up the South American marketing efforts? If we get access to the cheaper composite, where would be the best place to set up fabrication? Suppose we have the butterfly move its wings twice?"

Yes these are windows, but windows that let us look into worlds which otherwise we could not perceive: worlds that are complex, in flux; worlds that exist as perspective, not facts; but worlds that must be understood and managed for virtual operations to succeed.

Final Comments

The point of all this has not been to make readers technology experts. Those who are experts probably find these accounts superficial. The point is that those of you who are involved with virtual organizations and virtual operations need to know that there is technology out there with tremendous potential; technology that can free you to redesign operations to succeed in the virtual environment. You need to take your ideas to your IS and telcom professionals; they are your technology stakeholders. If they don't have the expertise, vendors of these applications are more than willing to show you their stuff and provide case studies. Instead of a sales pitch, create a collaborative situation where your team presents scenarios for workflow, modeling, and design support. Learn together where the "fit" is that Greg Oslan spoke of. There may not be one, but then again these technologies may become an important part of you virtual technology repertoire.

TRANSITIONING TO VIRTUAL OPERATIONS

In Part I we took an insider's tour of an organization that had run head-on into the new realities of the world around it, and responded by beginning its transition to virtual operations. Throughout the tour we had the feeling that we were looking at a work-in-progress: that the transition had begun but was not and might never be over. Grammatically, "transition" might be considered "the perpetual present"; indeed the brass ring in virtual operations is to develop the capability for continuous transition, rather than attaining a steady state of operations.

In this section we'll describe a process that can help your organization begin the transition to virtual operations.

Our approach is not the only way to do it; but in our work with distributed and virtual organizations we've seen each element of the approach work well, although no organization we know has by design gone through the process from start to finish.

We'll start in Chapter 11 with the strategic, upper-level management activities that must be initiated to sanction and create a supportive environment for the transition. While the energy to initiate this transition can come from anywhere in the organization, the executive level must spearhead the efforts. The strategic phase culminates in management's charging a leader/champion/project manager with a specification for business goals to be achieved through a prototype project, designed for virtual operations. We strongly believe that changes of this magnitude -- transitioning from traditional to virtual operations -- occur primarily through experiential, not just logical learning. In this case a team learns how to design and conduct virtual operations by designing and conducting virtual operations.

In Chapter 12 we focus on tactical activities: how the leader/champion/project manager selects and designs specific processes to prototype.

Chapter 13 is a reality check, pointing out some of the barriers that may be encountered during the transition. No quick fixes are offered to counter the barriers here; the collaborative processes of virtual work themselves will create the positive environment that can dispel both hidden and open objections to the transition.

Chapter 14 is an interlude, an interactive inquiry to determine the organization's general readiness to transition to virtual operations. This dialog will help the leaders decide where first to invest in virtual operations to provide the most learning as well as having the highest probability of success.

Later in Part VI, we'll move on to a walk-through of the actual design work.

And now to strategy.

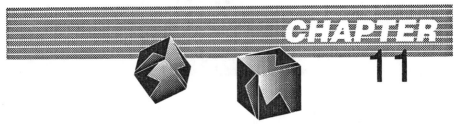

A STRATEGY FOR TRANSITIONING TO VIRTUAL OPERATIONS

Don't you just love it when a plan comes together?
Lt. Col. Hannibal Smith, *The A Team*[1]

Knowing that a problem exists is the first step to finding a solution, or at least an approach to a solution; but knowing the problem isn't enough, nor is just figuring out the solution. You need to do something, in this case, to transition from the current way your organization does business to increasing levels of virtual operations capability. Understanding the value and workings of the electronic information infrastructure, collaborative relationships with partners and suppliers, complementary competencies, and virtual reengineering all raise the probability of a transition happening. The actual implementation of these virtual capabilities requires action: high-level sanction, commitment, planning, prototyping, and scaling of prototype efforts throughout the organization.

The objective of this chapter is to outline a strategy that will help organizations design and conduct successful transitions to virtual operations; the underlying philosophy is that in virtual work, we learn best by doing. The strategy involves intense activity on several fronts, leading to the determination of a project/prototype candidate that will initiate the transition and to the nomination of a project manager to lead that first virtual effort.

---

[1] *The A Team*, NBC Television, starring George Peppard, throughout the 1980s.

High Level Strategic Activities

There are nine basic activities involved in creating the context for the transition to virtual operations. On the face of it these are sequential steps, but true to the realities of virtual work, they'll probably happen in parallel. Here they are:

1. **Engaging in the Virtual Situation** - Top management launches a formal and objective process to examine the organization's current situation and recognizes that their business exists in the virtual environment.

2. **Visioning** - Management collaboratively creates a vision of what the virtual future looks like and the role the organization will play in it. This vision is shared with the rest of the organization.

3. **Making the Decision to Go Virtual** - Executive management, in the context of moving from the current state of affairs toward the vision, decides upon and commits to transitioning to virtual operations.

4. **Building a Transition Constituency** - Management concentrates on getting the word out and building a consensus among the key influencers in the organization, including managers, technical gurus, human resources professionals, and key contributors.

5. **Engaging the Entire Organization** - Management develops and initiates a process to introduce the concept of virtual operations to the entire enterprise. This will involve dialog on the challenges and potential of the virtual opportunity, as well as basic training in the fundamental virtual processes: work tasks, teaming, communications, and learning.

6. **Building a Planning and Designing Ethos in the Organization** - By example, training, publicity, and on-site leadership, management raises the organization's awareness of the value of a planning and design approach to work.

7. **Sensing the Readiness of the Organization to Begin the Transition** - Key indicators of organizational readiness are examined by management to gauge the current state of the organization and guide the project specification and select the leader.

8. **Creating a Specification for a Virtual Operations Prototype Project** - Management selects two or three "pain points" in the organiza-

tion's performance that may be traceable to working in the virtual environment without the benefits of designed virtual operations. Then management develops a specification for a prototype project that would need to use virtual operations to produce something of value while meeting aggressive and "therapeutic" business goals. For example, if synchronizing the efforts of various departments was a habitual problem in a company, upper management might specify the development and delivery of a product or part that demanded order-of-magnitude improvements in distributed work processes. The project constituencies -- marketing, personnel, development, manufacturing, and support -- would need to collaborate in designing those processes.

9. Commissioning a Virtual Project Leader - Simultaneously, management identifies a project manager to lead a virtual team in the design of the new processes and propose prototyping that would meet the specification. The leader would lead the team through prototype project to deliver both the product specified and new knowledge about the design and performance of virtual operations.

Now for a closer look at each of these strategic transitioning activities.

1. Engaging in the virtual situation

Management must be willing to look at its existing work paradigm and determine if the organization's ability to create value is operative or seriously flawed: Will projected performance keep them in business? They must commit to an in-depth analysis of their environment, their markets, customer needs, and essential relationships. They need to look at their competition, then determine their own position in the race -- ahead, realistic contenders, or gasping for air at the beginning of Heartbreak Hill. If change is indicated, they need to begin understanding what those changes are.

A few years back, the US Navy did the unthinkable. Word from the top came down to every ship, every base, and every person that the complexity of worldwide naval operations had become overwhelming and there was a need to get a grip on what the Navy in its entirety was actually doing. The decision was made to briefly "stop the world and get off" for one day - to cease all operations for 24 hours, stand back, and take a hard look at the players, their equipment, and activities. Corporations have done this too: recall Greg Oslan's advice about not jumping into some new management technique until you've reflected on its fit to your situation; or the organizational practice of freezing hiring and job shifting for a couple weeks to better understand who's on board, where they are, and what value they're adding.

Jumping off the carousel for a moment isn't a bad idea for any organization, especially when what used to be occasional crises suddenly start to run together to megacrisis. Crises will not disappear, but organizations can build the capability to anticipate crises, not just react to them. Contingencies make up most of what is called knowledge work, and the performance of a knowledge-based organization is a function of how well that organization handles change. For example, the best travel agents are those who can handle itinerary changes; the best surgeons deal well with complications; the best managers constantly tune their work systems to handle external and internal disruptions. Anyone can do the "by the book" routine work; the ability to handle contingencies separates the knowledge workers from workers.[2]

But back to our point. When organizations take the time to reflect on their own situations in the context of the world situation, they may see that there is a virtual environment and they are players in it. But what's more important, they may realize that their performance is not what it should be and that they're playing without the tools and processes of virtual operations. They haven't adapted to the new environment, the new contingencies.

A case in point. Ray McCann is the Chief Executive Officer of Management Research Group, a New England consulting group. MRG helps the top executives of organizations identify the management and leadership attributes and behaviors needed to guide their organizations through the shoals of the chaotic business environment. The group has long perceived its core competency to be in developing leadership and management assessment instruments: to determine where an individual is on a spectrum of management and leadership skills, where they want to be, and where the company needs them to be. "Ours is a strategic process that looks at a company's human resource development. We help the development of those individuals, create criteria for succession planning, provide guidance for people to become better leaders, managers, and workers for the organization."

One day, after dropping in on a short presentation on virtual work, Ray asked, "What do you folks mean by 'virtual'? To me its just like what

---

[2]Harold Garfinkle and other posit the significance of "contingency" in their system of "ethnomethodology." There is nothing of interest happening as long as things go according to plan. Learning begins when contingencies come up. See Harold Garfinkel, *Studies in Ethnomethodology* (New York: Appleton-Century-Crofts, 1967). Also see Lucy A. Suchman, *Plans and Situated Actions: The problem of human machine communication* (Cambridge University Press, 1987).

we're trying to do here every day." As he listened to the response, a thumbnail description of the virtual environment and virtual operations, he suddenly, intuitively, recognized that MRG was a virtual organization. But they certainly weren't performing like one. MRG had the need, the intention, and the potential to succeed in the virtual environment, but something important was missing.

Ray began describing a successful but painful project that involved a virtual relationship with another organization located in Canada. Pressed for specifics on how well everyday work of the project went, what processes and technologies supported their communication and information intensive work, he began to see the project more and more through the lens of virtual operations. Ray next called in the project manager and asked if she could elaborate on that project's day to day activities. What followed was a litany of things that could have gone better:

- Planning was cursory and the team quickly came to expect the unexpected.
- Communications, largely phone and fax interactions were random and fell short of providing the support needed: they all knew they had to work electronically, but hadn't thought much about how to do it.
- Clarity of vision and process was lacking - a problem in any situation, deadly in a virtual one.

The virtual epiphany had happened. MRG was beyond doubt a virtual organization, engaged in the virtual environment. What they did not have, however, were the processes, competencies, and technologies to support virtual operations. Ray knew what the next step had to be for MRG: understanding how they could support their work with virtual processes.

The point here is that the first step to going virtual is not only to recognize, but to engage consciously in the virtual environment: to accept the situation and the challenges and begin taking the path to full enfranchisement as a capable virtual organization.

2. Visioning

Visioning is important for at least two reasons: first, a vision will create a shared image of the virtual future that the organization sees for itself. Second, the visioning process can help executives and managers change their mental models about the "raison d'etre" of the organization and the environment in which it operates. Shifting mental models to accept change is not easy: This is where egos hit the road, and where past decisions stand out and scream for defense. Visioning is a process that enables executives to confront and share their own beliefs about the world in a non-threatening venue. As its name implies, "visioning" involves "seeing," or "envisioning" in the fortune telling sense, as well as "visualizing" in the sense of visually perceiving imagery, not just reading words or adding up numbers.

For executives and managers in virtual environments, the ability to lead and contribute to the constant refinement of the organizational vision is a key competency. People who are moving very fast need a clear sense of where they are headed. They need a strong sense of destination, or at least direction, plus skill in piloting: adjusting course according to landmarks and environmental conditions.

Airplane pilots at one time navigated by dead reckoning. By looking over the rim of the cockpit at the ground and searching for prominent and familiar landmarks such as the outline of a city, the bend in a river, a water tower, or railroad tracks, they determined the route to their destination. They operated "situationally"; if there was a lot of fog in the valley they climbed and looked for a familiar mountain top. At all times they kept a destination in mind: home, a delivery, a new speed record to a far off place. That was their vision, or mission.

By raising the profile of visioning as value-adding activity and emphasizing managers' responsibilities in developing, maintaining, and disseminating the organization's vision an organization can build an effective visioning culture. Organizations can sponsor visioning sessions, facilitated by experts who use visual mapping techniques to enable executives to create and share meaningful imagery about their direction, hopes, feelings, and expectations. Such sessions help people break out of the rigid and structured left-brain dominated thought patterns they depend on daily to design and manage their work.

The vision itself should be cast in the virtual mode, supported by electronic media, by shared screens and audio, computer, and videoconferencing.

It should provide more than a single lens focus on the organization, bringing in the perspectives of the stakeholder community.

As a sense of the vision develops, the next challenge is deciding on the form of "declaration." Some visions are stated as clear and clever mottos: "NUMEX - Calculators you can count on"; or cryptic ones: "SYSCO - The Leading Source." Some visions are more lengthy and introspective, like the virtual vision implied in this excerpt from an annual report:

"The word partnership has many meanings, but common to all
is this: a partnership is the sharing of the responsibilities and
rewards of a relationship. At Detroit Edison, we believe both
our business and the prosperity and growth of communities we
serve depend on the give and take that distinguish successful
partnerships. We have developed partnerships with our customers, communities, suppliers, shareholders, governments
and regulators, employees and the environment we all share.
Such partnerships lead not only to sharing responsibilities
and rewards, but to mutual understanding -- a cornerstone for
success."[3]

This report then goes on to describe the mutual benefits of and specific initiatives in each partnership area.

Structured visioning provides an excellent setting for collaborative
learning about the organization itself. Consider this real visioning experience at a very profitable division of a computer chip manufacturer;
we'll call the company ARTX, Inc. Executives and managers of ARTX's
Onboard Chip Division were struggling with improving the performance
of their work systems.The overall problem seemed to be that there was
no clarity to their overall work flow and the strategy behind it. Before
leaping into reengineering, the group participated in a visioning exercise
to clarify their purpose.

They used various right-brain visualization techniques, ranging
from wall charts with lines and arrows, to stick-on figures on a cartoon-
like map of the organization and the environment. These figures and
other symbols represented constituencies, barriers, resources, expectations and goals; lines representing relationships connected the symbols.

One element of the process involved gathering input from various
stakeholders on their personal visions for the organization three years in
the future. The results were tremendously helpful to the group in giving
multiple dimensions to the statement of its future direction.

For example, one category of expectations dealt with the division's
performance. The following is a list of the organizational behavior that
the various stakeholder groups each thought OCD should exhibit in the
visualized future state:

• Sales and Marketing: "Sustains real-time communications.
Delivers on time, with flexible production. The Division deals
quickly to resolve shortages of product."

[3]*Detroit Edison Annual Report for 1994.*

- Factories: "Assures up to date information and communications between design, build, marketing, and sales teams. Fast decision making."
- Customers: "Reduces time-to-product. Is responsive to issues and requests."
- Competitors: [OCD will probably] reduce cycle time - "time-to-money"
- Upper Management: Reduces cycle time - "time-to-money"

Interestingly, the only stakeholders who did not mention speed at all were the employees, who had another perspective on organizational goodness:

- Employees: "OCD helps us develop long-term goals for our jobs. Pays attention to employees' advancement, rewards, and security."

This too was valuable input; it was clear that promises of shorter cycle times were not motivators to the workforce. Employees were certainly as much a part of OCD's knowledge community as any other constituency and their interests needed to be represented in the vision.

3. Making the decision to go virtual

It's a pretty good bet that most organizational leaders, after they've gone through the visioning process and seen the vision from multiple perspectives, will know whether or not the virtual operations model has the potential of addressing their needs. We say potential, because the relationships between organizational purpose, culture, customers, environment, and operations is so complex that you can't really predict success. The exercise itself will have built a core group of influencers, a critical mass whose beliefs will support each other and very visibly represent the vision across the organization. So, if based on the evidence at hand, plus intuition, plus what the experts are saying, virtual operations look right, then a formal decision, backed by the sanction of the highest levels of management, should be articulated and spread through the organization.

But just as technology is not enough in virtual operations, words are not enough in announcing a decision to "Go Virtual." There's a discipline in linguistics and sociology called Speech Act Theory. The concept is that speech is more than just words, empty puffs of air; that in certain cases speech constitutes action. For example, "I now pronounce you Husband and Wife"; or, at the other spectrum of anticipated harmony "We declare war!"[4]   But usually, especially in organizations, not only isn't speech an action, but it doesn't precipitate any action. Not only do our organizations operate more through influence than command, but too often people don't really understand what a declaration means or how to go about acting on it. "We will delight our customers." "You are empowered." "We build systems." Noble thoughts all, but they don't give people a lot to act on.

The decision to adopt virtual operations must be supported by visible demonstrations of what is meant by the statement, by training, and by gradually bringing the workforce into this new work medium. One excellent way to simultaneously develop a collaborative understanding of virtual operations and test the hypothesis of virtual operations for the organization is by trying out a limited set of virtual operations in a real, yet low-risk project environment: a prototype virtual project. And this will be our approach. But first the emerging champions of virtual work need to build the constituencies that will lead and support the overall transition effort.

4. Building a transition constituency

Multiple constituencies are involved in the transition to virtual operations. The first level is the executive team that originally reflected on the state of the organization, sanctioned the visioning exercises, and made the decision to go virtual. The second group includes the stakeholders who control the assets and resources needed to design and complete prototype work projects. This includes all levels within the organization and extends to the partners, suppliers, and other contributors to the value chain. It includes customers who, because of the nature of virtual operations and the capabilities associated with the electronic exchange of information, can now play an active role in various processes. In some cases constituencies include individuals and groups who have influence within the market such as the press, consultants, and other recognized gurus.

These groups will not only need to be convinced of the viability of virtual operations, but convince others in the workforce, the third constituency, to radically change the way they work. Changing work habits will not be easy: Workers identify personally with their work processes. The stakeholder constituents must be wholly in the fold when the transition begins if they are expected to take others through the hurdles of change.

[4]Speech acts are linguistic statements that communicate intention, like commands, questions, apologies and so forth. Some understanding of speech act theory is useful in understanding human dialog/multilog. "Producing" a speech act, like, "You're fired!" is considered a basic unit of communication. For an introduction to this large and complex field of linguistic inquiry see J.L. Austin, *How To Do Things with Words* (Oxford, 1962)

In most cases active commitment should be sought across all constituencies. Here are a few questions to ask to begin the work of identifying the core constituency:

• What groups need to get started first?
• Are there leaders within the groups that can be singled out
  for special attention?
• What is the preferred channel for reaching these groups?
• Who are the opinion leaders that can influence others?
• Who should be the messengers?

Once communication about the virtual transition has begun, the
process of engaging the rest of the organization can begin.

5. Engaging the entire organization

Next, a persuasive case for virtual operations should be developed and
communicated to the organization as a whole. This message will serve
two purposes. First, it will be the rational, compelling logic that justifies
the need to change in terms that are relevant to everyone affected. Second, the message will provide a basis for executives to continuously examine their own convictions. If a persuasive case cannot be made for the
transition, in general or in some specific aspect, something is seriously
wrong and the audience is not likely to be convinced; with good reason --
the transition won't work.

To be persuasive the argument for virtual operations should be

• Logically related to the vision
• Understandable and expressed in language that each con-
  stituency of the organization understands
• Clear in the effect it will have on the organization
• Unambiguous in its demands
• Definite about benefits and incentives.

You can test the argument by asking the following questions:

• Has success clearly been identified?
• Are training or tools required, and is it clear how they will be
  provided?
• Are there metrics in place?
• Are the most appropriate delivery mechanisms being used:
  Face-to-face meetings, newsletters, video broadcasts, training?
• Is there a way to measure the effectiveness of the message?
• Is there a non-threatening feedback mechanism?

As the organization becomes engaged in the virtual opportunity, enough people will be energized to make it possible to go on to planing the transition.

6. Building a planning and designing ethos in the organization

While most of this book addresses virtual operations design, the planning process is equally important in conducting virtual operations. For simplicity, we define "design" as the collaborative activity in which key processes are conceptualized, structured, and supported. "Planning," again a collaborative process, relates more to articulating macro-level scheduling, resource allocation, and business development intentions.

Most of the individuals we talked to as we researched this book accept planning as an essential part of their job. But we were surprised by what we see as a disconnect between the various planning activities and the operations they enable. That is, plans are often centrally developed and thrown over the wall to operational groups, who, not having a context for understanding the logic of the plans, often ignore them. To be useful -- used -- plans must be developed collaboratively by all stakeholders in the project, especially the designers of the virtual operations. Furthermore, plans are living, not closed guidelines. They should be followed where appropriate and openly revised when the situation calls for something different: when a contingency appears.

In some high tech organizations, planning is often the work of just one individual, even for expensive, complex, long-term projects. For example, a lead engineer who understands the technology will plan the development of a new product. This proposal, drawn entirely from the engineering perspective then becomes the basis for budgeting, documentation, marketing, manufacturing, logistics, and everything else associated with the life-cycle of the product. Because other constituencies are not included in the planning activity, conflicts are buried throughout the plan. Either these land mines are unearthed at review time, causing consternation, cost and loss of time in loopbacks, or they simply explode at some untimely moment during the project. Exclusionary planning inevitably leads to crisis management in virtual operations.

There are good reasons why planning has a bad name. We can all identify with the following truisms about traditional planning:

- Executives, managers, and workers spend an inordinate amount of their time planning, occasionally there's more time spent planning than there is in doing the work that's planned.
- Plans are weapons of delay. No one does anything until the plan's complete; plan revision stops all work.

- Most meetings are consumed with planning.
- Plans are ignored after work begins.
- The more formal, or top-down the planning process is, the less likely it is that the plan will make sense or be followed.
- It is extremely difficult to change plans that have been approved by senior management.
- Some of the most creative efforts in projects involve shaping results to look like the plan.

On the positive side consider the following points:

- In most organizations there are people who have the skills, experience, and knowledge to plan the best, fastest, and most cost effective way to get work done. Fortunately, they are often the same people who have signed on to do the work.
- When the right people come together, it doesn't take long to make a plan.
- Given the right conditions, it's possible to plan for the majority of changes and contingencies.
- If plans are flexible and publicized, they will be followed.

In the context of virtual operations, planning and design are ongoing, flexible processes that constantly readjust the projects to the changing realities of the situation. While everyone likes stable rules and objectives, with the current rate of change these rules and objectives must be constantly reassessed. Circumstances change: the market shifts, new legal constraints are announced, economies of materials change, new competencies are needed -- so are replanning and redesign. This constant change is a fact of life, although it can be minimized by keeping virtual projects relatively short.

But flexibility has its dangers. Teams and organizations get tired of being refocused (i.e., jerked around), and wonder: "Why bother planning at all? Why not just forge ahead and see what happens?" The problem is that with distributed, cross-organizational teams, randomness can be devastating. By building appreciation of flexible, participatory planning into the organizational culture, a balance can be struck between planning and discovery, sticking to plan and revising, spending too much time on planning and spending none.

The following are guidelines for organizations that wish to develop a strong planning ethos:

- Inclusiveness - Planning is not the fiefdom of upper management, of central planners, or of one or two favored functions, like marketing or engineering. While inclusion of people who represent multiple perspectives may increase the time of planning process, the time saved downstream will more than make it up. Besides, good facilitation can keep planning meetings on track, avoiding the "rat-holes" that arise from relentless pursuit of particular perspectives.

• Structure - The planning process, like any other key virtual process, should be designed. Indeed, planning is a good "generic" process for transitioning organizations to prototype. The planning process is useful throughout the organization, and building the process helps develop planners and knowledge of teaming and communications.

• Communication - Planning is a mainstream activity, and plans in-progress should be electronically available, in real-time, to all stakeholders in the project.

• Concurrency - There usually isn't time to run a lengthy planning process and then go about filling in the resource slots for the virtual initiative. Planning and other work, such as process design and prototyping can go on concurrently, even though people don't know exactly where they're going when they start. Furthermore, the planning process itself should be concurrent, with teams addressing aspects of the plan in parallel, electronically, and sharing their unfinished work with each other.

• Flexibility - Planning is a process, not an event. It does not stop as soon as the first released plan is published. Like all other virtual tasks, planning is a Day 1 activity: it starts at the beginning of a project and continues, either monitoring the environment and the work, or actively revising plans throughout the duration of the project.

From one perspective, everyone potentially is a planner. As work tasks become increasingly complex and changeable, we are often advised against central planning: "Those who plan, do," goes the admonition. In planning, an organization will probably find itself somewhere on the continuum between the empowered work team and the planning suite. No matter what the policy, it is important that all planners have a good understanding of the work and skills in the planning process.

Good planners exhibit the following characteristics:

• Competency - Planners are chosen because their competencies and perspectives provide essential input into the project plan, not by inheritance, position, or enjoyment of the sport.

• Commitment - The contribution of planners is needed over the life-cycle of the project; their commitment to make planning a reasonably high priority is required for that entire period.

• Collaboration - Virtual planning is not a competitive sport. The idea is to work for the team goals, to raise the probability of project success through careful allocations of time and resources. Everyone should care about everyone else's planning issues and work to satisfy the needs of all stakeholders.

• Skills in Negotiation and Influence - In their work, planners should use their competency-based influence, not position power to negotiate scheduling and resource tradeoffs. This is a practical issue, not an ethical one; a VP may dismiss the Support Group's lead-time needs as unwarranted, but that VP isn't going to answer the Customer Service calls when they start rolling in to unstaffed phones.

We've gone on a bit about planning to emphasize its important role in virtual operations. The point here has not been to suggest replacing your organization's preferred planning processes, but to provide ways for you to develop positive attitudes toward planning, and to augment your current methods with some tailored for virtual situations.

7. Sensing the readiness of the organization to begin the transition

Before going on with developing a Specification and choosing its leadership, management should develop a fuller picture of the current level of virtual capability in the organization. This is closely related to the process of finding out "what you really know," as opposed to "what you think you know" (this will be discussed further in Chapter 18). Reflection and questioning of the "As Is" condition of the organization will give management a better feeling for

• The extent of the virtual transition needed
• The capabilities and shortfalls of virtual skills within the organization
• Where the highest leverage processes are that could be specified for virtual reengineering
• Who can best lead, and follow, in the critical early prototyping projects.

Because of the importance of this reflective process, we have devoted Chapter 17 to a discussion of organizational sensing, providing guidelines and checklists to aid you in determining your own organization's levels of virtual competency.

8. Creating a specification for a virtual operations prototype project

The next strategic step in the transition process calls for executive management, the management level that has the responsibility and authority to commit financial, personnel and physical resources, to formulate a specification outlining aggressive business goals for the first virtual prototype project. We offer the following specification development model as a guide for creating a comprehensive and formal tasking document that will

- Inform and authorize a project manager to convene the key stakeholders
- Launch the formulation of detailed project plans
- Provide a benchmark to evaluate the specifics of the proposed virtual project, as well as the completed prototype.

The Specification has five segments, each contributing to the next:

- Business Objectives

A clear statement of business objectives prompts management to link the project with strategic business objectives. This statement ensures that management's expectations are clearly associated with value producing activity. This section also sets management's priorities for the project in terms that will guide the project manager in resolving issues, conflicts, and deal with possible strategic changes. If business objectives include internal or external special interests or considerations, they are identified here: minority inclusion, special quality programs, and so forth. Business objectives should map to technical, administrative, and support requirements.

- Goals

Establishes quantified management metrics for monitoring progress. Sets performance requirements such as time, quality, cost performance relationships.

- Constraints

Sets parameters and boundaries for the project manager, stakeholders, and team members. Constraints that exist in technology, people, processes, and schedules are identified. If the project manager is authorized to appeal the constraints, the process for doing so should be outlined.

- Special Issues

This segment provides for the definition of issues beyond the normal scope of the organization's activities. These include political issues, organizational issues, marketing considerations, materials considerations, government regulations, customer and supplier relationships, approval/decision authorities who are not included in the core constituency (directors, investors, regulators, associations, etc.).

- Metrics

Metrics instigate most virtual initiatives:

-- Short cycle times mean you need to find ready-made competencies, inside or out; also, you do not have time to move people about but need to develop a virtual teaming ethos and practice to succeed.

-- High customer satisfaction means an inclusive product design process that needs to be supported by electronic communications.

-- Cost realities mean sharing risk with outside partners.

Metrics are the challenge, but not the enemy. They are road and destination signs that must be put in a language that customers, virtual teams, technologists, and management find appropriate and can mutually understand.

9. Commissioning a virtual project leader

In this final step of strategic design, management specifies the person or persons best qualified to lead the prototype project, as well as the start-up activities that will launch the initiative. Specifically, management identifies and authorizes the following:

- The project manager and champion and the limits of his or her authority
- The timing of the project design process
- Stakeholders critical in meeting the business objectives
- Physical assets necessary for the design activity
- Any other specific instructions for launching the prototype activity

Final Comments

As was pointed out at the beginning, this survey is not a sequential recipe for strategic virtual operations design. Many of the activities discussed here are probably ongoing in some form already in your organization. Furthermore, the activities are not really sequential, but parallel, interacting continuous processes. If undertaken with commitment, engaging in these processes can set the foundations for actual design and implementation of virtual operations and greatly increase the probability of a successful transition.

At this point we shift our focus to tactical design, led by the commissioned project leader.

TACTICS: LAUNCHING THE PROTOTYPE PROJECT

"I mean, how do you know what you're going to do until you do it. The answer is, you don't."
Holden Caulfield, *The Catcher in the Rye*
J. D. Salinger[1]

With strategic planning and preparations in place, it's time to actually engage in the virtual operations design process. So don't tarry in fine tuning the strategic side; begin a prototyping project in parallel, even though you don't know everything you need to know to finish it.

Tactical activities pick up where the strategic effort left off, with handing off the Management Specification to the commissioned virtual prototype project leader. In a way, the tactical steps are more focused versions of the strategic activities mentioned in the previous chapter, so there are no real surprises. The stages are listed here:

- Building a committed team to plan, design, and carry out the prototype project
- Understanding (engaging with) the management specification
- Envisioning the virtual processes that will meet management's goals
- Assessing the team's current processes and capabilities
- Designing in the virtual spin for the key processes: work tasks, teaming, communications and learning
- Creating a financial model for the virtual initiative
- Presenting management with a prototyping proposal

---

[1]J.D. Salinger, *The Catcher in the Rye*, (Boston, Little, Brown Company, 1951), p. 211.

- Conducting the prototype project
- Evaluating the learning from the prototype project

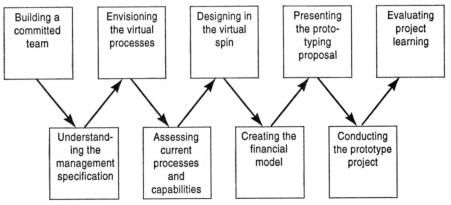

Figure 12.1   Tactical Steps in Transitioning to
Virtual Operations

Keep in mind that as with the strategic program, the steps in this transition are not linear; the process should be viewed as one of simultaneous development, interaction, and loopback. For example, planning, visioning, and understanding the specification are concurrent tasks, each having an influence on the others. Discoveries in the prototyping stage may require re-building the constituency to include representation for new key competencies. As the interval between interactions shrinks, activities become virtually simultaneous: Transitioning becomes a set of simultaneous, interrelated activities, instead of a sequential passage.

It's also important to understand that there are two agendas operating here: the need to design a project that will deliver the results specified by management, and the application of virtual spin to various project activities to provide the energy and learning needed to fuel the organization's overall transition to virtual operations. These agendas operate in parallel, and it is the responsibility of the project manager to ensure that the design team keep both balls in the air. As we discuss each stage of the tactical process, we will reinforce this distinction.

Now we'll take a closer look at some of these tactical activities. Again, the concepts and procedures aren't new, but have a different spin in the virtual context and bear emphasis. The point isn't to prescribe a different project management technique for your organization, but to focus your project planning capabilities in ways that will have high payback and lower risk in transitioning to the virtual model.

Building a Committed Team to Accomplish the Prototype Project

The first step for newly commissioned virtual project leaders is to engage the key stakeholders representing the competencies that are essential to meeting the commitments to management. By following a formalized planning methodology, these first efforts can be very focused and efficient. They result in a plan that will, in turn, focus the collaborative preparation of detailed designs for work process flow, teaming activities, and the communications and learning protocols that will launch and sustain virtual operations.

Understanding (engaging with) the Management Specification

Again, this is a reflective, not a reactive process. The specification should be studied (not just read) and clarification effected through interaction with the team that wrote the spec. Since the project manager will have been part of that team, the relationships should be in place to make communication easier. One excellent way to clarify a specification is to put it on-line, structured by section into a computer conference. The on-line dialog concerning each section, along with continuous revision can last a week or two, but other tactical work can proceed in parallel because it won't be necessary for everyone to show up for endless review meetings.

Envisioning the Virtual Process

With a common understanding of management's objectives, the stakeholder team can brainstorm about the ideal virtual system that can accomplish these goals. This assumes, of course that a high level of awareness of virtual operations possibilities has been developed during the strategic stage. This activity, along with all collaborative designings should be done in an open, rather than restricted mode. Some groups go so far as to use a "need not to know" model. Here, "need to know" does not have to be proven for a stakeholder to participate; only explicit reasons why the person should not "know" can be used for exclusion.

A general sense of a "To-Be" virtual systems provides the foundation for the next step, a determination of the team's "As-Is" capabilities.

Assessing Current Processes and Capabilities

The project leader needs to establish the levels of virtual competence in the prototyping team, and to assess the existing processes across the organization to determine the most likely candidates for reengineering as virtual processes. The sensing activities described in the following chapter can generate much of this information.

Designing in the Virtual Spin for Key Processes: Work Tasks, Teaming, Communications, and Learning

Designing virtual work is the responsibility of the project management team: the project leader and key stakeholders. The technique we suggest is based on interaction between the project leader, key stakeholders and others they feel represent special and essential interest or resources key to the success of the project. Designers can use a process design checklist that helps them superimpose issues that are important in virtual operations over the specific design activities that are needed to derive specified results. The "virtual" agenda may be addressed by the entire project management team, or by the leader and a sub-group that have special knowledge and experience in the use of complex information and communications processes. However, in order to ensure commitment to carry out the new agenda, the entire team should have input into the design process and ultimately accept the design as the team's work model.

The design activity can be directed by the participants themselves. Sometimes, especially in the early stages of an organization's transition to virtual operations, it helps to bring in an outside expert familiar with the design technique and able to provided an objective perspective. Whether chaired by the project leader or facilitated by an outside expert, the project leader is in charge. The leader must make certain that the final proposal/plan is supported by the entire team. If there are disagreements that prevent full consensus and cannot be resolved by the team, the leader must involve top management to arbitrate and resolve the issue. The goal is that this group will complete a virtual operations design that will, in their judgment, successfully and with manageable risk, deliver the required results as specified by management.

The basic virtual designs include the following elements:

• Work Task Design: designing optimal work processes for the distributed, electronic, information based, teaming environment.

• Teaming Design: establishing the proper mix of individual competencies, cultural norms, management relationships, and technical support for sustaining effective cross-functional, distributed teams.

• Communications Design: ensuring that distributed workers have the capability to share knowledge, resolve issues, and create a trusting work relationship using a networked electronic information infrastructure.

• Learning Design: creating an environment that will stimulate innovation and creativity, provide continuous learning opportunities, and facilitate problem solving.

Overviews, guidelines, and checklists for actually accomplishing these designs are the subjects of Parts V and VI.

Creating A Financial Model for a Virtual Initiative.

At some point a senior manager will ask for financial justification. "So we spend the money, take the time, train the people, invest in more technology...how do we know we will get a favorable return for these investments?" What follows is a technique to help designers model the most significant cost elements associated with virtual operations in order to have a basis to make valid comparisons.

To calculate the Return On Investment (ROI) for virtual operations use the final process design determined to meet management's specifications. Select a sample from those tasks that were designed using virtual operations techniques, technologies, and processes, and estimate the anticipated cost for these activities. The principal costs will be for people, facilities, and expenses, and for additional tools and competencies needed to meet essential performance requirements.

Consider and assign a value to the intangible results expected from virtual operations such as

• Reductions in the time needed to deliver results
• New capabilities and skills developed by team members
• Cost savings by reduction of process overhead:
  -- less travel time, expense, work disruption
  -- less time lost in periodic reporting
  -- less "back to the drawing board" rework
  -- improvement in change management
  -- more efficient team and/or individual replacements
  -- faster and more effective distribution of decisions

-- better support services through stakeholder involvement

• Value of tested virtual relationships with participating suppliers, collaborators, and customers.

From the above calculate a ROI and include the team's justification for each component of the calculation. The values representing the intangibles will be estimates at best, but if they are the considered and experience-based judgments of the stakeholders, and if they are held constant wherever they are used, they can be quite accurate and revealing. Management should use these estimates as part of their review of the proposal. These estimates would also be monitored by the project leader during the preparation, launch, and ongoing management of the project. Meeting these numbers is where virtual operations pay off!

Presenting Management with a Prototyping Proposal

The next step is to integrate the project planning and virtual operations design into the team's prototyping proposal to executive management. The purpose of this proposal is to present management with a clear recommendation for action: what should be prototyped, what it will cost, and what its payback is expected to be, to both the tactical and strategic agendas.

You know best what form a proposal should take in your organization. The proposal is a statement of intent, not a contract. It sets out your current state of knowledge of:

--the challenge: the virtual opportunity

--your prototype focus: designs for processes to be reengineered for virtual operations

--benefits of this redesign to the organization

--plans for schedule, cost, resources, and risk management.

In addition to being a statement of work, these completed plans and designs provide a feedback mechanism to allow management to re-examine their objectives based on realistic estimates of time and cost. If the project still meets the business needs of the organization, management can make an informed commitment to the leader, stakeholders, and workers to stand behind the team as they launch actual work operations.

The following guidelines can help in producing an effective proposal to management:

• Develop a comprehensive statement describing the work tasks that the team believes will satisfy management's specifications. A work process flow diagram can be included showing the physical location and organizational relationships that make up the virtual teams.

-- Will management be able to understand how the recommended process will meet their specifications?

-- Do any of the relationships firmly committed to require investments authorized by management?

-- Are there contingency plans for:

- emergency notifications and actions?

- natural disasters?

  sickness and accidents?

  schedule modifications?

- business changes?

- cancellation?

-- Does any part of the proposal require special explanation? Are people available to do this?

-- Do all leaders and stakeholders have access to the project's proposed information systems?

Are there detailed descriptions of the teams and the competencies they bring to the project?

-- Is everyone available for the duration?

-- If replacements are required, have plans been made for their rapid assimilation?

-- Should management consider any special incentives?

-- Does special training need to occur prior to launch?

-- Do all team members have access to the information systems selected for this project?

-- Is there a process for replacing team members for cause?

Is there a complete phase-out plan to mark the end of the project?

-- Is there an outline for the final report to management?

-- Are the steps for dissolving teams clear?

-- Are rewards and recognition processes acceptable?

-- Are processes in place to capture and distribute learning within and outside the organization?

Has prototyping been recommended and justified?

-- Are prototype suggestions and the expected results clearly identified?

-- Do the prototype tasks include specific goals and metrics to be used to manage results?

-- Are special assignments needed for the prototypes, and have resources been recommended?

If the proposal development process has been accomplished with high levels of communication with management, tacit approval of the proposal will have been built concurrently with its development. Now only formal approval and commitment of resources are needed to launch the project.

Conducting the Prototype Project

The objective is to treat the prototype project as a high visibility, carefully managed operation that will highlight the results, impact, and value of virtual operations. Additionally, prototypes can be used to test capabilities and competencies that are believed to exist in or outside the organization. The extraordinary monitoring that prototyping allows reduces the likelihood that misinformation or faulty expectations will go unnoticed for very long. Prototyping is a good way to mange for success.

Prototyping can be accomplished following whatever organizational process is currently operative. In addition, the following activities should be integrated into the process:

• Pick a qualified and motivated leader and core team of stakeholders that understand and accept the concept of prototyping.

• Develop a virtual work process plan for the selected activity that includes additional monitoring and intervention opportunities that may be needed to ensure success.

• Follow all the virtual design processes, and be continually on the lookout for ways of applying the virtual spin.

• Make sure that the work team will have all the capabilities and support to complete the prototype.

• Select appropriate metrics and rewards.

• Prepare a formal and detailed schedule for task completion, management reviews, and learning.

• Plan to celebrate successes, make sure that everyone participates.

• Include a publicity plan.

Once they get started in prototyping virtual operations, most organizations don't stop. Prototyping becomes a continuous activity as the scope of potential and challenge of virtual operations becomes more apparent to the team. But projects must have closure, so each proposal, formal or informal, must have completion criteria, points at which the specific task is deemed complete. Here the learning, tactical and strategic, is announced and publicized. The newly discovered virtual operations are now rolled out into the organization's ongoing operations, as well as into follow up prototyping efforts.

Evaluating and Reporting the Learning

Prototyping is an experiential learning activity. The team will emerge from the prototyping effort with virtual operations knowledge in their heads, in product or part they produce, in the processes they create, and in the on-line record of the prototype work. The point of all this isn't to create an island of excellence in the organization, but to spread virtual capabilities throughout the organization.

Make project learning available both in real time, as the project is conducted, then more formally at project end. Don't just publish reports: run demos, give away processes, hold gripe sessions -- at all levels of involvement.

Final Comments

There is just one more step: do it again. Not to be flippant, continuous prototyping is the best way to sustain reengineering for virtual operations. The first one is the hardest, requiring great leaps of faith, arm twisting and courage in the face of the unknown. It doesn't get any less challenging, but it does get easier.

Now to the design of virtual operations.

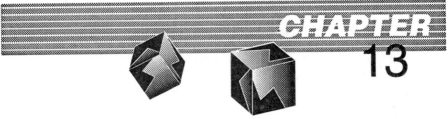

BARRIERS
AND NEW REALITIES

Eusa sed, How menne Chaynjis ar thayr? The Littl Man sed, Yu mus no aul abowt that I seen yu rite they nos. down in the hart of the wud. Eusa sed, that riting is long gon & aul they nos. hav gon owt of my myn I doan remember nuthing uv them. Woan yu pleas tel me how menne Chaynjis thayr ar? The Littl Man sed, As menne as reqwyrd. Eusa sed, Reqwyrd by wut? The Little Man sed, Reqwyrd by the idear uv yu. Eusa sed, Wut is the idear uv me? The Littl Man sed, that we doan no til yuv gon thru aul yur Chaynjis.
Riddley Walker, Russell Hoban[1]

"Peace. War. It makes no difference. You are talking about change and we just can't have that!"
Pontius Pilate to Jesus, The Last Temptation of Christ[2]

To this point we've presented arguments for virtual operations, discussed somewhat the nature of those operations, and suggested a transition strategy. Our intention has been to convince you that this exciting new operations paradigm has already arrived and is available to organizations that decide to make the commitment and investment to learn the virtual ropes. Of course, we expect to hear loud audience approval. So let's get on with it; where do we go from here?

Experience tells us that even the best thought out and tested concepts will not convince people and organizations to change to drastically new modes of operation. There are barriers, natural resistance to change. And

[1]Russell Hoban, *Riddley Walker*, (New York: Summit Books, 1980), p. 36

[2]*The Last Temptation of Christ*. Screenplay by Paul Schrader, based on the novel by Nikos Kazentzakis. Directed by Martin Scorcese. Produced by Barbara De Fina. Universal Pictures & Cineplex Odeon Films, 1988.

we speak here of "people" or cultural barriers, not barriers of technology or process. Certainly technology falls short of perfection, but there's plenty to get started with. Likewise, we've seen enough good virtual operations to realize that there are breakthrough processes available to us today. The barriers that inhibit the transition to virtual operations will be based on fear of change and trust in the existing system: the beliefs, knowledge, skills, and experience that have brought success until now. The purpose of this chapter is not to address methods of change, but to look at some of the factors that inhibit change. Developing an understanding of these inhibitors will make it easier to identify and address barriers on the road to virtual operations.

Many of you, satisfied with the way things are going in your own organizations, would be hard pressed to think of any reason to change to virtual operations or anything else. "Look, we've always done things this way and we're still in business. Why fix what's not broken?" So it's unlikely that organizations, or more precisely people, will change by being told to change.

The ways in which Detroit automakers reacted to the inroads of Japanese cars into US markets in the '70s and '80s illustrates this first category of resistance. Successful in selling high-margin, large, and loaded automobiles in the past, executives showed no interest in following the lead of Honda, Toyota, and Subaru with their economical, durable, smaller models. There's the now legendary story of a high-level GM executive pointing out his penthouse window to the corporate parking lot and remarking: "Where are all these Japanese cars I hear about? I don't see any Japanese cars. What's the problem?" The problem was of course that it was career suicide to show up for work in a foreign car; besides, employee discounts on their own brand made loyalty very economical.

Others may accept the potential of virtual operations, but only for the other guy: the "Not Invented or Particularly Useful Here" perspective. These folks might like the sound of virtual operations, but doubt the relevance to their own circumstances. "Those ideas may be OK for high-tech but they won't work in banking." We don't encourage the trendy belief that all industries can be run the same way; it's important to know your product. We do argue that industries can learn from one another and there are virtual opportunities for all kinds of business and organizations.

A very popular way to resist change is to avow that

1. Your organization is working so hard it doesn't have time to change.

2. It costs too much to invest in the transition.

Both arguments carry weight in the short term: "Everyone in the streets; we need Q4 revenue." But such attitudes foretell doom in the longer run. What's called for is investing in the future; not as some optional ivory tower activity, but as part of the organization's work—which is to keep building capability.

Most resistance, however, will come from experienced, reflective individuals who accept the validity of the virtual responses with unseen nods, but finally say: "So what? We're already doing that stuff. We have information and telecommunications systems; we use E-mail. We have teams, alliances. We groom strong leaders. What's your point?" One reason this is such a common source of resistance is what Ben Shneiderman calls proactive interference: when you've used a word to mean one concept for a long time, it's difficult to understand and accept a new concept attached to that same word.[3]

A manufacturer of large computers got on the "systems" bandwagon several years ago, announcing one day: "We build systems." These were the days when barbells were being replaced by fitness systems, apportioned food purveyors were creating meal systems, and your TV and Stereo were being integrated into entertainment systems. "Systems," in the corporate lexicon had always meant a complete computer hardware product: terminal, workstation, mini or mainframe. In the new definition, "system" meant a compete solution to an organization's or a user's computing needs: hardware, software, documentation, support, training, and so forth. It became politically correct for everyone to claim they were in the "systems business," which made the strategists happy because they assumed they had by decree turned the corner to becoming a user centered provider, and left the designers and developers pleased to continue doing what they had always done. The discontinuity was discovered before too much time passed, but it took years of transition to really move into the "systems" business.

In this chapter we'd like to address all three modes of resistance to change:

- "Don't Fix What Isn't Broken."
- "Not Invented Here."
- "So? We've been doing that for years."

These objections aren't frivolous, mean spirited, or lacking in insight. And they won't be overcome by preaching and haranguing with a lot of "Haftas," as in "You hafta do things this way or else....." The approach here will be to explore, open up, annotate the virtual perspective enough to begin the conversion of more resistant readers, and clarify key aspects of virtual operations to those who already see its general benefits.

---

[3]Ben Shneiderman. *Software Psychology: Human Factors in Human and Information Systems* (Cambridge, MA: Winthrop, 1980), p. 199.

Argument #1: "We're doing fine; don't fix what isn't broken.".
  (or, "I see what I believe.").

We've mentioned that people in organizations, in societies, in cultures are generally most committed to the way they DO things, rather than to some lofty principle, group goal, or even job description. There, in the way a person works, is where his or her sense of personal value resides, where an emotional link exists between the individual and the group's business. You can make any number of rational arguments to convince people of a better way to work based on yield -- higher quality automobiles, more potatoes per acre, faster customer service -- but self-interest lies in the work process, where the individual or group has expertise, control, and experience; as well as strong beliefs, substantial knowledge, skill, and experience.

We have seen, however, that the situation in many organizations today is far from "fine." Days are marked with panic driven downsizing (how arrogant to call it "right sizing," since results are beginning to show that a lot of organizations haven't yet taken the trouble to figure out what's right -- where to cut, where to move, or where to add). Many "lean and mean" organizations display an inability to deliver products on time, and are assailed by disgruntled customers as well as by ruthless external and internal competitors. The morale of the workforce is severely shaken by the turbulence. Executives, like those GM folks who didn't believe there was foreign competition for their auto markets, often are the last to let go of the trees they've been hugging.

The need for change is being recognized throughout industry. Inciting and managing organizational change gets a lot of play these days. Books, audio tapes, videos, and articles tell how it's done. Take your choice. The best of these acknowledge the dangers of change resistance and propose to overcome the barriers through role playing, simulation, or prototyping techniques, rather than just through rational arguments, paeans to systems thinking, or threats of dire consequences. Realistic scenarios and exercises enable individuals to help develop and simultaneously experience both the new ends and the new means of their work. Learning how to change by changing. That's our bias; we hope that trying out the approaches suggested in *Going Virtual* will *cause* change, not just be *about* change.

Argument #2: "Great! You do it!". . .
  (or, "Not Invented Here, nor Useful in My Backyard").

The concepts of virtual organizations and operations are not an abstract idea about clever ways to work in the future. Rather, they are part of a new paradigm evolving from the ways a wide variety of organizations have begun to respond to today's business opportunities. Highly respected corporations have already launched virtual efforts: Ford, MCI, Apple, and Ameritech Cellular, all with track records in directing alliances, have naturally put on the mantles of driving the paradigm by initiating virtual initiatives. These organizations aren't really "early adopters"; they are innovators, creating the paradigm as they go along. Others, frequently partners in these alliances, are adopting the principles of virtual operations in order to play in the main events.

Everyone is a potential partner, if not a potential leader of virtual alliances. "Followership" is the term that comes to mind, but with no derogatory connotations. There is nothing negative or passive about developing and sustaining the capabilities to play in this virtual field being staked out by industry leaders. Yours does not need to be the lead organization in a virtual enterprise; but if you develop some of the competencies mentioned in Chapter 4, it could a very attractive partner for someone leading a virtual project. Many companies in diverse industries are already finding themselves left out because they don't have the processes, infrastructure, relationship skills, and, most importantly, the commitment to go virtual.

In recent years many small and mid-size manufacturing suppliers have discovered they're losing orders because they don't have Electronic Data Interchange (EDI) capabilities that allow them to exchange and process various business forms electronically. Some pull back and keep looking for customers who still do business the old fashioned way. This is the classic "pursuit of an ever increasing share of a diminishing market." Others react positively. They make necessary investments in technology and process reengineering, they adopt and master international standards such as ISO 9000 to develop the capability to compete in the worldwide marketplace. They develop their own Just-In-Time logistics capabilities, or form alliances with manufacturering representatives who already are electronically linked to the worldwide business network.

In the biomedical industry, forming virtual alliances has become an article of faith. The rate of change is too high, work too complex, times too short, and financial risk too high to depend on going it alone or even setting up traditional partnerships. In the biomedical game virtual rules are the fact of life; no buggy whip makers need apply.

Even in advertising, that bastion of competitiveness, secrecy, and person-to-person relationship building, the virtual model is being recognized. Already major ad execs worldwide are using computer conferencing to foster continuous communication and mutual learning about industry issues that affect them all. This dialog leads to relationships and helps develop capabilities that enable them to participate as virtual stakeholders with global clients in delivering worldwide media programs.

Virtual business is in the air, the same air that everyone breathes. Every organization that has a competitive competency is in the virtual game. Every organization should know what virtual skills it will need to develop to make its "core" competencies marketable.

Argument #3: "So? We've been doing that for years!" (or, "Nothing different here. It's just semantics.").

The last type of objection to virtual operations comes from those to whom virtual operations seem extremely familiar, and therefore not very interesting. This is a particularly potent demon in the world of managing change. "If it looks like a duck, walks like a duck, it must be a duck," we are told. Looked at a wristwatch lately? It may look like a watch and sound like a watch, but this watch does spreadsheets, sends E-mail, and calls Dick Tracy away from the dinner table. The old bottle, or name, makes it difficult to really appreciate the new wine! For whatever reason, the "there's nothing new here" barrier to transitioning to the virtual model seems to be the major point of resistance. For that reason, we'll look closely at the causes and effects of these hard-to-shake beliefs.

New Virtual Perspectives

Several years ago we watched some engineers from a major New England computer manufacturer look at an Apple Macintosh personal computer for the first time. The immediate reactions were very revealing:

1st Engineer: "Huh. It's a toy."

2nd Engineer: "Jeez. We built one of those back in the 60s."

3rd Engineer: "We can do that."

They saw what they wanted to believe, something trivial from the fantasy coast, and their collective wisdom was to ignore the personal computer fad and stay with industrial machines; the company never has become a serious competitor in the personal computer-centered market, and their corporate health has suffered.

So one of the ways to dismiss something new, something that will require you to change, and even admit you're behind the power curve, is to identify it with something you've done or been doing. Here are a few typical responses to our suggestion that virtual operations might be worth trying:

• "We know about change. And we've always managed to keep up with it. I don't see what virtual operations can do for us."

- "Of course the customer's a stakeholder; we've been doing TQM for years."

- "Tighter development cycles? You're talking about concurrent engineering; that's been in our blood since 1980."

- "Metrics? You think Metrics are new?"

- "We've always shared information here. Doesn't everyone? We communicate through E-mail. If that's virtual operations, great, we're already there."

- "Alliances? We been doing alliances for fifty years. Our company already has processes to tap outside resources; what we need is help in making our partnering work!"

Against such arguments we maintain that virtual operations is much more than business as usual. This is not merely old wine in new bottles. There are qualitative differences between the traditional and virtual versions of these widely accepted business practices. We'll discuss some of these differences next:

1.Dealing with Change

2.Customer Satisfaction

3.Time Management

4.Information Sharing/ Electronic Communication

5.Alliances.

We'll look at each of these concerns in terms of their place in the traditional paradigm, why this traditional interpretation inhibits virtual operations, and what the context is for each in the virtual environment.

1. Change: In the environment, in the organization

Academic and trade journals are fond of describing situations in which companies "hit the wall." For these organizations business as usual has not met their needs, and without significant change in the way they operate, the very survival of the company is in doubt. We have seen enough cases in the automobile, computer, banking, pharmaceutical, and aerospace industries to dramatize this condition. We saw it in the ZYX virtual tour; their products were better than ever, but customer needs changed and ZYX missed it. So they went all out to recover their place in the market.

Change is a fact of life, but the phenomenal rate of change today is unprecedented. As rate of change increases, the traditional management responses of reaction and damage control cannot cope with its effects. The result is crisis management as a way of life.

Over the last several months the largest and apparently most stable organizations have gone through enormous changes. Corporate downsizing has reached epidemic levels. A sampling of cutbacks announced in 1993 included: Xerox, 10,000; Philip Morris, 14,000; Bell South, 10,000; Woolworth, 13,000; Martin Marietta, 11,000; IBM 100,000; Sears, 50,000; Boeing, 31,000. These numbers have continued to grow.

IBM has begun reorganizing their extremely bureaucratic and monolithic organization into several autonomous and flexible business units. AT&T is forming strategic alliances with Japanese trading partners to jump-start the production of new computer products. Boeing, in addition to downsizing and production cutbacks, has initiated programs to cut unit cost by 25% by 1998 and to speed delivery time for new airplanes from twelve months to just six months for some of their models. Most organizations, regardless of size, industry, or strategic position, have initiated outsourcing; Total Quality Management, reengineering, and any number of other equally sweeping, but destabilizing, management programs.

The problem with these internal reactions to external change is that they focus most of the company's energies on crisis management: morale suffers, risk taking is avoided, research and development investment is reduced, and creative work ebbs. The bunker mentality today merely accelerates organizational demise.

The challenge today is not necessarily to manage change, but to build the systemic capabilities to turn continuous change to competitive advantage. This can be accomplished through reengineering for virtual operations. But organizations first must let go of their last paradigm "managing change" beliefs and build a new culture of working with change.

The key virtual operations process that helps build this capability is virtual learning, a way of using the virtual infrastructure to support continuous learning that may not stay ahead of change, but will anticipate the effects of change. For example, some political event, like granting most favored nation status to an emerging country or withdrawing it from another may change a company's export strategy. Tracking the progress of such events, perhaps through daily news updates in the network, and conducting on-line sessions in how to do business in new foreign markets can position the organization to act quickly when the opportunity arises. Simultaneously, the organization will be building its skill as a virtual learning organization.

Change, then, because it has been anticipated, becomes an ally, making the organization more competitive than the rest of the crowd, which merely reacts.

2. "Of course our customers are satisfied, or else they wouldn't be buying our products."

Many businesses are doing quite well today, with a happy, satisfied customer base. This base could disappear tomorrow if another company came up with a better, faster, cheaper solution. Brand loyalty works in "high-image" products and services, like sneakers and fast food, but more complex offerings are wide open to the competition from a customer base that is more concerned with value than past reputation of the producer.

In the 1980s the "voice of the customer" began to be heard throughout the land in thousands of TQM initiatives. Over the last several months, business has yet again rediscovered customers. Dozens of books and seminars and hundreds of articles call for new relationships with customers, declaring the urgency to respond to customer needs and interest. We are seeing a call to respond to crisis caused by change. Many argue for improving existing relationships, a few suggest that it may be time for entirely new kinds of relationships. Boeing, for example, has launched a "pleasing the customer" initiative to improve their market performance. In the past, Boeing did not set a high priority to responding to customer request for changes in aircraft design. Often, weeks passed before requests for modifications were even acknowledged, let alone acted upon. But customer preferences didn't go away, they just landed further on in the project, when changes had become orders of magnitude more expensive. Costly and time consuming change orders at advanced stages of production convinced Boeing to initiate a program to accelerate the response to customer inquiries by establishing a seventy-two hour response goal. Results were fewer last minute, "unexpected" production changes, and happier customers.

But the concept of virtual operations involves even deeper, more dynamic customer engagement. Customers, in the process of buying, make the final judgments about value. For this reason the virtual model requires that customers be interactive stakeholders continuously throughout the product or service research and development cycles, not just at opening requirements time, or episodically when they request changes. As we heard in the Tour of ZYX, it can take years to serially get customer feedback on the way a complex product or service contributes to a customer solution. These responses must be heard in parallel to the development process, with customers helping guide change in real-time, to assure the right product for the right customers at the right time.

Today's customer is quite capable of playing this new role:

• Customers have become very sophisticated in areas that have traditionally been the private preserves of experts. They increasingly know what they want and why they want it.

• Customers believe that they can add value, so why shouldn't they?

• Customers are more vulnerable to mistakes made by vendors and suppliers, and in today's economy, mistakes can be fatal.

• Technology has made it possible for customers to be involved, and they know it.

However, inclusion of customers in the value creating process is easier said than done. Most work processes have been designed within a quite different, exclusionary atmosphere:

• "There's us and there's them -- we know what is best for them."

• "Don't ask for input from customers; they'll each tell you something different.

• "Customers can't be trusted to keep our secrets."

• "This stuff is too complicated for them."

• "They don't need to understand how any of this works."

• "Make sure customers can't find out what we're really doing, what our investment is, and what our margins look like."

These beliefs must be buried if organizations hope to achieve aggressive "time-to-delight" customer goals.

The best way to address this form of resistance is to give customer input a try. TQM has lead the way for bringing the customer's priorities into product design. Now is the time to extend customer participation to full-stakeholder, process design level. Run a project -- a prototype -- with full customer participation. See how it works. The risk can be controlled and the initiative might yield very positive and illuminating results.

3. "Time. There never was enough time."

These days everyone feels stretched. Work days are consumed in the pursuit of people, information, meetings, and customer opportunities. As victims of Xeno's Paradox, we keep halving the distance to the goal and are surprised when we never reach it. Work has becomes a bizarre race, a combination marathon-steeplechase, run at the pace of a 100 meter dash. The market, customers, and competition sets the pace. Better, faster, and cheaper products and services won't do; only the best, the fastest, and most cost-effective need apply.

Time compression has begun to threaten even the most resilient organizations. The normal, routine, traditional ways of coping with time pressure are no longer viable. Even the quantum time management solutions refined over the last several years have begun to reach their event horizons. Just-In-Time logistics concepts did relieve pressures on inventory systems -- for a while. We now know that there are limits to the JIT logic; like an earthquake that temporarily relieves geological stress, the solution itself has introduced risks that create new dangers. Companies that had refined JIT to near real-time inventory management found themselves in crisis when the Mississippi decided to alter its flow as well as the flow of truck and barge transportation during the floods of 1993. Just-in-time became wait-till-summer, and inventories were back in vogue.

A flood of other "just-in-times" have followed JIT, all aimed at managing, or even just moderating the impact of time compression on organizational activities: Just-in Time Learning, Just-in-Time Supplies, Just-in-Time Marketing. Many of these could more aptly be called "Barely-in-Time," but the intentions are good. The problem is that most of these new approaches still center on old beliefs about dealing with time.

To save "product cycle" time -- how long it takes from the drawing board to the delivery truck -- traditional approaches address subcycles in the overall process and seek to reduce them: compress the research phase, compress the specification review phase, and so forth. All this does save time in the serial process of getting the work done, but it also can be hazardous to product quality. Saving time on the individual work process cycles isn't the point, saving time in the overall cycle is the goal. And one doesn't necessarily yield the other. The problem is complexity and change. By shortening the conceptual design phase of a new Personal Video Player you get to final design more quickly, but if new and better/cheaper composites come on the market, or if the FCC rules change, or if the market wants video/personal assistant combinations, you'll need to loop back from wherever you got so quickly and regenerate conceptual designs.

The systemic, virtual approach to working within time constraints is to sustain simultaneous, networked, full-project length subcycles, instead of trying to manage time by compressing it. Virtual operations make this possible through the use of electronically supported access to the competencies you need when you need them. All competencies, all cycles start at "time zero" of the project and continue until closure. In this model, the time to complete a project would be the time necessary for the longest task, and each stakeholder would be engaged all the

time, though continually, when needed, rather than continuously.   In
virtual operations stakeholders can know in near real-time when exceptions demand intervention. They have the power to negotiate resolu-
tions to problems at the time, on the spot, without waiting for a monthly
status/action meeting.

Virtual operations breaks down traditional time based barriers by
reaching out for world-class competency rather than taking the time to
develop home-grown capabilities, by reengineering work processes
around the potential of electronically formatted and distributed information, rather than relying on face-to-face meetings and paper document
exchange, and by removing the need for the "stop-and-go-and-loopback"
overhead of serial processes. If you are networked into the scene of the
action, you don't need to spend as much time preparing, presenting,
reading, and acting on reports. The virtual paradigm provides new
options to address time management, and solutions that deliver breakthrough efficiencies convert rapidly into competitive advantages.

4. Information sharing and communication

Lots of organizations today are wired. People send E-mail to each other
on proprietary networks and to the world through the Internet and rapidly proliferating private world wide systems. These same organizations,
with their specialized matrix management structures, assume that a
great deal more information sharing exists than is actually the case. In
spite of connectivity,   a network of filters exists in information and communications channels that operate very effectively at blocking the passage of information.   Senior executives are often told what others feel
they want to hear, not what they need to hear: 100% effective filter. As a
result, they may not be aware of confusion, ambiguity, or even anger in
the ranks. On the other hand, these senior managers feel it their responsibility to make sure subordinates know only what they need to know, to
shield them from uncertainty, from instability, from change.   Be happy,
keep smiling, no problem.

Digital Equipment Corporation is arguably one of the most thoroughly wired organizations in the world. Two decades ago the computer
company invested in an information and network infrastructure that
would enable the majority of its employees to electronically communicate
with each other, access and share information openly anytime, anyplace,
anywhere. In addition to standard business traffic, the company encouraged employees to use the network for social reasons as well, to enhance
team cohesiveness and to exchange information that would improve the
quality of their private lives. There are thousands of computer discussion
forums available on line to any employee

This is an environment where, theoretically, nothing should hinder the open flow of information. And in some cases this is very true and Digital has the success stories to prove it. Worldwide work teams have been able to to form virtual relationships effecting orders of magnitude breakthroughs in time and cost reduction as well as quality. However, Digital also has many examples of failures and missed opportunities. Enough of these, in fact, for us to conclude that a ubiquitous information infrastructure will not generate, encourage, or support virtual operations simply by its mere existence. However, in situations where work is designed around the organizing principle of openly shared electronic information, and people believe in and are committed to sharing electronic information, spectacular results can occur.

The key here is design; design of processes that utilize the richness of the information sharing competencies mentioned in Chapter 4. Processes founded on the beliefs, knowledge, skills, and experience of using electronic information collaboratively to build joint value. Wires alone can 't do it; virtual operations design can.

5. Alliances, partnerships, joint ventures. "We do them all; how do you think we've been able to be an international corporation for so long?"

Business alliances are so common today that many companies have departments exclusively dedicated to the care and feeding of "external" relationships. Despite their similarities, alliances in the traditional environment are very different in form and substance to their counterparts in virtual operations. The conventional wisdom is that alliances are a means to an end, a convenience. The selection of partners is usually based on location, cost (of whatever the partner is going to provide), or habit.

However, virtual alliances are based on the competency needs. Virtual alliances are more than just a means to an end, they are the essence of current and future success of the virtual organization. They must form faster and dissolve more quickly than traditional alliances. They are more complex, as one corporate entity may be involved in thousands of alliances, each to gain needed competencies. An organization may gain desktop publishing competency from one small unit in a large company. That company may be involved in numerous alliances with competitors in the same industry. More than once an executive, flying back from making a deal with a major telecommunications corporation, has heard an in-flight recording of how his company is involved in a virtual alliance with a competitor of that same company. Another benefit of seat belts! A communications design for upper management is definitely called for.

Final Comments

In this chapter we have addressed some of the underlying reasons why the concept of virtual operations is frequently misunderstood, often mistrusted, and sometimes mistaken for the status quo. We've spent some time in trying to point out how several high-visibility virtual phenomena, such as alliances and customer involvement differ from the models we've been accustomed to. Hanging on to the traditional ways in which these concerns have been defined presents a barrier to developing the competencies and processes required by virtual operations. One way in which many of these barriers can be overcome is through hands on, collaborative design, implementation, and exercising of real virtual operations. Just how that can be done will be the subject of Part VI.

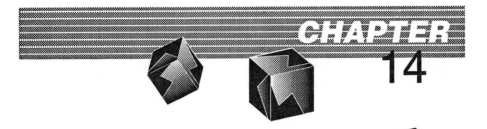

GETTING STARTED: ASSESSING CURRENT ORGANIZATIONAL CAPABILITIES

So [said the doctor]. Now vee may perhaps to begin. Yes?
Portnoy's Complaint, Philip Roth[1]

This chapter is addressed to the champions of virtual operations within the organization: these individuals can be executives, middle managers, or project leaders. The activities suggested here certainly do need some level of management sanction, and that comes more easily the higher in the organization the champion is placed. But that sanction can be obtained through influence and persuasion; what's important is that the person driving these assessments be knowledgeable about and committed to virtual operations.

As we mentioned in Chapter 12, the first step at the tactical level of moving to virtual operations is not really a step, but a reflective pause: finding out where you are. Usually it's difficult to hold up at this point: your vision's in place, your business goals are clear, launch a prototype project! Experience indicates that the best thing to do is not to take the leap, but to assess your readiness to make the leap. Specifically, get a feeling for what your organizational capabilities really are, as opposed to what they may appear to be; overconfident assumptions about your own state of knowledge and skill will severely impact your ability to get on the learning curve you need to develop project competencies.

Don't worry about painting too bleak a picture of your organizational readiness for virtual operations. An honest calibration will help you focus on developing the competencies that will contribute both to the projects at hand and to your capabilities for building project competencies: As you design and implement virtual operations, you will be increasing your capabilities to

[1]Philip Roth, *Portnoy's Complaint* (New York: Vintage Books, 1994), p. 274

design and implement those same kinds of operations. This is what Doug Engelbart calls bootstrapping: Increased capability feeds itself, boosting your ability to gain more capability.[2]

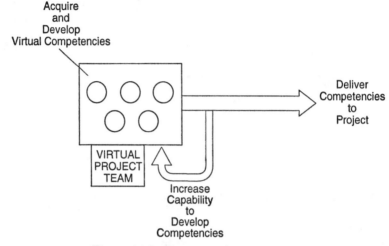

Figure 14.1   Bootstrapping

For example, if improved communications is required to meet the objectives of management's specification, and only two or three individuals on your virtual team have used electronic mail, electronic communication would be a good first capability to focus on. Get the team all on E-mail ("take away their pencils"); the value return will be threefold:

- The team will be able to design the project more quickly
- The project objectives will more likely be met
- Experience in electronic communications will be built and made available to the rest of the organization for future projects

To help you determine the base level of virtual capabilities for your organization, we offer here a series of sensing exercises. They are designed to elicit information from the team's participants concerning their current operational capabilities, preferences, and culture. We find that the processes of uncovering this information in a collaborative environment has an interesting side effect: participants get a better feeling for the perspectives of various team members on the organization's current capabilities, for those perspectives can vary wildly:

- "We have 'open door' communications." (upper management)

[2]Douglas C. Englehart, *The Bootstrap Institute*, Fremont, CA.

- "No one talks to anyone." (middle management)
- "Communications? They're one-way around here. Management tells us what to do." (line contributors)

The sensing process becomes an opportunity to understand and begin to resolve differences early in the transition process. This is especially important when multiple organizations or companies are involved and perspectives are even more divergent. Left undiscussed, assumptions can be time bombs as projects progress and become stressful.

These sensing lists we offer are informal. The discussions about them can be informal as well. Talk about them in cafeterias, on airplanes, in the local pub—wherever. The main requirement is that people feel empowered to be open and honest, that revealing one's perspective isn't a career threatening activity. Be prepared for a few surprises: managers, especially out-of-touch managers, sometimes fall out of their chairs when they hear what the troops think. In one sensing session we participated in, the senior manager was absolutely shocked to hear that every one of her direct reports felt that the group had no clear direction. The problem was that she was following her intuition on what was the right direction, and assumed that since her managers were all bright people, they would see the same future. Not so. After the revelation, the team and the manager began a continuous (electronic) dialog to help clarify signals from the top.

Besides providing a basic understanding of the knowledge, skills, and experience of the organization, the sensing exercises can reveal whether there is sufficient understanding and personal commitment on the part of executives, managers, and potential leaders to support and sustain virtual operations. Unless these key individuals are solid in their commitment, virtual operations are high risk. By being engaged in this exercise, they become aware of the sensitivities that will be required to function in their virtual roles.

A final bit of advice: This is not Jeopardy. The important thing is not a list of quantified, right answers, rather the intent is to develop multiple perspectives on the current organizational situation and capabilities: where you really are and where you should be investing for the highest virtual operations payback.

> ## Virtual Operations Organizational Environment Assessment

1. Thinking virtual

Everyone in the organization should be aware of the following aspects of virtual operations. While total understanding, agreement with, and support of these principles can only come with time, it is essential that the team at least be thinking about them and grappling with their implications. The aspects include the following:

• Management's role and responsibility to establish clarity, scope, and purpose to all individuals engaged in virtual operations

• The relationship between project expectations and the organization's key business strategies and objectives

• The need for dedicated leadership for the full project schedule

• The concept of electronically enabled work processes and the need for reengineering processes for virtual operations

• Continuous change and the need for dynamic, real-time management of the effects of change

• The need for special training and preparation for virtual operations, including:

-- virtual meeting techniques

-- team and alliance building

-- sustaining concurrent stakeholder participation

-- documentation and knowledge transfer

-- metrics and rewards.

2. Identifying and assessing barriers

Assess the organizational climate for virtual operations and determine what serious barriers exist within the business and social culture of the organization that could compromise the virtual initiative. This short list can stimulate thinking about barriers; for a fuller coverage of barriers refer back to Chapter 13:

• Do individuals generally oppose participation in joint efforts?
• Do individuals or groups resist taking direction from outside their established chain of command?
• Is turf protection a major cultural factor?
• Are contributors arrogant about their knowledge in ways that would sabotage competency alliances?
• Can the team members stand high-profile, high-performance heat?
• Have many, or any, of the team worked in virtual teams before?
• Is open communication practiced?

- Are there stovepiped loyalties?
- Are there rigid political relationships that would influence objective decisions?
- Do any of the key players have personal ambitions that would make it difficult for them to credit team activity?
- Do any players have a history with an external competency provider that could pose problems of friction, distrust, or lack of confidence?
- Are there language barriers? Are they being addressed? How?
- Will there be significant differences in the equipment and systems available to various teams and work groups?
- Are there radically dissimilar processes or applications in use?
- Are there resource shortages that will compromise any team or work group?
- Are there outstanding or potential labor issues?
- Are there financial concerns, or potential issues?
- Is job security an issue?
- Are there political or other stressful factors?

3. Assessing managerial culture

Determine how various managers and leaders ensure clarity within their areas of responsibility and communicate purpose and direction:

- Where do they get their information? How?
- Do they rely on subordinates to communicate and explain policy?
- Do they have formal and consistent techniques for communicating different kinds of information and direction?
- Do they empower subordinates to assume responsibility and to make decisions?
- Do they make participative decisions; do they get and accept feedback?
- How do they make sure that everyone gets the word?

4. Understanding the real organizational drivers

Examine the most important business, financial, or operational values driving the organization; for example, quality, cost management, time sensitivity, volume production, customer/employee satisfaction, continuous improvement.

• Does any program overwhelm everything else, and what is the relationship of the virtual project to this or other high priority interest?

• Is there a history of "flavor of the week" management priorities?

• Are there hidden agendas or masked drivers? For example, are alliances based strictly on competency or does tradition, friendship, or politics really underlie partner choices?

5. Is There any organizational experience with virtual or even distributed work?

• Are there established values, expectations, or history influencing established virtual activities?
• Are there published policies?
• Is there frequent publicity for successful virtual activities?
• Are there formal training programs to prepare individuals for virtual activities, and does this include virtual teaming?
• Are people rewarded for individual work as part of a team, or is the team rewarded? Both?

6. Alliance building

One way to better understand the nature of virtual alliances is to reflect on your own organization's current attitudes and perceptions *viz a viz* alliances. To stimulate this reflection we offer the following set of questions. The point here is not to find right answers, but to generate some insights into where your organization is on the spectrum between conventional and virtual alliances.

• Which term does your organization or company use to identify outside resources? (a) vendor, (b) supplier, (c) collaborator, (d) consultant, (e) partner, (f) stakeholder.

• Do outside alliances require the investigation, approval, and monitoring of your legal department?

• Are outside contributors allowed to communicate directly with counterparts in operational or line groups within the company?

• Are outside contributors allowed to have controlled access to the company's: (a) E-mail, (b) information network, (c) internal documentation, (d) meeting minutes?

• Does everyone in the extended organization (the virtual team) have full network and information system access? Internet access?

• Do outside contributors participate in: (a) planning meetings, (b) design sessions, (c) marketing meetings, (d) pricing discussions, (e) customer service, (f) project or phase reviews, (g) internal or external training?

• How do outside contributors participate in the decision process? (a) not at all, (b) made aware of decision elements and asked to provide input, (c) participate in discussions, (d) have a vote, (e) can make decisions that are as binding as those of internal stakeholders.

• Who represents the outside contributors? (a) a lawyer, (b) an executive manager, (c) a line manager, (d) someone recognized as having essential competencies.

• How are interactions with outside contributors conducted? (a) through an exchange of written memos, (b) through scheduled face-to-face meetings, (c) whenever and wherever the work is being done, (d) continuously through the open exchange of electronic information.

• How are outside contributors rewarded? (a) through payments based on contractual agreements, (b) by participation in future results of the relationship, (c) by receiving preferred status on future business, (d) by sharing in recognition and incentive programs equally with all stakeholders, (e) all of the above.

Your responses to these questions indicate how far along your organization is toward practicing alliances in the virtual sense: c's, d's, and e's suggest you've solidly begun the transition to becoming a virtual organization with supporting virtual operations; a's and b's suggest you have further to go to become a virtual player.

7. Teaming experience

Teams and special teaming processes are central to virtual work. Most organizations have experience in the use of dedicated teams, but few have adapted their teams to be effective in virtual environments. Further, the increasing complexity of the tasks teams must address under compressed time constraints requires that there be special training and support for virtual teams.

• Do cross-functional or virtual teams exist in the organization? Do existing teams have formal structures, practices, and management? Is there a communications protocol to ensure that distributed team elements can effectively work together? Have existing cross-functional teams produced results?

• Is there a formal team training process? Does the training program include skills needed for virtual team operations? Does the training include material designed for leaders and managers of virtual teams? Have the leaders and stakeholders been trained?

• Determine the results of previous team efforts. Were there processes in place to capture learning about the teaming process as the project matured? Are there audited results? Did teams publish final reports, and how and to whom were these reports distributed? Were the comments and suggestions of team members included in any reports?

• Is team performance called out in performance reports? Are team members rewarded for their successes? Has management created specific rewards for participation in teams?

• Were leaders of successful teams assigned to new team responsibilities where they could use their teaming skills? Are there indications that team members volunteered for new team assignments? Are team building and leadership training formally included in the planning of new projects?

8. Individual and team empowerment

Each stakeholder and competency leader needs the authority to fully represent his or her parent group. This authority includes the ability to commit group resources consistent with the expectations of the project plan.

• Individuals should know that they have the authority and responsibility to act within the boundaries of the project.

• Is there a strong possibility that their decisions will be challenged or overruled? By whom?

• Do the team members feel confident that they will be able to serve on the team for the duration of the project?

9. Team metrics and rewards

Virtual teaming and the accelerated schedules associated with virtual work projects generates intense stress and pressure, and requires total commitment from managers and workers. These conditions must be recognized and managed.

• How does the organization identify and value results and contributions? Is the focus on

- Output measured in terms of quality or quantity?
- Contribution to process, planned or ad hoc?
- Commitment to quality as an overarching goal?
- Individual or team accomplishments?
- Commitment to process improvement or product development?
- Adapting to changing environments or processes?
- Interpersonal communications skills?

• Is interaction with individuals and groups outside the organization valued?

• Do all levels of the organization participate in a reward/recognition process?

• Are the conditions and criteria for reward formal and widely publicized?

• Are there formal standards for measuring team performance?

• Are there special incentives for experienced team leaders and members to seek out and experiment with new teaming opportunities?

10. Assessing leadership skills

Project leaders need to be competent in their specialties, in the techniques and technical support requirements of virtual operations, and in virtual leadership skills.

• How did they acquire these competencies? If training is in progress, when will it be completed? If needed, is special training easy to obtain?

• Do leaders have authority over team members within the scope of the project? Will the team members know who is directly responsible for their work activities? Will they know who is in charge of the person in charge? Do they know how the team leader will communicate with them? Does every leader have the support necessary to access all project information?

• Are there limits on open access to project information? Who established the limitations? Does the communication plan include the location and access protocols for all project information? Can everyone who needs to access the information? Why not?

11. Attitudes toward change

Virtual operations requires significant changes from well established individual work habits, behaviors, and performance metrics. If there is strong resistance to change within the organization, the transitioning to virtual operations will be difficult. On the other hand, where organizations are more comfortable with a constantly changing environment, establishing virtual processes can be streamlined.

Determine whether change management is reactive or pro-active.

• Are there examples of recent changes and evidence of processes in place to manage the changes?

• Do the examples indicate that the change was a response to a problem -- reactive; or an opportunity -- pro-active?

• Does the organization resist or encourage change?

• Are there any official statements from top management concerning their position on change?

• Do existing planning documents recognize change and include activities to control the impact of the change, for example: training programs for new technologies, demonstrations of new processes, internal publications which explain to workers the reasons for making necessary changes?

• How many of the key leaders and stakeholders have been formally trained in change management?

• Are line level individuals trained?

• Does the organization have an "early warning system" to identify potential or future situations that will require change?

• Are there different responses to change through the various organizational levels: worker, management, executive?

How does the organization respond to crises?

• Are there formal processes for dealing with crises?

• Are there courses in crisis management?

• How many of the key leaders and stakeholders have been formally trained?

• Are line level individuals trained?

• If there are no formal processes, how are crisis situations managed?

• Are there different responses to crisis through the various organizational levels?

12.   Knowledge building and information access

Knowledge and knowledge sharing fuels virtual operations. It is critical to determine the organization's valuing of knowledge and its attitudes towards knowledge sharing.

• Are formal processes in place that focus on electronically building, preserving, and accessing organizational knowledge and intelligence?

• Does the culture reward knowledge sharing or knowledge hoarding?

• Are there training programs to establish knowledge building techniques and processes? To build knowledge sharing teamwork?

• How is organizational knowledge distributed throughout the organization? Determine if the flow is both up and down and across functional divisions.

• Does everyone have access to organizational knowledge in forms that will enhance his or her job performance?

13.   Decision making processes

The decision processes practiced in the organization can have critical impact on the pace required for virtual operations.

• Is there an effective, predictable decision process? Is decision making responsibility aligned with the level at which the competency to make the decision exists? How are issues resolved, and decisions made?

• Is the decision process open?

• Is the process dictatorial, democratic, or nonexistent?

• Are all stakeholders aware of the issues and options and do they have the opportunity to influence results? Are there easily accessible electronic dialogs to gather input for decisions?

• Are decisions made unilaterally by individuals or special interest groups?

• Do issues and decisions require formal review? By whom?

• Are issues and decisions recorded? Are they distributed? How? To whom?

• Are decisions permanent, or are they viewed as tactical expedients and revised as required by changing circumstances?

14. Information sharing

Virtual operations require an environment in which information flows throughout the stakeholder community. This does not exclude provisions to control or manage the flow of information which may be required for security or efficiency.

• Is information currently controlled or managed?

• Are the control decisions predictable, based on a specific and understood rationale, or are they simply "go by the book" general policies?

• Do key stakeholders have full electronic access to all project information?

• What are the procedures to deal with information security, information overload, information access, and user navigation through information and knowledge resources?

15. Meeting protocols

Meetings are the most common instrument for team information sharing. Face-to-face meetings are extremely important for launching projects, gaining commitments, publicly praising performance, and other communications purposes. To be effective, except for brainstorming or discovery oriented meetings, meetings should be structured rather than haphazard. We've all left what we thought were action meetings feeling as though we'd lost ground on the situation at hand.

The point here isn't to discuss the protocols for face-to-face meetings but to simply make the point that electronic meetings require infinitely more structure than do face-to-face meetings. So if no tradition of meeting protocol exists in the organization, special efforts will have to be made to build in that tradition for electronic meetings.

Indeed, electronic meeting protocols are so important to virtual operations that many organizations choose to develop these protocols in their first prototype efforts.

• Are meetings currently designed or ad hoc?

- Are meetings considered part of work, or an interruption of work?
- Does the organization routinely use meeting agendas to ensure productive and predictable use of time?
- Is there a standard format for meeting agendas?
- Are agendas distributed to attendees prior to the meeting? How?
- Are agendas easily changed or modified?
- Do agendas include the time to be spent on each item?
- Are agendas generally followed?
- Is there a method for ensuring that the right people are identified and included to participate in meetings?
- Is there a process for documenting, communicating, and accessing meeting results?
- Are electronic meeting aids available and used: audio, video, or computer conferencing; fax; electronic whiteboards, etc.?
- Is there formal training in meeting techniques and in the use of meeting augmentation tools?
- Do all levels of the organization accept and use virtual meeting techniques?

Final Comments

Our objective here has been to share an effective technique for preparing for the virtual transition, while minimizing the discomforts, distractions, destabilization, and chaos that usually accompanies major organizational change. By taking the time to find out where you are, you reduce the risk of catastrophic underestimation of capabilities, and the ensuing drain on other resources to shore up the initiative. In short, you can continue to run the organization -- earning revenue, keeping the best people, and making customers and suppliers happy -- while you deliberately go through the change process.

These lists are by no means complete, either in scope or in detail. But they should stimulate a dialog that will give everyone a deeper insight into what the organization knows and doesn't know. Specifically addressing aspects of your organizational environment will create a greater sensitivity to virtual issues, enriching participants' mental model of virtual operations.

Having taken some time -- a couple hours, a day, a week --to reflect on the "As Is" state of the organization, now you should be prepared to begin the actual design of virtual operations for your organization. This will be the subject of the final two Parts of the book.

VIRTUAL OPERATIONS: KEY PROCESSES

Chapter 15: Virtual Work Tasks
Chapter 16: Virtual Teaming
Chapter 17: Virtual Communications
Chapter 18: Virtual Learning

Until now we have concentrated on the business trends that make virtual operations a likely business strategy, and the new roles, cultural realities, and technologies that recommend it as a viable one. Now we will introduce the four virtual processes that are at once the most highly leveraged change agents in transitioning to virtual operations, and the foundations of all future virtual work.

- Virtual Work Tasks
- Virtual Teaming
- Virtual Communications
- Virtual Learning

In each of the next four chapters we examine one of these fairly traditional processes in its new virtual context. For example, we will talk about teaming design as it applies to the design and support of virtual, not traditional teams.

We begin with the planning and design of virtual work tasks: the activities that support the physical work the organization must accomplish to be successful in developing of new products, improving the quality of existing production, service, or

administrative processes, or launching new organizational initi
atives.

The next focus is teaming. Teaming is ubiquitous today, but virtual teaming is in many ways quite different from the traditional teaming model. For example, virtual teaming involves tapping into world class competencies whereever they can be accessed, electronically. We see this demonstrated every day when news networks assemble ad-hoc teams of experts to provide us with real-time commentary and analysis on the latest breaking news. The perspective on teaming here includes specific beliefs, knowledge, skills, and behaviors that must converge for a team to work successfully to overcome time, distance, and cultural barriers.

In Chapter 17 we examine the essence of "virtual" communications: the characteristics, techniques, and technologies available to support the virtual work system. Any number of studies have concluded that communication, or the lack of communication, causes over 80% of collaborative work problems (probably closer to 90% for virtual operations). In many business situations communications is episodic and often initiated only by crisis. The success of the virtual operations model depends on the availability of open, predictable, robust, electronic, multimedia communications.

Finally, we look at learning. Earlier chapters have made the point that today's fast pace, the increasing complexity of products and services, and the impact of technology have stressed our traditional work models to the breaking point. Learning is the key to getting back on track and keeping up with change, but it turns out that traditional learning systems are just as threatened. Continuous learning is the route to improving existing competencies and developing new ones. Learning builds teamwork at the worksite, but in a non threatening way. And virtual learning—learning that is conducted through the same network and information infrastructure that supports virtual operations—situates learning in the context that it will be used: the electronic network.

The design is the responsibility of the project management team: the project leader and key stakeholders. The technique we suggest is based on interaction between the project leader, key stakeholders, and others they feel represent special and essential interests or resources key to the success of the project. They can be guided by a process design checklist that superimposes the virtual spin over the specific design activities (see Chapter 19). The "virtual" agenda may be addressed by the entire project management team, or by the leader and a subgroup that have special knowledge and experience in the use of complex information and communications processes; however, the final design must be accepted by the entire team. Remember, the best way to develop the commitment required to change work and behavior is to involve everyone in the design effort.

The design activity can be self directed by the participants, although, especially in the early stages of an organization's transition to virtual operations, sometimes it helps to bring in an objective outside expert familiar with the technique to facilitate the activity. Whether chaired by the project leader or facilitated by an outside expert, the project leader is in charge and must make certain that the final work process plan is supported by the entire team. If there are disagreements that prevent full consensus that cannot be resolved by the team, the leader must involve top management to arbitrate and resolve the issue. The goal is that this group will complete a work process plan that will, in their judgment, successfully and with manageable risk, deliver the required results as specified by management. Work task design, high performance teaming, designed interpersonal communications, continuous learning -- none of these is a new idea—all have unique properties in the virtual paradigm. The following chapters examine each of these virtual leverage points in some detail, preparatory to Part VI, which provides summary checklists for designing each process.

While these processes are quite different from each other, they are also closely intertwined; like the competency elements in Chapter 4, the key virtual operations "quadruple helix" relationship. To reinforce this interrelatedness while focusing on the unique qualities of each, we follow the same general sequence in each chapter:

1. Introductory comments, including definitions and benefits
2. The "virtual spin" that differentiates the virtual form from the traditional
3. Example
4. Specific barriers
5. A design approach.

Now, to Chapter 15 and Virtual Work Tasks.

VIRTUAL WORK TASKS

I love the logic of reengineering. My approach is to take a process, examine it very carefully and identify everything that is happening, then figure out what you want that process to actually accomplish. Then design a new process that only accomplishes what you need, and gets rid of all the rest.
John McClellan, President, McClellan Inc.[1]

I don't want step functions of improvement; I want a staircase. Better yet, give me an elevator to breakthrough.
Senior Executive, International Aerospace Consortium[2]

In business today, process redesign, or reengineering, is the conventional prescription for survival. Redesigning work tasks for virtual operations has the same goals that drive all organizational redesign efforts -- improving quality, reducing time and cost. However, the characteristics of virtual processes are dramatically different from those of traditional processes, even recently reengineered ones. In this chapter we'll consider the nature of these new processes that can lead an organization to breakthrough virtual capabilities.

Definition

We suggested earlier that most organizations are playing new games with old sets of rules. For example, conventional wisdom dictates that business processes are designed as a set of complimentary tasks

---

[1]Conversations with the authors, New Hampshire, 1994.
[2]Conversations with the authors, Belfast, Northern Ireland, 1992.

needed to produce desired results. Typically, when these processes are modeled, they reveal the physical flow of materials from raw input, through various refining processes until the final product rolls out the door. Logic suggests that tasks should occur sequentially, the results or output of one task feeding the next and so on until the entire process is completed: design a widget, manufacturer the widget, market the widget, sell the widget, service the widget.

Virtual operations are founded on a different set of assumptions, based on the nature of today's organizations (virtual), raw materials (information and knowledge), people (knowledge workers), offices and factories (the network), tools (telecommunications and information systems), markets (demanding, fickle, global), and products and services (complex, information based). Now widely separated virtual teams smoothly work together electronically, developing financial services, writing major systems integration proposals -- for other virtual organizations -- and designing "world cars." The benefits of these virtual work processes are becoming more and more evident.

Benefits

At a high level, virtual work processes contribute both to value generation and cost reduction in organizations that find themselves trying to compete in the virtual environment. Early results have shown that by reengineering basic business processes for the virtual environment, organizations are achieving results like these:

• Producing high quality, knowledge, products and services, by enabling the collaboration of geographically separated leaders, stakeholders, and competency- based teams.

• Reducing project cycle time up to 50% and more by bringing serial work processes into parallel. Simultaneity is achieved by providing ubiquitous access to information across geographies, disciplines, and cultures.

• Reducing travel related expenses for these virtual collaborators by up to 50% and more.

• Providing management with real-time windows into projects, bringing the ability to make immediate adjustments to change, rather than waiting for periodic reporting to trigger interventions.

• Providing comprehensive and easily accessible audit trails, and the ability to capture valuable learning and share it throughout the organization -- to advance the learning curve for the next project.

More specific benefits will become apparent through an example used in this chapter, the redesign of an Engineering Change Order system for the virtual environment.

The Virtual Spin

It's important to understand the characteristics of virtual processes in comparison with conventional ones. In time these virtual process attributes will not need to be called out, having become an integral part of the organization's thinking of the virtual mental model. But, at the risk of stating the obvious, we'll begin building that perspective now, first by simply listing some differences between virtual and traditional work tasks, then by discussing in some detail the more significant attributes of virtual work tasks.

Traditional Processes	Virtual Processes
Co-located resources	Widely distributed resources linked electronically
Serial work	Parallel work
Periodic communication	Continuous communication
Face-to-face interaction	Electronic interaction
Physical objects	Electronically generated and processed information objects
Information distribution	Information access
Information on paper	Electronic information
Sharing completed work	Continuous sharing of incomplete work
Knowledge/Information hoarding	Knowledge/Information sharing
Transparent Processes	Computer-visible processes
Commodity work	Unique work
Upper management decisions	Point-of-work decisions
Downstream focus	Whole process focus
Hard prototyping	S/W simulation and prototyping

Now we'll look at some of these key transitions in more detail:

• Process Resources - From Co-location to Competency

Traditionally, managers have felt it was important to have all the people on a project work in the same building. This enabled concentration of tools and materials, facilitated communication, and provided a certain amount of control by the presence of management. One manager we know always fought for office space contiguous to his own manager; the logic was that every time the senior manager walked by she would be reminded of the existence of his group—no small help at budget time.

In projects supported by virtual work processes, participation has less to do with location, or even organization, than it does with competency. A senior manager may have responsibilities for projects whose people are spread all over the world, connected through electronic networks: seeing them at work isn't likely, nor is it worth much, since the value of virtual work is results, not activity-based. However, virtual processes bring with them the capability to make work and through it people, visible in the network. These "windows in to the work system" are already being formalized in project management software, management schemas of databases, and comprehensive situation, or war rooms for complex projects.

• Process Time - From Sequential to Simultaneous

Physical development and manufacturing processes have traditionally involved sequential fabrication and assembly processes; they still do. Even early information-based work processes such as research, administration, and design were based on sequential information flow models. The serial model had drawbacks in that people had to await the arrival of the work and developed no perspective on the whole work system. Furthermore, errors or unacceptable input to one stage in the process were extremely disruptive, causing major "loopbacks" in the system. Of course, a great deal of time was wasted waiting for the work to show up.

Virtual work tasks are not monolithic, but are broken down into sub-tasks that can be performed simultaneously. Sub-tasks continue in parallel, with information objects being continuously exchanged between the teams involved. Some have suggested that this resembles the relay-race model of passing the baton, as

opposed to the assembly line model of waiting for a part to arrive
before starting work.

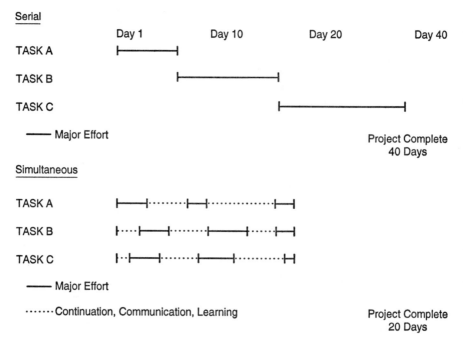

Figure 15.1   Serial and Simultaneous Work

Since virtual work tasks are designed around electronic information access, rather than sequential flow, people can see the work
developing and contribute to it as appropriate. They can perceive
the whole work process, can anticipate problems, and negotiate
solutions while the work is still "upstream," eliminating loopbacks.
For example, in the sequential model of a document development
process, the text is shipped by E-mail or file transfer to an illustrator. She might then discover that the text provides no call-outs to
the illustrations. In the simultaneous model the illustrator has constant access to the text as it's being written, perhaps in shared
database or computer conference. She can spot the impending problem during the writing stage and cue the writers to build appropriate lead-ins into their text in near real-time.

• Process Information - From Completeness and Paper Distribution, to Incomplete Electronic Sharing

These characteristics of information in virtual processes are
implicit in the previous paragraphs, but need to be called out. The

tradition of publishing complete information on paper is a long one. There is a sense of closure, permanence, and professionalism embodied in the formatted, crisply printed page. But in the virtual environment the goal is to collaboratively create a final "information object," not to provide groups with opportunity to create attractive reports, specifications, or even designs. As we mentioned in Chapter 5, professional standards need to be reset: Value lies in making useful information electronically accessible, not in printing a definitive document.

• Technology - From Data Flow to Information Access and Interpersonal Communications

Technology is no longer considered a solution, but rather an ingredient of a solution. In virtual operations we need to take the view that technology can be found to support most virtual processes. Through file transfer, scanners, and database access almost any information can be made available in digitized form. Wireless communications and a worldwide telephone system make access ubiquitous. Multimedia communications and presentation applications provide bandwidth that supports everything from ASCII characters to full motion 3-D graphics and video. The challenge is to design virtual processes that utilize the potential of existing technologies, and can evolve to use new technologies as they emerge.

Remember, these are general points of contrast between traditional and virtual work forms; any one of these characteristics may or may not be apparent in a particular virtual process. Of course, the boundaries here are arbitrary. Traditional, face-to-face, paper-based concurrent engineering has taken the simultaneous view for decades, and virtual initiatives usually embody some traditional characteristic, and virtual initiatives usually embody some traditional characteristics.

Candidate Virtual Tasks

In order to raise the probability of designing a task or work process that embodies the virtual mental model and makes a significant positive impact on organizational performance, the process should have certain characteristics. The most promising candidates would be

• Information and communication intensive -- Look for processes that have a high information content. Information is easily moved and processed electronically, within and across organizations

• Distributed and cross-functional resources -- Processes should require assets that are widely distributed, within and outside the organization. Really, the process constituency should be a mini-virtual organization.

• Competency-based -- Look for processes that require expert or specialized input. There's no need to settle for available competencies; you can go for the best wherever it resides.

• Subject to Change -- Managing change is often the most demonstrable feature of virtual operations. Processes that define highly stable, extended operations may mask the benefits of virtual operations.

• Complex -- Look for processes that qualify as complex systems, composed of sub-processes that can be performed simultaneously. Here is where the greatest reductions in cycle time can be achieved.

Engineering Change Orders: An Example of Virtual Task Design

Consider the following real, but anonymous example. A major aerospace contractor, under pressure from the US government to drive cost overruns out of an ongoing missile program, set out to reengineer key processes to help bring performance in line with government expectations. At the same time the organization hoped to gain some insights into where they needed to invest in technology and get more return from the technology already on hand.

A cross-functional team, with representation from executive, line, and supervisory management, looked into various processes whose improvement could dramatically reduce the overruns. They used traditional systems analysis approaches to see where the waste lay, finally settling on the document review and release process as a candidate for redesign. Review and release is the formal process by which all project documents, including specs, drawings, change orders and so forth, are validated, verified, accepted, and officially released for implementation. This process had many of the virtual hallmarks cited above, but as currently implemented made little use of the information network. Most work was carried out on paper, face-to-face.

In any system development effort, whether the system in question be a product, service, or organization, the project document generation is complex, time consuming, error prone, and therefore, expensive. When late or erroneous information is released it results in downstream loopbacks that incur order of magnitude costs in time and resources. Back to the drawing board. This team chose review and release, because it was a key task that, through virtual redesign, could dramatically reduce project cycle times and therefore costs.

The team decided to focus on just one kind of review and release, then apply the learning laterally to similar processes in the organization. That way an immediate benefit could be derived from the redesign of the target process, and more strategic value gained from wider application.

The specific organizational process chosen was the Engineering Change Orders (ECO), the activity that managed significant changes to key documents relating to the complex system (i.e., product) being built: the component, the missile, the aircraft. The ECO process included activities ranging from the detection of the cause for change, through dissemination of the information describing the change to the right people, to negotiation support, to formal decision/approval/release.

The process in place was very structured, but relied heavily on paper media and face-to-face meetings. This caused problems because the information involved was, until the final approved Change Order, very tentative and flexible. To constantly print, publish, distribute, edit, and revise documents repeatedly took enormous support and time. More importantly, key people were invariably off on assignment to other sites around the world when the need for their competency arose. The meetings generated huge costs in time and dollars to bring all these people together face-to-face. Scheduling and traveling were a nightmare; often stakeholders missed parts of the deliberation because of conflicts, and either meetings needed to be rescheduled, or went on without key participants. In sum, the existing process consumed time and resources and sometimes resulted in flawed decisions because of the inability to sustain communication among all the stakeholders.

At the same time, the ECO process had all the hallmarks of a good candidate for redesign as a virtual process, being:

- Information and communication intensive
- Requiring participation from distributed resources
- Competency-based, involving many experts
- Extremely complex: composed of sub-processes that could be performed simultaneously
- Change-related.

Having decided on a specific target, management empowered an experienced virtual team leader to develop a proposal to reduce project cycle times through reengineering of the ECO process. The major constraint was that the new process had to be based primarily on available or quickly and economically procurable information technologies.

First, using simulation software (but any systems analysis methodology will do), the team learned where the real "drivers" of time and cost lay in the current performance of ECO tasks. Then, using this information as a reference point, they conceptualized a new process, based on designed-in virtual processes and technologies, that would avoid the pitfalls of the current system. Systems analysis revealed these key phases of the process:

1. Detection of the exception, the prime cause of the change order. Anyone at any level could spot a design or process problem; the challenge was to be able to raise the visibility of the problem and to begin looking for solutions quickly.

   For example if a structural engineer realized that the current landing gear was too weak to handle new payload configurations, that person had to be able to note the problem and do something about it; in this case it meant convening a team of experts in materials, stress, business planning, and so forth who could assess the problems, model various alternatives, and propose a fix.

2. Continuous dialogue support for the team that would propose the solution, the actual Change Order. The team addressing the problem would without doubt be distributed, probably all over the world. The challenge would be to provide a platform for review and structured dialog.

3. Notification of all known product and process stakeholders who had an interest in the change or its effects on the rest of the system. For example, sturdier landing gear might be proposed, but that could affect other aspects of the product, like fuel consumption and internal cargo space. Those responsible for those areas needed to be real-time participants in the stakeholder review process.

4. Making available all relevant information to all potential stakeholder/reviewers. Not knowing everyone who might be affected, wide access to review information needed to be provided. There was no time to wait for closet stakeholders to accidentally find

out that a change was being made that would impact their own areas of responsibility.

5. Support for deliberations and negotiations among the reviewers

6. Support for final approval, release and dissemination of the Change Order.

Like ZYX Corporation, the organization already made extensive, if random use of local area network based E-mail, computer and audioconferencing. The team looked very carefully at their current capabilities and considered what improvements they could make with moderate additional investment. They reengineered the ECO process to have more structured communication protocols. In most cases the protocols were supported by the already in-place technologies:

The Virtual ECO Process:

1. E-mail distribution lists prepared to announce the need for an engineering change and to convene the review process. All milestones in the review process to be announced through E-mail

2. Automatic start-up of an expertly facilitated computer conference for each change proposal. The conference to be accessible by Internet/Telnet and through high-speed 800-line dial-up. Threads in that conference would be dedicated to

-- Posting of relevant documents, including situation descriptions, proposed changes, standards and so forth

-- Dialogue about defects and problems, as well as proposed changes

-- Clearing house for input from stakeholders affected by the proposed changes

-- Posting of decisions.

3. Professionally facilitated audioconferencing for real time, voice resolution of specific issues. Follow-up with written documents in appropriate conference thread.

4. Face-to-face approval/signoff meeting

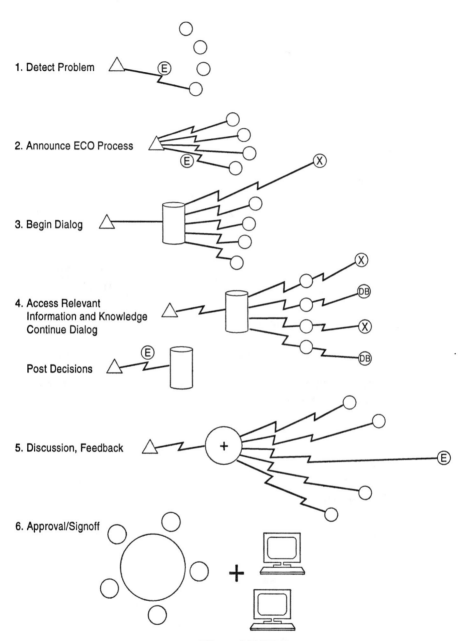

Figure 15.2   Virtual ECO Process

The advantages of the virtual process included the following:

• Dramatic reduction in the time needed to process a Change Order—This resulted from acceleration of document development, support for continuous communications, elimination of time lost for distant stakeholders to access new information or travel to a meeting site, elimination of need to reschedule face-to-face meetings, elimination of need to pull people together from all over to handle a real-time crisis.

• Increase in quality of decisions—With all stakeholders having clear access to documents and input to the dialogue, problems and solutions were better understood and less likely to cause later problems. The continuous dialog among stakeholders introduced the presence of a phenomenon called "the phantom reviewer": this was a personification of the collaborative viewpoint, different from any single person's, that arose from the continuous on-line deliberations.

• Reduction in costs—Wasted time and poor quality are major cost drivers. Accelerating the process and delivering right decisions saved both present and downstream resources.

Barriers to Virtual Work

While virtual processes such as the ECO process seem to be obvious improvements over conventional processes, there are of course barriers to implementing and sustaining virtual work. As expected, most barriers involve the people who execute the processes. While people issues are not the focus of this chapter, a few words need to be said about creating an environment in which people will be comfortable—can we hope for eager—to use the virtual approach.

Many people are reluctant to use the electronic infrastructure to do their work, which may be highly communicative, knowledge intensive, and ego-involved. They communicate best face-to-face, like to persuade over the phone, are resistant to wide-spread electronic information sharing, and don't like the planning and formality that are required to make virtual processes work.

Using distributed resources can also be a problem. The normal convention is to have all resources physically collocated. This way you can see when things begin to go wrong and you can step in and do the right thing. When the link between resources is electronic, many hands-on managers feel they will lose control. Information sharing is difficult at best even within a single organization, and distrust goes up exponentially as resources begin to include outsiders and, in some cases, organizations that might have been or could be competitors.

Experience has shown that the best way to address these barriers is through

- Encouraging people who perform the processes to be part of the design effort; "Those who plan, do" is a powerful and empowering motto.

- Making visible the goals and advantages of the process

- Training people in virtual operations and virtual teaming

- Rewarding those who experiment with the new virtual processes.

Indeed, the collaborative Virtual Operations Design approach does a lot to encourage people to become proponents instead of resisters of new virtual processes.

Designing Virtual Work Tasks

We've had a look at what a specific designed virtual process looks like. Now we'll suggest a general methodology for virtual work task design. It's important to keep in mind that the virtual redesign effort does not simply set out to automate, or even informate, existing or traditional work processes; rather, the design focus is driven by what management specifies are the "desired results." In many cases the result may be an "electronic information object": a plan, specification, 3-D product model, schedule, or a combination -- like a 50% reduction in the time it takes for document review and release.

In *Systems Thinking, Systems Practice,* Peter Checkland defines, develops, and demonstrates an approach to analyzing and changing complex human work systems that is remarkably suited to the design of virtual work processes. His conceptual basis is interesting for us because it incorporates formal systems design as well as the realities of business process redesign. Uniting these disciplines gives strength and reality to the approach. We don't go into the full methodology here, but modify and summarize the approach to adapt it to the challenge of virtual process design.[3]

Stakeholders in the design process can approach the task by following these basic steps. Here the steps are presented with little expansion, but obviously each step requires a great deal of knowledge input, information access, dialog, negotiation and decision making:

1. Become immersed in the Situation. Participants in designing the work process should understand the existing process in the larger context of the virtual environment and the organization's business goals: the role it plays in those larger complex systems.

2. Understand, describe, and display the ideal virtual work task from multiple perspectives. Stakeholders can reveal the many interlaced, non-linear processes and problems involved, including sub-processes, communications paths, activities, teaming relationships, and learning needs. They can keep in mind the "virtual spin" that gives power to these processes. It is useful to represent the process as a transforming system that changes various inputs to outcomes.

3. Construct a full conceptual model of the To-Be or Could-Be virtual process. Show information access and flow, show transformations.

4. Compare the ideal conceptual models with the systems apparent in the situation; do a conceptual model of the As-Is situation if desired. The comparisons can "structure the debate" as to the accuracy and appropriateness of the conceptual models.

5. Look for the Delta between As-Is and To-Be.

6. Decide if the As-Is system can be "virtualized," or if an entirely new virtual process needs to be developed

[3]Checkland, Chapter 6

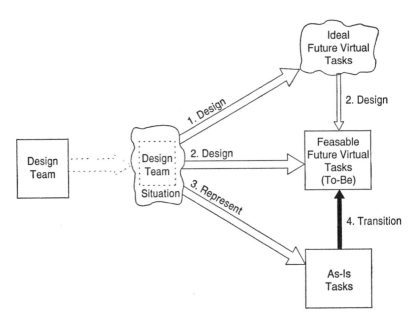

Figure 15.3   Virtual Task Design

In order to appreciate the elegance of this approach it's helpful to run through a couple of process scenarios with which you are well acquainted. For example, consider the common enough process of document generation. Choose an appropriate sub-process: generating and submitting a major proposal to an inside or outside organization. Anyone who has done this knows that it has all the hallmarks of candidacy for virtual work:

• Information and communication intensive

• Involves distributed and cross-functional resources

• Competency-based

• Subject to Change

• Complex.

Describe the system using whatever systems analysis techniques your organization favors. This analysis will provide all the information you need to design a conceptual virtual process. The next steps would be to actually design the protocols and technologies that would implement the system, keeping the virtual spin in mind. After you have run through a couple "desk" (or workstation) examples, doing the task redesign for real should pose no show-stopping problems.

Final Comments

The intent of this chapter has been to introduce the concept of reengineering work tasks for the virtual environment. We want to emphasize that the technique your organization uses in the design or redesign activity is not as important as paying constant attention to the virtual spin. Here we have addressed these virtual characteristics at a general level, to give you a feeling for the nature of virtual work tasks. In Chapter 19 we will provide prompts and suggestions that provide more detailed guidelines for the task design process.

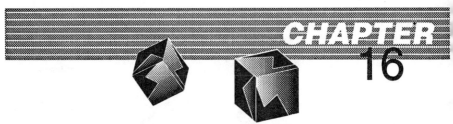

CHAPTER 16

VIRTUAL TEAMING

We need to work together as if we were all in the same room, although we're not.
The common plea of modern managers.[1]

Teams are in vogue today: sports teams, business teams, military teams, fashion teams, writing teams. Teams are the norm, not the exception. So we won't ask you to endure yet another treatise on traditional teams. But we do hope to provide insight into the nature of virtual teams and virtual teaming, the heart of virtual operations.

Definition

There are obvious differences between traditional teams and virtual teams (OK, we will talk about teams!). The most obvious distinctions are physical. Virtual teams are not co-located, although we have seen examples of virtual teams operating within a single building. There are no uniforms or offices to help define the teams. Teaming members come from a variety of organizations. They may share very little except a common purpose, but this purpose becomes the emblem, the unifying icon of the team.

Usually virtual teams are project focused. Because of the stress of virtual work, projects are of relatively short terms, six months to a year.

---

[1]We have heard this bit of "thinkful wishing" from all levels of people in all kings of organizations. This plea underlines the fact that with all our advances, today's processes and technologies give us less communication than we used to have in the old four-wall days. The goal is, of course, to have more.

As always there are exceptions, some virtual teams become permanent teams. Digital's Larry Walker has already described the situation that led to his multi-national chip/code design team. This is an example of a team that has adapted to the realities of the physical situation and, using virtual techniques, has turned what could have easily been impossible barriers of distance, time, and culture into positive virtues. However, virtual teams normally exist only to perform a specified task as efficiently and as effectively as possible, then they disband.

Both traditional and virtual teams are expected to reach higher levels of achievement than would individuals working independently (recall the phantom reviewer in the last chapter).

Benefits

While virtual teaming is difficult to initiate and sustain, the benefits to organizations that find themselves in the virtual situation are impressive. Virtual teaming

- Effectively deals with the realities of time compression, distributed resources, increasing dependency on knowledge-based input, the premium on flexibility and adaptability, and the fact that most of the information we use today is in electronic form

- Enables the recruitment of the best competencies available, not just those in the organization or the neighborhood

- Takes advantage of the electronic infrastructure, enabling the teams to

  -- work in parallel rather than serially

  -- have continuous access to the latest and best knowledge and information

  -- participate from their home-sites, without abandoning other threads in their multiplexed work and home lives.

  -- bring new team members up to speed through the online record of the ongoing work

  -- capture their learning electronically making it easy for other teams to access this learning, often in real-time.

Keeping these benefits in mind, let's turn next to those attributes that characterize virtual teams.

The Virtual Spin

As with virtual work tasks, there are definite contrasts between the characteristics of traditional and virtual teaming. Some of them are listed below:

Traditional Teams	Virtual Teams
Members from same organization	Members from different organizations, companies
Members trained and often certified against established standards	Members selected because of demonstrated competence
Roles and expectations per job title	Expected to perform by situation
Hope for trust	Require trust
Work processes rigid and defined	Work processes flexible and adaptive
Position authority	Knowledge authority
Persuade through power	Persuade through influence
Assert one's perspective	Negotiate, make tradeoffs
Stable work environment	Environment continuously changes
Formal communications minimized	Continuous structured communications
Members work together -- together	Members work together -- apart
Hierarchical	Hierarchical and Networked

These attributes of virtual teaming are not just options or desirable traits; they realistically represent the capabilities and behaviors needed to succeed in complex knowledge work in virtual environments. We believe that as the virtual ethos becomes more pervasive, these teaming characteristics will become the norm.

Proposal Generation: An Example of Virtual Teaming

At the end of Chapter 15 we referred to the process of proposal generation to illustrate an aspect of virtual work task design. The case from which those comments were drawn stands as an excellent example of virtual teaming. In 1991 a major computer products and services company set out to develop a proposal to become the "Automation Systems Integrator" for an aerospace organization. This organization was forming a joint venture team to design and manufacture a new commercial aircraft, and the systems integrator would be a risk-sharing partner in the venture, not just an outsourced competency.

The initial proposal team consisted of about forty stakeholders from different groups within the proposing company. By the time the proposal project got into full swing, over 200 people were involved either directly or indirectly. These people represented four companies, located in over a dozen states and six countries. Team membership was always in flux, with competency needs changing and people moving to new jobs.

The overarching goal of the team was to deliver a win-win proposal by the deadline date, which turned out to be six months. Win-win was an important constraint. These aerospace and integration companies would be in a partnering, not a vendor-supplier or outsourcing relationship. Investment risk in people, equipment, and delayed payments was being shared, so neither "beating the customer" or writing a great losing proposal were alternatives. This fact set the policy that the customer actually would be part of the proposal team, as far as was ethical and fair to the competition.

Time would reveal that to achieve the goal several challenges had to be met. They included

- Creating and keeping together a closely knit team, representing all required organizational, technical, and administrative competencies
- Keeping executive management informed of progress
- Avoiding or neutralizing turf wars
- Meeting an aggressive time schedule.

We'll look at how the team and its leadership approached each of these challenges to successfully accomplish virtual work.

1. Creating and keeping together a closely knit team

The Proposal Team was convened by a triumvirate of leaders:

- A Project Manager, who had overall responsibility for the project
- The Process and Technology Manager, representing the engineering and work process perspective
- A Business and Relationships Manager, who took a business

perspective on the proposal and facilitated the relationship between the team and the "customer."

The initial, or kick-off meeting was held in a facility near the customer site. About forty people from various organizations attended the meeting; they got there by invitation or just showed up. Organizational affiliation was not an issue, only demonstrated competencies in the areas that the leaders agreed on as a first cut at the problem. The team agreed to the goals of the project and went on to discuss how they would work -- what the teaming would look like.

It was decided that teams would be created in ten key skill areas. Each area addressed a critical part of the customer's situation and each would be a key section of the proposal. These areas included the following:

- Program Management—lead the interactions between the Project Team and the customer, and between the Project team and its executive management.

- Technology Team—developed the technical aspects of the proposal.

- The Organizational Capability Team—addressed the virtual work processes, teaming, communications, and learning elements of the proposal, and addressed those same areas for the proposal team.

These were multiorganizational teams. Besides the customer and the proposing company, several other companies were involved at various times proposing applications for inclusion in the technical sections of the project. Communications was obviously the greatest barrier to having such a widely dispersed team work together.

At a key point in the meeting, communications specialists were invited by the leaders to present the case for using electronic communications to support the team. They did so, convincingly, and the proposal team empowered the specialists to develop communications infrastructure that would address the teams needs. They did just that; we'll discuss this plan in Chapter 17.

With designed communications and protocols in place, team members were able to do a great deal of work at home base, on the road, or at the customer site. Since pulling the proposal together involved each team's knowing what the others were doing, a "cascading" model was used, where each team would keep track of the activities of one other team, reporting relevant activities or output back to his or her own team. We'll see exactly how this was done when we discuss virtual communications in the next chapter.

2. Keeping executive management informed of progress

This meant that the right people would know what they wanted to know and should know in near real-time. Virtual windows were designed into the workflow to allow the executives to see what was going on at all times. In addition, individual team members were matched up with specific executives--from both companies--as the liaison to the work.

Team members also were identified to cultivate "friendlies" and neutralize "hostiles" in the executive ranks. This was not done cynically, but pragmatically. This was after all new and risky territory; some executives avoid risk. The goal was winning the contract, not working feverishly only to be stopped by disgruntled management.

3. Avoiding or neutralizing turf wars

Since this was a discovery project, rather than a routine undertaking with a clear set of players, "ownership" was expected to be an issue at both the competency and management levels. The best competencies were not always found in the organizations chartered to provide expertise in certain areas. The leaders usually went over demonstrated experience, rather than theoretical knowledge. It was important that team members had both the specialist and lateral virtual competencies we spoke about in Chapter 4. Team members would be "working with" the customer, not just throwing a proposal over the wall. They would be working with persons from a wide variety of internal organizations. Therefore all team members needed to be skilled in working, electronically in many cases, with outside as well as internal organizations.

4. Meeting an aggressive time schedule, while the aerospace project itself was being defined in parallel with the proposal

At the start the team accepted the challenge of designing its virtual operations: parallel work processes, teaming culture and protocols, continuous communications, and an integral learning system. For example, work tasks were designed to be carried on in parallel:

- Gathering input from the customer; testing solutions
- Finding what the state of the art solutions were for emerging needs
- Writing the skill area proposal sections
- Designing the final proposal
- Managing management
- Constantly improving the team's virtual operations

With these sub-processes going on simultaneously, the team was able to meet the schedule, with no burn-out. This general overview only scratches the surface of the whole effort involved in supporting these teams. What is important is the virtual framework: keeping focused on the competency approach to reaching an agreed goal, without accepting geographical or organizational constraints. Oh yes, in looking back three years later many of the participants considered this leading edge virtual experience as a personal work triumph and learning experience that has helped them immensely as more of their work goes virtual.

Barriers to Virtual Teaming

In designing the teaming process, keep in mind that barriers will crop up and hinder the effectiveness of work. For example, information overload will inhibit the success of an E-mail based solution. Barriers have a secondary effect beyond lost time, inter-team arguments, and so forth. That is, the barriers and their effects cause stress, which is itself a barrier. Stress, from mild annoyance to burnout can wreck a project. It feeds on itself and is contagious if not managed.

There's a formal model for describing stress in a system.[2] At the risk of being overly structured when talking about people's behavior, we'll use this model to show how barriers create stress. Furthermore, the model illustrates how stress creates a positive feedback loop that increases work barriers and can neutralize the positive effects of virtual work. Actually, the stress loop is the reverse of Engelbart's capability increasing Bootstrapping model, mentioned in Chapter 14! The stress model looks like this (Figure 16-1).

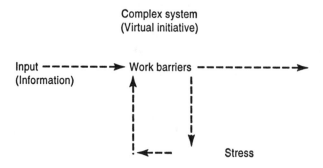

Figure 16.1   Systemic Stress

[2]This model was suggested by Piotr Chadzinski, of Digital Equipment Corporation's Simultaneous Development Process Program in 1990.

In virtual teaming situations, the following are *not* options to reduce stress:

• Changing output specifications (time/complexity relief)
• Increasing processing capacity by adding people
• Ignoring the situation

What follows *are* options for managing barriers:

• Educating and empowering leaders to raise workers' awareness of the potential and rewards of the new processes and of the nature and effects of the barriers and stresses.

• Provide proactive, situated learning in networking processes and technologies. This will enable the team to collaboratively confront barriers in a relatively nonthreatening learning environment.

• Remove old baggage: get rid of trees that are being hugged, like collocated groups, paper document-centered work, fly-in meetings —"Get rid of their pencils!" This may cause a temporary increase in stress, anger, and discontent; but if the teaming participants understand the value of the new ways of working to themselves and to the organization, they should be able to work through this particular kind of stress fairly quickly.

• Identify, build relationships with, and include people on the teams who have been through and learned to manage the stresses.

• Seek innovative uses of all forms of electronic communications to keep teams constantly in touch, addressing the barriers in work, in learning, and in informal communications. If team members are aware that they're not alone in feeling the stress, or dealing with the barrier, their chances of being able to work through the problems is greatly increased.

The following barriers are unavoidable in a virtual teaming situation; they will occur as a result of the cross-cultural, simultaneous, highly informated, and volatile teaming work. But they can be managed using the techniques just discussed, along with other organizational development, change management, and support systems the organization has in place. Team level barriers include:

• Resistance to changing to new ways of working
• Fear of the unknown
• Surrender of security, control, power, information through working with external organizations

Individual level barriers include the following:

- Complexity overload
- Day 1 thinking
- Information overload
- Continuous real-time interacting with others, some from other organizations
- Constant feedback/evaluation of work by others
- Individual responsibility for quality
- Uncertainty of team expectations
- Reversal of upstream/downstream roles
- Required changes in communications behavior
- Constant change, continuous redesign
- Social barriers in electronic workspaces
- Ever-changing, ephemeral electronic information objects (little paper to hang onto)
- Technology barriers in electronic tools/media
- Sharing rewards ("I'm doing/did more work than they did; but I get less credit")
- Trusting cross-functional/cross-cultural/external partners
- Major changes in belief systems:
  - -- stovepipe to team
  - -- individual contributor to group
  - -- serial to simultaneous work
  - -- perfection in work to early sharing
- Lack of effective distributed management.

Designing Virtual Teaming

As we noted earlier, there is a rich body of knowledge available for designing and supporting teams and teaming. We do think that it's useful at this point to draw off what we think are the major steps to effective teaming and point out how and where to introduce the virtual spin. More detailed guidelines will be presented in Chapter 20.

- Competency and Skill Requirement Assessment

This activity tries to determine what individual skills are necessary to accomplish the tasks. Besides generating a competency shopping list, this activity will provide the leaders and stakeholders with a macro view of how the skills and competencies group into logical relationships throughout the life-cycle of the project. This also provides the leader or facilitator with a sense of how well the participants understand virtual operations and the terms and concepts used in the design process.

• Teaming Barrier Identification and Assessment

As we have seen, barriers come with any new territory. It's a good idea to collectively confront, discuss, try to eliminate, work around, or otherwise neutralize barriers at the time the team is first convened. Addressing barriers at design time has several advantages over waiting for them to come up unannounced in the heat of work. Team members confronting barriers this early gain a realistic sense of the rigors of virtual work and experience in recognizing and dealing with barriers, but in a more controlled, risk-free environment than when projects get underway. Furthermore, barriers to accomplishing the design tasks themselves can be overcome: Work and learning can proceed together.

• Stakeholder Empowerment

This establishes the responsibility and authority of all key players. Because of the fast pace of virtual teaming projects, stakeholders must be clear about their relationships with their parent groups. Do they have the power to commit and act? In a way this is a go/no go sensing: If internal and external stakeholders cannot make the quick decisions need to keep virtual work on track, there's no sense taking the risk of starting off.

• Attitudes Toward Change

Virtual teaming generates significant changes to established processes, behavior, and individual work habits and performance. If there is strong resistance to change within the organization, the virtual teaming process will be difficult. Where organizations are more comfortable with a changing environment, the process of establishing effective teaming processes can be streamlined.

• Assessing Current Teaming Practices

This segment is used to determine the current status of teaming within the organization. It can be drawn largely from the organizational sensing activity described in Chapter 14. Most organizations have a wealth of practical experience in the use of dedicated teams, but few have adapted their teaming practices to be effective in the virtual, electronically supported environment. Further, the increasing complexity of the tasks teams must address under relentless time constraints require continuous modification of established practices and a positive commitment to special training and support.

• Decision Making Processes

How the organization typically makes decisions can have critical impact on the pace required to sustain effective virtual teaming. The team must agree to decision processes that will satisfy the needs of management, as well as keep the work cycle moving at virtual speed.

• Morale Management, Recognition, and Rewards

As we've noted, the accelerated schedules associated with virtual work projects and the lack of familiar interpersonal relationships generate intense stress on individuals. A continuous program to address this stress must be put in place. It should include

-- Sustained communication with management that will remind teams of the purpose and value of their efforts

-- Inter-team communications to remind everyone that they're not in the box alone

-- Strong support for training, continuous learning, and technology assistance

-- A responsive program to recognize and reward exceptional commitment and performance

The key here is to provide team support continuously, systemically, both in person and through the network. ¥

• Team Empowerment

This activity is designed to reduce confusion at start-up by ensuring that everyone is clear about expectations, commitments, responsibilities, and authority. Virtual teams are particularly vulnerable to start-up confusion because the members are not in direct physical contact. Additionally, this activity begins the trust building process essential to success.

Final Comments

Virtual teams are quite different from teams that are primarily co-located. They need to be able to achieve the same goals as co-located teams, while facing unique pressures from the nature of their work, social and cultural challenges, time pressures, and ever changing demands on their competencies. While there are methodologies for introducing the virtual spin into the consciousness of team members, action learning is the primary instrument in building virtual teaming competency. What we have offered here is start-up advice, with more specific guidelines to follow in Chapter 20. The real learning comes from doing, and the sooner your organization gets started actually using virtual teams, the sooner teaming capability will be achieved.

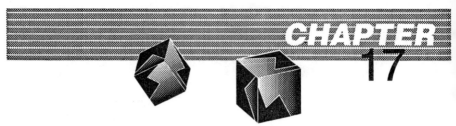

VIRTUAL COMMUNICATIONS

"Look! There's a fellow waving a little black flag...."
"That ain't a flag, is it? That's his coat...."
"So it is, it's his coat. He's taken it off and is waving it around his head. But would you look at him swing it!"
....
"What's the idiot with the coat mean? What's he signalling, anyhow?"
....
"Well, I wish I could make something out of those signals. What do you suppose he means?"
....
"Well, if he'd just signal us to try the surf again, or to go to sea and wait, or go north, or go south, or go to hell, there would be some reason in it. But look at him! He just stands there and keeps his coat revolving like a wheel. The ass!"

The Open Boat, Stephen Crane[1]

This is at once the easiest of chapters, and the most difficult. In a way this entire book has been about perspectives on communications:

- In leading and supporting virtual teams
- In sharing information and knowledge
- In collaborating
- In organizational functions and events

[1] Stephen Crane, "The Open Boat," *Men, Women & Boats* (Freeport, NY, 1972), pp. 38ff.

• Relating to the communications technical infrastructure and applications that enable people to "work together apart."

Here we will try not to be too redundant; we will focus not on behavior or technology, but on the ethos of virtual communications and the value of careful design of a virtual project's communication system.

Definition

It seems that most university undergraduates in the U.S these days are Communications Majors. Under this umbrella is a bewildering variety of specialties: telemetry, cultural anthropology, advertising, journalism, and building cross-functional teams. Now we add to the pot yet another variety, virtual communications. What makes virtual communications different from any other kind of communication?

There is a short answer, distinguishing virtual from traditional communications in terms of both nature and mission. We define virtual communications as a set of designed interpersonal communication protocols and technologies that support virtual work, teaming, and learning. The technologies are primarily electronic, (E-mail, videoconferencing, etc.) and the protocols are designed to capture the full potential of those technologies in support of the work at hand.

Benefits

No virtual project can succeed without well designed communications protocols and technologies. For example, we mentioned earlier that every virtual team needs to build a shared context, or culture, in which to work. That culture provides the framework, clues, expectation setting, trust, and language that helps the team members understand the web of communication that is so integral to their work. What's interesting is that the only way to build this shared culture that will support communication is -- you guessed it -- through communication. So the communication design, which is the subject of Chapter 21 needs to establish the start up communications environment, facilitate the communication necessary to build the common context in the cross-cultural team, and evolve a design that supports the work of the team.

Virtual communication also has the following characteristics:

• Builds trust between team members, especially in cross-organizational, cross-cultural situations; as that trust builds, better communication results; and the positive cycle continues as still more trust is built

• Ensures that every person who contributes to the value creation process is fully informed -- knows what is going on all the time

• Provides management with effective real-time awareness, command, and control

• Maintains channels for the creative expression of ideas

• Facilitates learning

• Allows people to express themselves in a timely way, to connect with anyone at anytime in a project, no matter how large. (This just-in-time connectivity reduces stress, saves time, and increases the quality of collaborative work)

• Supports the electronic synthesis of systems from components: product from parts, documents from chapters, solutions from information

• Enables global access to information and knowledge

• Facilitates simultaneous work

• Increases the probability of positive, quantifiable returns on technology investments

• Provides instrumentation to detect changes in the team, the organizations, the environment.

The Virtual Spin

When we say that communications is the heart of virtual operations, we are using a very rich definition of communication. Communication, in this sense, does not simply mean that data, or a message, was successfully sent from Point A to Point B with a minimum of noise. It means that a message sent from Point A was successfully *received* by Point B, and Points C and D if they were also addressees. We use *received* to mean understood. It doesn't do any good to get a message that makes no more sense to you than the whirling coat did to the shipwrecked mariners in the open lifeboat.

In the virtual context, communications involves the building, exchange, access, use, distribution, recording, change, and sharing of information and knowledge. Since information and knowledge are the not-so-raw materials of virtual work, communications in the virtual world is not *about* work, it *is* work, extremely complex work at that. The implication is clear: Virtual communications will not happen by accident, any more than the complicated work of building an oil rig, law brief, or TV set will happen by accident. Communications in the virtual environment must be designed.

That designed communication environment should accomplish the following:

• Connect everyone in the virtual project with everyone else, anytime, anyplace, anywhere. No walls!

• Encourage people to communicate. This is important to creating the common context within which work gets done. People need to understand enough about each other's mental models to anticipate their needs and the way they will understand messages. Teammates always have this edge: as surgical partners, as team players, as assembly line colleagues, as husbands and wives.

• Provide wide options for communications processes, to accommodate project needs and personal styles: phone, fax, e-mail, computer conferencing, desktop video, face-to-face meeting space, and facilitated travel. These last two are easily forgotten. With the emphasis on electronic communication it is easy to forget that a lot of work still demands face-to-face meetings and travel. It is important that easy-to-use procedures are in place for holding such meetings as well as for travel funding and approval.

• Create on-line templates that take the randomness out of routine communications. For example, on-line forms are an excellent way of setting up meetings, travel, or problem reports in collaborative settings. Such forms help categorize information and set expectations where specific information can be found. This can go a long way to addressing the problems of cross-cultural communications.

• Define communications support roles. These are not technical positions...they're not even positions at all. These are responsibilities that certain stakeholders take on to foster team communications. One role involves developing and maintaining distribution lists, creating templates, and designing audio-, computer and videoconferencing. Another is that of "circuit rider," a person who in addition to his or her teaming role takes on the responsibility of physically travelling from site to site to have personal contact with teaming nodes. This person carries the news, listens to complaints, takes on certain problem solving tasks, and generally keeps the network alive. These are not casual roles, but well-defined activities essential to the success of the project.

• Develop protocols for using *all* communications media. Even phone calls can have some structure to them. Team participants should agree on what media to use for various kinds of communication. And they should, as part of their common communications culture, agree on formats for communications, again to create a common set of expectation and categorizing that makes messages more understandable.

• Encourage structured and unstructured social communications, and set boundaries for appropriateness. A bulletin board on "Places to Eat" can

– Provide excellent social support and (help people learn about computer conferencing); but a real-time flash chat message about the newest restaurant in town, sent to a wide distribution list, can be irritating, even destructive.

– Provide constantly up-to-date purpose-determined distribution lists for all media. *Accessed* communications, such as computer conferences can be open to everyone. *Distributed* communications must get to the right people and only the right people.

– Support synchronous communication. Real-time processes -- phone calls, faxes, chat exchanges, video set ups -- enable fast response to situations.

– Support asynchronous communication. E-mail (usually) and computer conferencing support a more reflective approach to communications. People don't need to immediately respond, as in a phone call or face-to-face meeting, but can gather up information or just think about what and how to respond.

While some of these attributes are unique to virtual communications, some apply to any complex project environment. However, given the cross-cultural barriers to communication, the time pressures, the lack of face-to-face encounters to clarify faulty communication, the virtual environment requires orders of magnitude greater design, structure, and attention to its communication infrastructure and processes.

Proposal Generation: An Example of Virtual Communications

In the previous chapter we described a proposal generation situation as an example of virtual teaming. That same case is a good example of how designed virtual communications can help virtual teams accomplish their goals. We'll go back to the same general headings to frame our discussion here. We recall that specialists, with expertise in both the human and technology sides of communication, proposed and ultimately delivered a communications plan for the team. This was not simply a piece of paper, but rather an initial design for communications support for known team processes, and continuous redesign as new challenges arose. Many people contributed formally and informally to this living plan. Now we'll take a look at some of its key elements.

1. Creating and keeping together a closely knit team, representing all required organizational, technical and administrative competencies, regardless of organizational or geographic barriers.

   The primary communication facility for the skill teams was computer conferencing. A conference was designed and moderated to support each skill area. While face-to-face and voice communication went on as might be expected, any information or knowledge needed to be shared by the team was placed in the conference. All conferences were open to all members. It was suggested that one member of each team also read the conference of another skill group; that way each team could track all the other conferences -- a necessity in parallel work -- yet individuals could avoid the tremendous information overload that would be attendant to reading all conferences. In effect, the conferencing infrastructure enabled a cascading team structure.

   A special conference focusing on general issues of coordination was also established; this turned out to be the most active conference of all. In this conference all team related issues could be brought up with full assurance that everyone on the team would read the messages and many would reply.

2. Keeping executive management informed of progress. This

meant that the right people would know what they wanted to know and should know in near-real-time.

Virtual windows were designed into the workflow to allow the executives to see what was going on at all times.

Executives were invited to be participants in the actual work conferences. Instead of receiving a retrospective, abstract monthly report, they could actually witness the dialog on points that interested them. At one point a situation room, complete with modeling and visualization software, was established to enable executives in both the customer and proposer organizations to try extremely complex what-if scenarios with proposed solutions.

In addition, individual team members were matched up with specific executives -- from both companies -- as the liaison to the work.

A rationale and schedule for audio conferences and face-to-face meetings between counterparts were established. The plan did not limit communication, but established minimum standards so that expectations could be set on both sides, and in busy times communications would not irrevocably fall off.

Team members also were identified to cultivate "friendlies" and neutralize "hostiles" in the executive ranks. This was not done cynically, but pragmatically. This was after all new and risky territory; some executives avoid risk. The goal was winning the contract, not working feverishly only to be stopped by disgruntled management.

Here again there were lots of phoning and personal visits. Both hostiles and friendlies were brought out to the customer site and visited with the on-site team. Executives were given customer tours; in return, key executives from customer organizations were brought to the proposer's corporate headquarters, to build confidence in the already convinced, and help convert the "hostiles."

Avoiding or neutralizing turf wars. Since this was a discovery project, rather than a routine undertaking with a clear set of players, "ownership" was expected to be an issue at both the competency and management levels.

The communications infrastructure and the electronic work it supported helped bypass many organizational tiffs. The work went on, driven by committed contributors, as was evident to all who looked in on the conferences. By project end, with the proposal completed, some organizations were still holding endless meetings to decide how to get a piece of the action.

Taken together, the processes and infrastructure created by the communications plan enabled the team to go virtual. While the plan did evolve to reflect the reality of the ongoing work, it was clearly the upfront decision to address communications in the virtual environment head-on that made the difference in the project. Most of the systems used were simple, and individuals were dedicated to process and technology support. The systems never failed over the six month period and users always got the help they needed to communicate and work.

Barriers to Virtual Communications

In creating and sustaining virtual communications, teams run into two kinds of barriers, technological and cultural. The primary technology barriers are:

- Communications systems within the project that don't talk to one another
- Lack of technical support for specific information and communications media
- Limited access to the communications/information system.

Through advances in standards, multimedia, and wireless technologies, these barriers are being addressed. However, they must be recognized and minimized by the project leadership. One approach gaining popularity has cross-company virtual teams bringing in a virtual technology partner who will provide the communications services to all stakeholders. This eliminates the interoperability problem, reduces capital and support investment, and provides a common communications system upon which to base the evolving common culture.

But the most resistant barriers to virtual communications are the cultural ones: how people resist. We've indicated a few barriers early in this chapter, but here are some that should be addressed directly:

- Cultural Norms

In virtual operations different companies, organizations, disciplines, national cultures, and organizational levels are challenged to maintain the high rate of communication required to conduct the project. The virtual communications infrastructure must be rich enough not only to enable the construction of a shared culture, but to support the particular needs and styles of each of these groups and individuals. We've already mentioned the only way we know of overcoming this communications barrier, of creating a converged culture that can communicate: through facilitated communications.

- Language

There will be language issues. Real-time translation or agreement on a common natural language is essential. In many international efforts to build complex systems such as automobiles, deep-sea drilling platforms, and aircraft, a conscious effort is made to use graphics and icons as much as possible to reduce natural language barriers.

- Loss of Personal Contact

Teams that either partially or as a whole have thrived on face-to-face contact, may find it daunting to maintain electronic communication at the level required for virtual work. There are many reasons for this attachment to physical contact: habit, personal style, dominance, reading body language -- all valid. But there are overarching reasons to move to virtual communications. With the advent of desktop videoconferencing such teams can temper the loss of personal contact with periodic, even daily videoconferences to sustain information sharing and teaming energy.

Other personal barriers include

- Fear of change
- Technophobia
- On-line shyness, or hesitancy to communicate in fast changing situations (the desire to hold off until all the information is available—which is never).
- Mistrust of unseen, unknown communicants.

Most of these barriers should be recognized and continuously addressed through the communications system: communications begets communications. The communications plan, process designers, facilitators, leaders, and circuit riders all can make it their business to spot the barriers and take action. People can be encouraged to

- Take on-line courses
- Engage in "Water Cooler" or "Best Restaurants" bulletin boards

- Occasionally meet face to face
- Exchange pictures
- Not worry about spelling or grammar in informal communication
- Not worry about having a report co-opted by late breaking news. (Like sending E-mail badgering a draftsperson for the latest design, only to find it in your inbox.)

Virtual operations is tough enough. Communication should not be a threatening event, but a constantly available opportunity to tie into the team and the work.

Designing Virtual Communications

The communications design process leads to a plan that enables teams to initiate and sustain the quality and level of communications necessary to succeed in their work. The design addresses people's beliefs and skills, the demands of the virtual work processes, virtual learning opportunities, technologies, and communications support for both people and technology.

As with all design processes, this is a collaborative, not a competitive activity. The goal should be to serve the mission of the organization, not argue for the preferences of the design participants. The burden of sorting this all out, of keeping everyone focused on the goal of enabling productive virtual teaming through communications, falls on the facilitator. There is stress in this role, but it is expected that the organization will realize the importance of accomplishing a successful plan, and reward those who made it happen.

Indeed, the design process, as well as the output, yields many benefits that justify time and effort. The process can

- Demonstrate the synergy between virtual teaming activities and the electronic infrastructure. It can provide a graphic view of how distributed resources are electronically linked and can use these links to bond into an effective team, and to support reporting that can keep top management informed and pro-active.

- Identify where, and under what circumstances non-electronic, face-to-face interactions can and will be employed, even though emphasis is on the use of the electronic infrastructure.

- Promote teamwork; communications design can be the first virtual initiative

• Provide an opportunity for key stakeholders and leaders to re-
enforce the foundations of trust and collaboration. This is particularly true in organizations where there is a gap between the line
managers and the technical staffs.

• Demonstrate some of the communications techniques available
for the actual project. This is especially useful if key managers and
leaders have not had experience using electronic media. Using
these media can also serve a practical purpose to reach out and
include essential individuals who can not be physically present for
the design meetings.

Many of these benefits apply to communication in any context; but
taken as a whole they address, comprehensively, the unique demands of
the virtual operations environment.

Some of the major considerations of the kickoff session include:

• Timing -- The communications design should be started as soon
as possible after management specifications are delivered, and the
Process and Teaming designs have progressed to the point where
the work processes, and team resources are decided. The design
should proceed in parallel with the Design for Learning, which will
be heavily dependent on the communications infrastructure. Keep
in mind that any requirements that exceed the capability of the
existing infrastructure will take time to procure and integrate.
Also, user training will take significant advance time.

A prompt kick-off of the communications activity is not an
option, it is a virtual requirement.

• Participation -- Cross-functional, cross-organizational representation, including essential technical expertise must be included.

• Expectations -- The design team needs to be clear on what they
must produce as part of the design effort (See Design Output). In
some cases the physical artifacts are no more important than the
process used to create them. The virtual operations design efforts
are intended to stimulate creative insights and bring the virtual
communications spin to the consciousness of the participants.

The meeting should result in the drafting of an overview that sets
the framework for the work meetings that will follow:

• A map or schematic diagram of the project information infrastructure derived from available network and networking applications resources. Overlaid on this map will be the physical locations
of resources committed to the project and the "straw" communica-

tions protocols and ground rules set by the project leader and the key stakeholders.

• A list of available communications support systems, technologies and protocols to be used by all virtual teams.

• A specification of the protocols to be used for all meetings including minutes, distribution, technical support requirements, third party involvement, training, and any other details that will ensure that meetings are as productive as possible.

• Justifications for any investments top management is being asked to approve.

• Procedures for managing technical, administrative, and process changes to the final communications design.

• Specifications that define the flow of key information categories including who, what, why, how, and when.

• Procedures for journalizing and storing project information.

• Security and special handling procedures.

The first meeting should be scheduled and the facilitator, the nominated project leader, should provide a meeting agenda that addresses the limited objective of enhancing the visual overview.

At this first design meeting using the overview, the team can enhance the picture with templates that identify various communications protocols, technologies, scheduled events, progress reviews, and on-line training sessions. Succeeding meetings can bring in more dispersed team members, who can provide their perspectives using the communications infrastructure under design. The overview picture will eventually represent both the communications needs and the technical infrastructure for the life cycle of the project.

The team, using communication checklists such as those in Chapter 21, completes a communications plan for the project that includes all the necessary stakeholder commitments, and a listing of investment requirements if significant shortfalls exist that could jeopardize the project. Along with the other designs, the communications design is rolled into the final proposal and presented to top management.

Some tips that have proven useful in the facilitation of virtual communications design include the following:

• Use graphic aids extensively. Maps, graphs, block diagrams, schematics all help designers to envision the virtual relationships that their communications design will enable. Technical specialists also benefit from mapping exercises, which help them mentally shift from their inclination to use left brain logic to a more creative right brain mode. Using paste-on pictures of remote facilities to help planners see the situation from a holistic perspective. Expanding the map with imagery that represents exiting problems and proposed solutions also helps stimulate creative juices.

• Don't skip over tough issues because the right person isn't there—this is like starting to build a house before you buy the land! Ensure the right stakeholder representation, in person or electronically.

• Avoid the technology bias. Especially in work that involves extensive use of technologies, it is typical for people to go right for the (alleged) technology solution. Consider the whole picture: business objectives and constraints, as well as the process and people side of the equation.

• If possible, conduct some of the design proceedings using electronic interactive technologies. Bringing stakeholders together via an audio or video conference can uncover issues that can easily be overlooked without a test drive.

• Consider all available options. Very often organizations feel that they to have total control over communications and information facilities. Virtual communications plans should be short and dynamic. There is usually no need for massive infrastructure implementations. Public or leased services and facilities can often be procured just-in-time, and more important, shut down when they have served their purpose.

• Go for quality. Audioconferences, for example, can be of such poor quality that the agenda is completely lost if participants can't hear or spend all their time tweaking the equipment -- transparent technology is the goal!

• Always underestimate user competency. Training, using the communications technologies themselves, is usually the right approach.

• Expect change. Not only does technology obsolesce at a rapid rate, but users who commit to working with the electronic infrastructure become incredibly creative and demanding. As long as the mission gains, improving the infrastructure is a wise investment. Follow the example of experienced urban park designers, who put paths where they think they should go, then watch to see where people really go. These are called "desire paths" and wise designers recognize the reality of where people walk and put paths there. The unheeding put up with the mud ruts that result from paths being in the wrong place. Build flexibility into the plan; design the way you expect people to communicate, then see how they actually do communicate and revise the infrastructure accordingly.

• Make sure that the technical stakeholders stay connected for the duration. There is a need to feel that their value is continuous, not finished as soon as the project services are connected and tested. Technologists can and must become as passionate about the business objectives as they are about their systems. They will be needed on the next project and should share in the learning of the present initiative.

• Front load communications activities at the beginning of the project. Bonding and trust building take time; communications enables both. Use creative techniques such as circuit riding to bridge the gap between personal and electronic interactions.

• Never assume that people will intuitively understand the importance of communications. We all communicate, therefore we all consider ourselves to be good communicators. Communications protocols may seem irrelevant; the techniques are often complex and require skills that many individuals find personally difficult. Build in training and awareness opportunities. Encourage social use of the system and reward communications efforts as publicly as a production breakthrough.

• Add an implementation plan and schedule to the final design to ensure that investments, training, and any other pre-launch activities are identified and scheduled.

When the communications design is completed the management team should review the plan and incorporate it into their integrated management proposal. The proposal will include appropriate recommendation concerning essential communications investments, formal user training requirements and any schedule, quality, or financial impact that might be expected if investment recommendations are not approved.

Following management's review and approval of the proposal, the design team will be asked to make any required changes and finalize the communications protocols and systems assignments that will be used for the project. If required, an implementation plan and schedule can be added to the final design to insure that investments, training, and any other pre-launch activities are identified and scheduled.

Final Comments

Using these concepts as context, your organization should be ready to proceed with virtual communications design. Keep in mind that communications is at the center of all the other key virtual operations: tasks, teaming, and learning. The communications design should be conducted interactively with these other processes, reflecting their needs and presenting them with more opportunities to integrate the virtual spin. In a very short time it will become clear that the communications design is a living document that will evolve as the project develops; at the project's end that design will have captured an enormous amount of learning about how to work virtually. Plan to make it available for the next project in the organization and across the larger enterprise constituency.

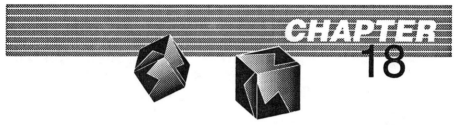

VIRTUAL LEARNING

Gentlemen, your business here is learning.
John Sloan Dickey,
Former President of Dartmouth College[1]

Today more and more business leaders agree that transitioning to a learning organization tops their list of priorities. It's become an article of faith, just like earlier flagship initiatives such as empowerment, systems thinking, and customer satisfaction. Of course, the concept of the learning organization makes perfect sense. Consider these pressures driving the spectacular demands for new knowledge and learning, in the business environment:

• Old paradigms are wearing out faster than cheap socks - remember matrix management, management by objectives, TQM?

• Decentralized decision making is putting increased knowledge burdens on people throughout the organization -- and across virtual initiatives.

• Organizations are challenged with exponentially rising product, service, and business process complexity: The more we know, the more we know we don't know. And the more we know we don't know, the more we don't know we don't know.

• New information is generated at unprecedented rates, and through networks and information systems is now available to everyone who is committed to obtaining it. Not to know how to reach out for this information can doom an organization.

[1]Matriculation address to incoming freshman, Hanover, New Hampshire, 1955.

• Peter Drucker has coined the term "knowledges" to describe the specialized competencies that will build value into the 21st Century.[2] While education can bring base levels of capability in these knowledges, only through continuous learning (not to be confused with continuous improvement - perhaps "continual" learning is the better term) can individuals and organizations keep up with their constant evolution and increasing complexity.

• There are no indications that any of these trends will stop or even slow down.

An environment characterized by increasing complexity, constant changes in processes and technologies, pervasive and shifting needs for boundary, or cross-cultural knowledge, and dependence on shared "knowledge assets," demands an accelerated, breakthrough development of capabilities. Continuous improvement of current methods and tools won't do it any more than continuous improvement of other virtual operations can keep up with accelerating challenges. Organizations that stay on the learning-as-usual curve will soon experience the disconnect illustrated by the dreaded "slip-sliding-away" chart shown in Figure 18-1.

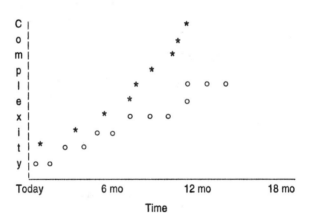

Figure 18.1   Need for Continuous Learning

A year out this virtual effort will be severely compromised by a lack of competencies. Only through breakthrough learning processes and accessing state of the art competencies from other organizations whose people are on an accelerated curve in specific competency areas can the virtual team's knowledge keep pace with the challenges of the virtual initiative.

[2]Peter Drucker, "The Age of Social Transformation," *The Atlantic Monthly,* November 1994, pp. 53-80

Definition and Benefits

Definitions of what exactly constitutes a high-performance learning organization vary wildly. To some managers, continuous improvement objectives and a forty hour per-year, per-employee training program fits the bill. Others seek the capabilities for innovating and anticipating constantly changing knowledge demands. Some organizational leaders see learning as an agent of personal, organizational, and business transformation. It's almost the reverse of the old cartoon showing the blindfolded sages naming the various parts of the elephant's anatomy: In this case we have managers with their eyes wide open looking at a collection of spears, snakes, trees and what have you, and calling it an elephant—or a "learning organization."[3]

They're all correct. For any organization, the appropriate learning model is the one that enables it to prosper in reaching its own goals in the current and future environment. That increasingly looks like a virtual future.

Enter the virtual learning organization, which uses virtual processes and technologies to keep its constituencies rising fast on their competency curves. Virtual learning is a designed, collaborative, continuous learning process through which individuals, teams of individuals, and organizations build the knowledge, skills, perspectives, and experience -- the competencies -- they need to

- Transition to virtual operations in a timely manner
- Develop and sustain competencies in specialities and in virtual operations
- Sustain organizational and cross-organizational virtual operations
- Build the higher levels of speciality and virtual operations capabilities needed to meet the increasing work demands of the virtual future.

The Virtual Spin

Virtual learning takes place through application of validated face-to-face and distance learning pedagogies, supported by the same information

[3]We support the concept of the learning organization, as we do support the various ways in which it's defined. But our bias is toward action, toward organizations actually designing and investing in the learning systems that will build the learning organization appropriate goals and vision.

and telecommunications technologies and processes that enable other virtual operations. In short, virtual learning builds the knowledge for knowledge-fueled virtual operations. It is not episodic, but continuous. It is accessible by schedule or on demand. It serves the people who "wage" virtual operations.[4]

The virtual learning community is a flexible, boundary-crossing amalgam of what would traditionally be considered teachers, students, guest experts, managers, workers, executives, auditors, librarians, consultants, facilitators, administrators, and any other category of learning-interested persons. With the network as their campus, experts worldwide as their faculty, computers and telecommunications devices as their desks and lab tables, and thousands of databases as their libraries, virtual learners access just-in-time training and learning on their own, in teams, as organizations

While traditional training is provided for specific individual skills, most virtual competencies need to be developed in teams, through the network. Here everyone becomes a teacher, everyone a learner. All share their knowledge and learn by working together in their common infrastructure, the network.

In addition, it is important to remember that members of the virtual community retain "home" organizational and role identities as well as their virtual roles. The learning system must not only bind them with their virtual teammates, but link them back to the fast growing specialities evolving in their home organizations.

For example, a packaging expert may be part of a virtual team developing a "World Toy." While she develops the designs for the logos and shipping cartons for the new toy she needs to keep up with the what the rest of the team is discovering from international market feedback. She also needs to know about shipping costs, specifications, and delivery times in various target countries. At the same time our expert must keep up with what's being discovered in her home organization: new composites for shipping, cheaper inks, faster printing, and folding processes.

But there's no time or energy for the shipping expert's shuttling back and forth between organizations to stay on all the learning curves upon which her competencies and career depend. The virtual learning system must somehow always connect her to these multiple learning sources, virtually placing her in the center of all the learning systems in which she is involved.

And yes, we'd like to know what the "World Toy" looks like too.

[4]For a comprehensive, enthusiastic discourse on the role of technology in learning see Lewis J. Perelman's *School's Out: A Radical New Formula for the Revitalization of America's Educational System.* (New York: Avon Books, 1992).

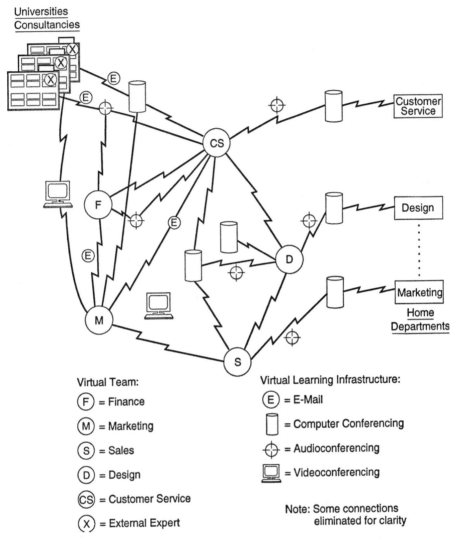

Figure 18.2   Multiple Virtual Learning Streams

Virtual learning has its roots in "distance learning," the capability to extend the reaches of learning experiences, such as classrooms, seminars, correspondence courses centers, to learners at remote sites. Distance learning has been shown to be just as or more effective than face-to-face instruction in many situations. And since distance learning can reach people otherwise shut out of the centralized learning community - in rural areas, hospitals, sub-cultures out of the mainstream educational circuit, travellers, and members of distributed teams - its value as a learning approach continues to grow.

However, distance learning has been used primarily as a delivery mechanism for traditional educational presentation. For fast moving virtual teams such packaged "course" approaches have the disadvantage of being generic and periodic, where the team needs specifics just-in-time. In addition, such courses usually limit interaction among the members of the learning community.

Virtual learning, on the other hand, brings new processes, or pedagogies, that capture the potential of the technology in support of interactive, networked learning. The virtual learning system, integrated by design into the virtual operations framework of the organization, in many cases using the same network and desktop tools.

Virtual learning is flexible, thriving in a network of knowledge providers; many individuals with a variety of institutional affiliations, can be teachers, or learners, or mentors, or coaches at any given time. Traditional boundaries of school, department, class, and teacher fall away under the same forces as those that freed virtual work from the purview of a single organization. Consider the following examples:

- Instructors use voicemail boxes to receive foreign language recitations, or team reports.
- Medical doctors check into lunchtime audioconferences for updates on new pharmaceuticals.
- College students submit exams through E-mail.
- Systems integration teams work with clients in computer conferences to collaboratively learn about the organization's situation and develop proposals.
- Design/build teams use videoconferences to learn about the potentials of new composites and designs, or to collaboratively review flaws in physical objects.

Nor is specialized knowledge the only subject matter of virtual learning; this approach is extremely effective in helping individuals and teams understand and appreciate the principles and practices of virtual work itself. Yes, a well designed virtual learning system can support teams of designers learning to understand and use new, collaborative CAD applications at their networked multimedia workstations: that's the content focus. In doing so, the designers learn the perspectives and skills of virtual teaming. They learn what it feels like to do collaborative, on-line design, experiencing the inevitable stresses of having a teammate electronically reach over and tweak ones "own" drawing or spec.

As another example, no better tool exists for helping virtual team members appreciate the value of over-, rather than under-communication in virtual situations than an informal, well-moderated, computer-based learning conference that requires a high rate of communication from participants. Virtual learning helps diffuse the resistance, stress, and anger that comes from working electronically with people you may not know, in an interrupt-driven environment where everyone has a better idea -- yet another way to improve what you've offered up on the network as your best try. In nonthreatening, noncompetitive learning environments the time-bombs of virtual work can be diffused and the work of building trust across teams begun.

Principles, Processes, and Technologies of Virtual Learning

Now we'll look more closely at the nature of virtual learning, at its principles and the application of those principles. First we'll look at virtual competencies in the context of learning, then move on to examine key pedagogical, social, and technical considerations. Keep in mind that the discussions that follow are primarily conceptual: They provide the framework and content for the design of the virtual learning system that can address your actual project needs.

We've stated that virtual learning is a designed, continuous process through which participants develop the competencies they need to transition to and sustain virtual work. As is the case with virtual operations, virtual learning requires acceptance of some nontraditional beliefs. There is little chance of sustaining a virtual learning organization without having these beliefs accepted by all stakeholders. The good news is that this belief system, this culture, can itself be built through -- you guessed it -- designed virtual learning.

What follows is an overview of some underlying principles of virtual learning:

• Competency, not Information

The argument has been made often enough that information *per se* does not have value. What gives it value is knowing how to use it. Competitive data and information are accessible over public networks, available to anyone willing to make a modest effort. But access to that information does not generate any value. *Interpretation* of the information and *action* on the basis of the information

are what brings results: The competencies in the "actors" trans-
forms neutral value information into a possible competitive edge.

This is a timely distinction: Some supporters of the Information
Highway tout "access to information" as the greatest good. We think
an equally valuable role is as the communications fabric of widely
distributed virtual learning communities, focused not on individu-
ally accessing information in the form of news, entertainment,
financial data, or encyclopedia entries, but rather on collaboratively
developing competencies for specific purposes.

• Continuous Learning Supplants Learning Events

Virtual learning occurs through the same technology infrastructure that supports virtual operations: the network. Earlier we
suggested taking the perspective of a project as a continuous meeting, conducted at various times electronically or face to face. Likewise virtual learning is continuous, supported by a system that
fosters learning through work, through collaborative research and
through learning process, such as lectures, classes, or on-line learning programs. As with network borne communications, learning is
always present - school doesn't close at 3 P.M.

• Unity of Work and Learning

In the early 1960s, Dartmouth's president was castigated by
many academics for using the concepts of "business" and "learning"
in the same breath (see the rubric that opened this chapter)—and
to impressionable freshman, yet. Today those objections have disap-
peared as business leaders tell their people, "learning is your primary task." Indeed, the boundary between business and education
continues to blur as expertise passes back and forth. Peter Drucker
speaks of the challenges that the knowledge era will pose to educational institutions; university professors tout reengineering as the
best thing that could happen to the Academy.

At the beginning of this chapter we pointed out some of the reasons why learning is valued so highly now. In virtual environments,
value is created as teams contribute their competencies toward a
mutual goal -- a service, product, mission, or activity. Stakeholders
learn their own competencies, then they learn how to apply those
competencies to the goal at hand. Learning is no longer an adjunct
or interruption to work, it is work.

By taking learning out of the classroom and to the desktop, or
the shop floor, or the airport lounge, virtual learning becomes a

partner in the work process: integrated and simultaneous with the work underway. Virtual learning replaces off-site education with learning as work is done—Just-in-time.

• Learner Directed, not Ordained by Curriculum

Granted, teachers generally have more specific information and knowledge about the subject at hand than do students. However, virtual learning is an access learning model, therefore the responsibility for engaging in the learning activity is the student's, and the teacher's responsibility is that the new information and knowledge be learnable by the student. Learning here is not a broadcast activity; the purpose is not to exercise a curriculum or keep a faculty engaged. The goal of virtual learning is to continually augment a virtual team's competencies through access to the best knowledge and information in the way that is best for the student: in ways that fit the student's needs and style of learning.

• The role of teacher, or instructor, or expert in virtual learning reflects the needs of the learning community, or team.

The teacher's goal is to build competency in the team, rather than merely provide information. The teacher uses his or her knowledge to

-- guide the team in electronically finding the information it needs

-- facilitate dialog across the team to collectively develop the capability to use that knowledge

-- interpret the dialog to help build team learning

-- contribute focused information and interpretation

-- learn.

As the teacher is also a learner, the other team members are, as their personal knowledge empowers them, teachers. Much as virtual teams are marked by multiple leadership and shifting followership, the distinction between learner and teacher is blurred, being defined by circumstance rather than title.

• Individual, team, organizational, and cross-organizational focus

Earlier we briefly mentioned "situated learning": learning that occurs at the workplace, with the same people and through the same tools that are used when the learned competencies are applied. It make sense to learn with your teaming partners, even when different competencies are involved. When learning a new process control skill, for example, it pays to learn in the same venue and at the same time as another person learning a different skill related to the same process. Since each learner uses his or her knowledge and information in the context of everyone else's contribution, a certain amount of "boundary" learning is essential. Teaming partners must know the capabilities and expectations of those in other competency areas to sustain high rates of simultaneous workflow. Finally, the collective learning process has an interesting side effect: It accelerates the trust and communication among team members faster than any artificial process can.

• Success-based evaluation rather than graded learning

Just as virtual learning is user centered, it is also purpose centered. In some situations the purpose may be a high grade; or 3 credit hours; or just another requirement for the MBA. But more often learning will be less formally tied to an academic system and driven instead by the need to develop competencies. So what's the point of a grade? Grades have very little predictive value beyond signalling how well you would do in the future, taking the same kind of course in the same place in the same manner. (We do admit that this position is not universally accepted.)

• The University as the Virtual Learning Stakeholder

The virtual learning model provides a significant opportunity for universities to enter virtual alliances with organizations, with industries to contribute to the design and delivery of learning. Partnerships between education and industry are not new, but being virtual teammates will help the flow of knowledge from the academy to the shop floor become systemic, predictable, and much sought after, enabling both parties to fulfill their missions.

Processes, or Pedagogies

Desire and technology are not enough to support virtual learning: Processes and pedagogies must be adapted to each specific situation. Pedagogy is an awful word; it's, well, pedantic. But we need a word to refer to those concepts, structures, and processes that have informed the earliest successes in virtual learning. It is important to note that these educational considerations and approaches are not unique to virtual learning: They have been validated in both face-to-face and in distance learning environments.

Addressing both "purposive," or content-directed learning, and learning for discovery, virtual learning is not limited by the traditional boundaries discipline, course, curriculum, and term; or to the customary roles of teacher and student. Learning is an act of potential realized, of knowledge moving from where it exists to where it is needed: assimilated and put into action.

What follows will only touch on the process foundations of virtual learning. The point is to introduce the more innovative of these concepts as to guide the Design for Virtual learning described in Part VI.

• Traditional Classroom, or Lecture Hall - Nothing new here; a necessity we all have gone through. Not often appropriate for virtual learning, since the context of face-to-face interaction with an information provider teacher has limited relevance in virtual situations.

• Computer Assisted Training - This can range from on-line help to programmed learning in design, mathematics, writing, and a variety of other disciplines. With interactive, multimedia technologies becoming more available, these training packages have become quite sophisticated, teaching everything from Russian culture to topology theory with game-like, interactive, graphical user interfaces.

A drawback to most computer assisted training is that it reinforces the individual contributor model, not collaborative work and learning. This is what the "p" in personal computer used to represent: personal. Now the personal computer is more often used as a device for communicating in collaborative environments than as a personal computing device.

• Distance Learning - Distance learning began with the use of telecommunications to take classroom learning situations to remote learners - at home, at schools, at businesses, at community centers. It includes the use of instructional TV, paper correspondence, audio-, computer-, videoconferencing and E-mail to obviate the necessity of all students coming together to learn face-to-face. It is also called the "electronic, or virtual classroom."

• Networked Learning - Perhaps the key concept in virtual learning is that of networked learning. The hypothesis of networked learning is that in certain learning situations, such as when a community of learners have fairly well developed competencies in related areas, learning proceeds more quickly and effectively if each member of that community functions as a teacher as well as a learner. A formal teacher or teachers may be included in the network and may provide knowledge in the traditional manner. But more importantly, the teacher orchestrates, or moderates the inter-

actions in the network, guiding the discussion, re-capitulating dialog (or as Michael Schrage calls it, gigalog), drawing conclusions
and eventually closing off the discussion.

To illustrate the acceleration of learning effected by networked
learning, consider a network of ten learners and a teacher. Traditionally, even in an "interactive" classroom, there would be twenty
learning paths: a two way path between each student and the
teacher, with occasional student to student interaction (usually dis-
couraged). In a networked learning situation paths would exist.
Granted, some of the paths would carry fairly weak learning signals
compared with high powered teacher to student messages.

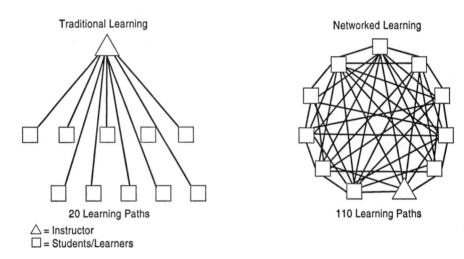

Traditional Learning   Networked Learning

20 Learning Paths   110 Learning Paths

△ = Instructor
☐ = Students/Learners

Figure 18.3   Networked Learning

But the advantages of networked learning far outweigh the drawbacks:

-- everyone has access to everyone else's knowledge

-- the ubiquitous learning paths enable continuous interaction

-- everyone can ask everyone else questions, not just direct
them at the teacher

This sounds a lot like the seminar model many of us have experienced probably more times than we like to remember. However,
networked learning is not an event that happens off in some confer-

ence room once a week; it is a continuous process that is designed to permeate the work environment.

It is obvious why networked learning is a natural for virtual teams: The learning paths are collaborative, and they can be supported by networking technologies, such as computer conferencing, providing connectivity between learners at their desktops. The network can support a variety of technologies adaptable to learning; or rather, in addition to their supporting communications and information access, these technologies double as the backbone of a learning system. We'll get to those technologies shortly.

• Situated Learning, Action Learning - These closely related processes are based on the belief that the knowledge one learns is inextricably integrated with the context in which the learning takes place (see classroom learning, above), and that knowledge is acquired more quickly and integrated better through active learner participation.

This is a key belief for virtual learning. Only if learning takes place in the same environment (the network), with the same tools (electronic communications), by learners performing work or work-like processes will the learning deliver the competency to work in virtual situations.

• Structured Learning - This kind of learning is designed to accomplish specific learning goals through specific processes: curricula, courses, scheduled lectures and computer-aided learning packages. Here "what the learner knows he or she doesn't know" drives the content and form of the course.

• Random, or Discovery Learning - A virtual learning system must also accommodate random learning, allowing the team to discover and share new knowledge that they weren't particularly looking for: "What they didn't know they didn't know." The challenge here is to have a system that enables people to recognize that new knowledge and make it accessible to others.

In the virtual world random learning can be accidental discovery of solutions or combinations of information in the network; the physical world counterparts would be overheard hallway discussions, eye-catchers in discarded newspapers and the like. Of course, these too are valuable in the virtual environment, but only if they are somehow categorized and journaled in the network to allowed shared access.

Learning Technologies

Five years from now I don't believe there will be a single school in the country that will not have the talking motion picture as the basis of education.

Walter Wanger,
Paramount Pictures Production Chief, 1930[5]

OK, OK. The promised benefits of technology in support of learning are usually oversold; obviously Mr. Wanger saw what he believed. We do not offer technology as a panacea here. But the virtual age is inextricably caught up in technology; both the cause of and the solution to the increasing complexity of life and work in the last decade of the 20th century. Technology *will* be a chief agent of learning.

The technologies most used in virtual learning are

• Personal computers and workstations
• Audioconferencing and videoconferencing facilities
• Information and telecommunications networks
• Computer conferencing and E-mail
•Shared document, drawing, and modeling systems

Other technologies are emerging to join this field, for instance, wireless technology is providing a mobility to virtual learners that lets them join the "class" from their portable offices. Teams have found hand-held personal assistants valuable as "note takers" for electronically recording actions and their implications at a worksite, or for later sharing with management or other teams. One can argue that there is nothing quite as useless as an exhaustive list, but we think it's valuable here to suggest at least a partial list of learning technologies that can be instrumental to Virtual Learning:

• Classroom, Seminars, Workshops, Courses - The traditional learning technologies now can be extended to become "virtual classrooms" through distance learning programs. They are usually high on information providing, and lower on learner to learner interaction.

• Audioconferencing - An easy to use and unobtrusive technology that has the highest return on investment of any learning/communications technology. Audioconferences can be periodic or ad hoc.

---

[5]Quoted in the *Dartmouth College Alumni Magazine*, (Hanover, N.H., August 1994).

Regular lunchtime talks can keep busy professionals abreast of the latest developments of their craft, and weekly meetings let virtual teams share their discoveries and pose issues for the next "box talk."

• Computer conferencing - The best collaborative, networked learning process and technology available. As an asynchronous application, conferencing allows participants to learn and interact with teammates when they want to, and from anywhere accessible by their personal computers.

• Electronic Mail - Excellent for one–to–one or broadcast discovery learning. "Hey. Did you know that....?"

• Videoconferencing - A favorite for many organizations who have a strong tradition of doing business face-to-face. While the in-person meetings are still required, professional videoconferencing can regularly fill predictable learning needs. Recently, the capability to use low-cost digital phone lines is making videoconferencing increasingly cost effective.

Of course, the evolution of all of these is towards supporting, or combining to support multimedia. There are a few caveats to introducing these technologies:

• Each technology, especially in virtual environments, requires certain shared beliefs, knowledge, skills, and processes to be successful: to help the learning virtual organization reach its goals. Training, cultural integration, and support are essential.

• Each technology has particular strengths and weaknesses that must be considered when designing the learning system. Misuse of a technology can be costly and destabilizing. For example, forcing the use of videoconferencing slows down work as people constantly prepare for the formal presentations. And being informal in video-conference, while permissible in some organizations, is usually considered an annoying waste of time and money.

Examples of Virtual Learning

1. Proposal generation

In the last chapters we have referred to the development of a systems integration proposal as a typical candidate for virtual operations reengineering. Here we'll continue that thread by looking at the virtual learning aspects of such a redesign.

In many ways the proposal generation project itself was a collaborative learning venture, jointly undertaken by the customer and proposing organizations. The final proposal was an abstracted snapshot of their accumulated knowledge. However, from Day 1 all the dialog, modelling, testing, in other words the work, that went into the proposal was also captured in detail in computer conferences. They became permanent records, learning instruments, of the project's knowledge building, decision making, virtual strategies, and dialog. The records were made available to newcomers on the project and to other teams undertaking similar work, current and future.

The planned communications helped executives continuously learn what was happening; this is an absolute necessity in innovative initiatives, where nervous executives often find it easy to reject something out of hand rather than face difficult and time consuming learning curves.

Much more could be done in formalizing the learning processes for such projects. As we shall see in the next examples, learning is more directly addressed by organizations that recognize learning in their missions and operations. But we are confident that the worlds of learning and work are converging and that in the near future, virtual work teams in many situations will see the learning challenge as clearly as do these learning-dedicated organizations.

2. Border learning

A small virtual business team has been commissioned to quickly bring a new consumer product to market in the border area of southern California and Mexico. On the team are American, Mexican, European, and Far Eastern nationals. Some are on-site in San Diego, others are working remotely from their organizational homes. Many of their work processes will be supported by continuous computer conferencing across the Internet. In addition videoconferencing facilities have been made available for periodic international project reviews. All team members have personal computers, phone, and FAX connectivity.[6]

[6]The learning/work described here has been going on for over ten years, since the inception of the BESTNET Virtual University program. The border project that is the basis for this account is being led by Dr. Miguel Cardenes, Executive Director of the International Training Center, and Dr. Frank Medeiros, Executive Director of Telecommunications and Program Development, both at San Diego State University's College of Extended Studies.

As the stakeholders begin to design their virtual work processes, they identify areas in which the team needs episodic and ongoing learning: customs regulations, advertising principles and distribution options for the border area, languages, new technologies, new science. In addition, pure "training" needs are evaluated. Since many teams are part of the maquiadoro community, where change is rapid and turnover is high, the virtual techniques are valuable for the more structured delivery of training materials, often in both Spanish and English.

The team invites experts in these areas to be "learning stakeholders" in the virtual initiative. The experts are located primarily at universities in California and Mexico, where joint, bi-lingual seminars are already offered. But the network of potential expert stakeholders extends as far as the Internet can reach: worldwide. These learning stakeholders are given access to the team's computer conferencing system, where conferences are set up for on-line seminars and courses in specific knowledge areas. One subject area is "Accessing Information using Internet," in which teaming stakeholders can collaboratively learn how to make productive use of worldwide information access and communications tools such as Worldwide Web, ftp, gophers, listservers and bulletin boards. Another addresses import-export regulations, with continuous updating of tariff structures and dialog about their implications for the project at hand.

Other courses include "Business Spanish" and "Business Chinese"; here computer conferencing is augmented by simple but effective telephone technologies: students dialog in audioconferences and submit their narrative assignments to instructor voice mail boxes. Periodically, a professionally produced videoconference module on a key area, such as "Financial Models for Border Alliances" is presented to the team from an academic site that specializes in packaged learning modules for business. Real time translation is provided in these videoconferences. On a weekly basis, management, the experts, and the team holds a "clearing the air" seminar supported by a carefully designed, highly interactive audioconference. Finally, as part of each module, instruction in the use of all the technologies involved and associated protocols is delivered through the technologies themselves.

Virtual learning, integrated into the work processes of this far-flung group, brings key knowledge to the group throughout the project, with minimal disturbance, expense, and time wasted in travel.

3. The World Design Forum

In February of 1994, a group of about twenty executives from a wide variety of disciplines gathered for three days and nights at an only moderately earthquaked hotel in Los Angeles to discuss an issue of mutual interest: "How could a coherent, collaborative art and science of design be developed to handle the complex systems of the global environment?"

To decode this a bit, this multidisciplinary, multicultural group, which included social and political researchers, telecommunications and information systems professionals, multimedia experts, professors of design and communications, pioneers in distance and networked learning, cinema sound designers, artists, and software engineers, felt that in spite of the rapid emergence of new technologies, the complexity of today's problems, or situations was far beyond our capability to solve, or even approach with a high-probability of success.

Examples of the complex systems they had in mind were health care and telecommunications infrastructures in emerging nations; international finance; models for global virtual enterprise and for virtual enterprises (joint ventures); scientific research, accelerated learning, and population management. As a look at any newspaper will tell us, the world is generally in a "coping," rather than "design" mode in many of these areas because these areas have gotten too complex to handle given our current knowledge, skills, processes, and tools. If we have trouble keeping up now, how can we hope to control the forces of complexity and chaos in the future?

From this three day meeting emerged the World Design Forum (WDF). The mission WDF undertook was to "...bring together worldwide leaders experienced in complex systems and dynamic organizations to explore collaborative design processes." This group would, over time, define the processes and technologies needed to support future design and they would accomplish this design work in an electronic network: WDF-NET.[7]

This network would be their office, lab, shop floor, board room, and cafeteria. Information, knowledge, and communication would pass freely through the network. Starting with a basic E-mail and conferencing infrastructure, they would define the future WDF-NET as their needs became clearer from the contingencies they encountered in their work.

At this writing, WDF has developed into a world-wide virtual learning organization. Participants from Europe, Asia, South America, and North America have electronically collaborated to design two major face-to-face conferences; the first in Maine, the second in Beijing, Peoples Re-

---

[7]The founders and principals of WDF-Net are Dr. Beryl Bellman, Professor of Communications at California State University Los Angeles, Dr. Ulf Fagerquist, Senior Consultant and Visionary for AT&T Global Information Solutions, and Hans Gyllstrom, Senior Manager also at AT&T GIS. Dr. Bellman is also founder, along with Dr. Armando Arias, BESTNET Program cited above.

public of China. The agendas of these meetings focus on discussion and design of networked processes and technologies that will support world-wide design efforts. The testbed for these new processes and technologies is WDF--NET itself.

From our perspective of virtual operations and virtual learning, this group, its mission, and activities, is interesting for several reasons:

• In formulating its mission, WDF has integrated work and learning (actually, virtual work and virtual learning). Because its focus is learning its intents and actions give us a particularly rich picture of the potential of virtual learning.

• WDF is dedicated to discovery of new global, collaborative design capabilities. Only through collaborative design can we conceive of, express, create, and support complex enterprises, projects, artifacts, or organisms. The mission is achieved through development, sharing, and application of knowledge. The World Design Forum is by nature and intent explicitly a virtual learning organization.

• WDF participants agree that knowledge is best acquired in context and through work, rather than by aggregation of theory in a neutral site like a classroom. Initiatives from which knowledge is already emerging are underway in projects addressing Mexican Health Systems, telecommunications infrastructure development in the People's Republic of China, environmental protection, and issues in international manufacturing.

Learning, even learning how to design its own network system, comes through work in the network.

• Multiplexed knowledge workers, from a variety of disciplines, with worldwide organizational affiliations adopted a virtual teaming approach to focus on the mission.

• Workers are committed to situated, reflective learning in the virtual workplace. WDF is pioneering the global network as a workplace. Semi-annual meetings at venues around the world are events within a continuum of work and learning through structured and unstructured dialog within WDF-NET.

At its earliest stage, this network provided access, via Internet, to a set of computer conferencing and information access facilities housed at California State University at Los Angeles. Today that network is evolving to support rich, information-sharing capabilities, such as multimedia communications, process flow and active

modelling, and dependable worldwide access. WDF is collaboratively developing networked design principles through WDF-NET
and learning how to work within networks. This is exactly the
approach we recommend for transitioning to virtual operations.

• Appreciation of the co-evolution of knowledge within the triple
helix of people, process and technology will prompt WDF to examine the full range of information and telecommunications technologies that support rational work processes, in this case "design," in
the context of high levels of self-mastery, competency, and shared
beliefs. Technologies to be investigated include networks, computer
communication applications, multimedia, hypermedia, object-ori-
ented visualization systems, wireless communications, and virtual
reality. We share WDF's belief that people's capabilities, technologies, and work processes must co-evolve.

Again, while WDF is by mission dedicated to learning, it
remains a model for the critical learning thread in any organization
that is trying to stay on the knowledge curve in these times of
mega-change. Whether the product be shoes, mobile faxes, or
knowledge of design, the same challenges and approaches to those
challenges pertain.

Virtual Learning's time has come: there is awareness of the
need, shared knowledge about learning processes, and abundant
available technology. What's needed to get virtual learning integrated into an organization's work system is no different from any
other critical stream in virtual operations: commitment, planning,
design, and development. Learning is good business.

Barriers to Virtual Learning

Most people who are engaged in complex work relish new learning. The
main resistance to virtual learning comes from an unwillingness, on both
the supply side and consumer side, to surrender traditional education
modes: the classroom, the textbook, the lecture. There are, of course,
issues of using new technology and of moving to a continuous instead of a
period learning mode. There also can be a reluctance to take on the
responsibility for acquiring the competency knowledge one needs, by
whatever available means. Many miss the structure of a fixed curriculum and required courses. But people eventually recognize that the purpose of virtual learning is not for credit, for degrees, for promotion to a

next educational level, or for getting to a new salary bracket. Rather, the objective is to keep up with what you need to know now and to build your competencies into the future. Usually this is motivation enough, and with good leadership and coaching, most accept virtual learning fully as part of their work, not just something else to do.

Designing Virtual Learning

To begin the actual design of virtual learning capabilities we introduce an artifact we call "The Strategic Learning Model (SLM)." This fairly simple model can help you structure the dialog leading up to the Design for Virtual Learning (Chapter 22), as well as framing the design process itself.

Each of the four stages in the learning design process can utilize the SLM:

1. Identifying needed competencies

2. Inventorying current competencies

3. Identifying gaps

4. Identifying systemic, pedagogically sound ways of developing the knowledge needed to fill the gaps and ensure future capability for virtual operations.

The basic SLM looks like this:

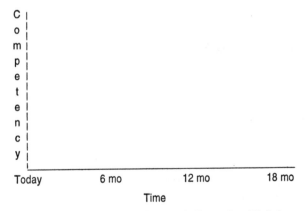

Figure 18.4   The Strategic Learning Model

The vertical axis represents increasing levels of competencies (and by implication, project complexities) required/in place, and the horizontal axis represents linear time in a project cycle. By the looks of things, we must consider both axes as infinite.

In this instance of the SLM, the data points represent relative stages of knowledge (or "knowledges") in a virtual initiative:

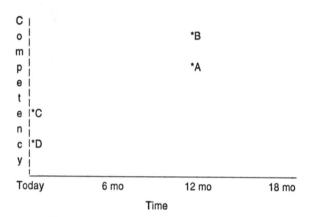

Figure 18.5   Knowledge Points-Concept

The knowledge points indicate the following:

A= What you (the team) think you need to know to complete the project

B= What you really need to know

C= What you think you already know

D= What you really already know

The model addresses several fallacies in the way we usually plan "training" for any mission oriented activity, fallacies we cannot tolerate in the virtual climate of accelerated change.

A= What you think you need to know

While history provides some guidance about what knowledge is needed in a new initiative ("We go with what we knew for the last project, then some."), given the rapid rate of change, dramatic new knowledge needs will surely arise. Fixing only on expected needs will ensure that there will be surprises along the way: a continuous improvement learning curve won't get you where you want to be.

B= What you really need to know

Of course you don't know everything you need to know until you discover you don't know it. Usually our anticipated knowledge needs fall quite short of reality. For this reason virtual initiatives require learning systems that support "discovery" of new knowledge needs, as well as filling out the anticipated curriculum of competencies.

C= What you think you already know

Even after assessing what an organization knows, the *real* knowledge is usually far less that the *reported* knowledge. At the launch of a new aerospace project, a training manager reported that twenty-one engineers had CAD systems training. After the project got underway, it was discovered that the full experience of eighteen of those people was in exercises involving drawing floor plans of houses using a simple personal computer application. Using complex, distributed team-based airframe design CAD systems was far beyond their reach.

D= What you really already know

Since we never underestimate our competencies, it's necessary to cover the delta between espoused knowledge and actual knowledge by careful sensing of the current competency state. This will greatly improve the chances of designing a learning system that will support the learning rate the project requires.

Interpreting the relationships between these data points reveals some interesting facts of life about initiatives:

• The differences between espoused levels and actual levels of knowledge (Δ BA, DCD) define what you don't know you don't know. These are the project killers. Surprise! Expense! Lost time! Failure! A realistic sensing of competencies possessed and competencies needed is essential for success. The Design for Learning will provide those safeguards.

• The learning curve CA, which is the one you think you're on, will fall very short of taking you where you need to go in developing competencies. The real rate of learning you need to sustain is expressed in curve DB.

And if you think DB has an aggressive slope, wait until you see the next project's learning requirements, "E"!

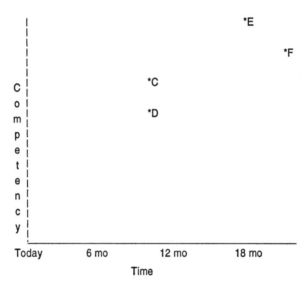

Figure 18.6   The Next Project Learning Curve

If you actually start from C and go to F you'll fail. If you don't reach C in the first project and start from D to reach F or E you'll fail sooner: either you'll get to the wrong level of competency (F), or burn out by following an impossibly steep learning curve.

The right road is, of course, CE. It won't be easy, but if the learning from the first effort is captured in close to real-time, and an appropriate virtual learning system is put in place in a timely manner, CE is the best chance you have; And it is possible to attain.

Final Comments

This has been an unabashedly analytic discussion of virtual learning. As such it is self-limiting, ignoring many of the affective and cognitive aspects of learning that make the discipline so exciting. We realize how important those areas are and by no means exclude them as key considerations when establishing learning processes. We have presented the concepts and elements of virtual learning to provide an introduction to the potential of virtual learning processes and technologies, and the necessity for designed learning in virtual operations. We expect that growth of knowledge about virtual learning will be accelerating as more organizations address learning as part of their work, and work as a main ingredient of their learning.

DESIGNING VIRTUAL OPERATIONS: GUIDELINES

This last section moves from the world of conceptualization and description to a bare bones enumeration of tips, guidelines, and checklist items that help you keep virtual operations design on track.

Since these chapters are essentially checklists to be used as real-time guidelines in the design processes, their format is somewhat different from that of earlier chapters Specifically, they consist mainly of hints and lists and do not close with Final Comments. We feel that this structure better fits the intent of the chapters, which is to assist in actual design, not just provide information about design

In keeping with the tone of the next four chapters, we'll move right to into these guidelines for work tasks, teaming, communications, and learning. As with everything else in the virtual world, these designs are best undertaken simultaneously, with progress in each, enabling higher reach and higher capabilities in the others. In our experience, however, many organizations, already somewhere on the road to virtual, first address their communications needs. Communications Design has immediate returns in supporting ongoing work and in facilitating the design processes themselves; and in many ways virtual communications is the soul of all of the other processes.

The Epilogue describes the kind of virtual reality we've alluded to all through this book: that the virtual revolution is upon the organizational world, and it is less of a question *whether* to make the transition as it is *when*. We are not looking at a future opportunity, we are in the midst of it.

So, as the good doctor said, we begin.

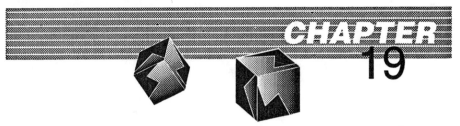

CHAPTER 19

DESIGNING VIRTUAL WORK TASKS

When designing virtual work tasks -- using whatever approach the extended team is comfortable with -- it is critical for the team to build and sustain a virtual perspective. The guidelines in this chapter can assist the leader or facilitator in keeping the task design virtual and on track.

The Task Design Event

Here we will assume that the Checkland model, discussed in Chapter 15, is used as a framework. The leader or facilitator and stakeholders can approach their analysis by following the steps outlined below:

1. Participants should understand the existing macro and sub-processes in the larger context of the virtual environment and the organization's business goals. This can be provided (electronically) as advanced materials, or by an executive at a kickoff meeting -- a great way to get everyone's attention!

2. Develop a model of the ideal virtual work tasks that can help achieve these goals. Describe the virtual processes involved, including sub-processes, communications paths, activities, teaming relationships, and learning needs. They can keep in mind the "virtual spin" that gives power to these processes. The model provides a good way to formally visualize the big picture.

3. Using the guidelines that follow, expand the conceptual models of the project to show information access and flow, transformations, and other process options.

4. Test the ideal conceptual models against the traditional processes currently in use within the organization with the systems apparent in the situation; do a schematic representation of the As-Is situation, and discuss the accuracy and appropriateness of the conceptual models.

5. Look for significant Deltas between the As-Is and To-Be.

Indicators of Virtual Spin Opportunities

Highly leveraged candidates for virtual spin application generally have the following characteristics:

- Information intensive
- Communications intensive
- Involve distributed and cross-functional resources
- Consist of discernible sub-processes that can be performed in parallel
- Competency-based
- Highly changeable
- Complex.

Virtual Options

As you design the work for your virtual prototype project, follow these guidelines:

- Ignore geography; go for the best competencies no matter how widely distributed.

- Break down work tasks into sub-processes that can be performed concurrently by virtual teams. Schedule all sub-processes, or tasks, to begin on Project Day 1.

• Assume continuous communication capabilities. Go for break-through processes, counting on the ability of the team to stay hot-wired to each other throughout the project.

• Base as much of the work as possible on electronic interactions: interpersonal communications and information access.

• Shun physical objects; design process outputs to be electronic information objects. Use electronic simulation, modelling, and pro-totyping wherever possible.

• Base processes on information and knowledge access, rather than distribution. Your electronic communications infrastructure will support this paradigm well.

• Ration paper. Demand very good reasons why anything, save a final product, should be put to paper.

• Avoid black boxes. Sub-processes should be visible to teams working in boundary areas and to management. This allows nearer real-time communications and helps eliminate the serial process of reporting, explaining, and bringing up to speed.

• Instrument tasks and sub-tasks for continuous evaluation, adjustment, and improvement.

• Design tasks so that leaders can monitor, encourage, and reward creative inputs from workers.

• Design in decision points at the work task, not the upper man-agement level.

• Always keep the whole life-cycle of the task in mind. Provide continuous electronic access to the state-of-the-work to upstream and downstream workers. The project should be a fast moving pond rather than a raging stream.

• Plan to capture the dialog and processes of the electronic work to share as learning with other teams.

• Keep replication of information at a minimum. Wherever possi-ble use shared databases to hold all project data and information.

With effort and persistence the process designs will begin to take on more and more virtual spin. As the stakeholders begin to "think virtual," the virtual options will become a natural choice: the advantages to the organization will be so clear that barriers to this new way of conducting work will diminish.

Virtual Task Design Checklists

The leader or facilitator can use these prompts to help the design team identify and evaluate virtual techniques and options. This design activity has two specific purposes: the first is to design a process that will deliver the results specified by management, and the second is to accomplish the process using virtual operations tools and techniques.

1. Selecting and calibrating the design team

All critical stakeholders, including representation from executive management and outside organizations, should be represented because the work process design will cover the entire life-cycle of the project. It is also essential that everyone participating in the work task design be fully empowered to make decisions and commitments:

- Are we certain that we have representation from all stakeholder interests needed to begin, complete, and wind-up this project?

- Who is missing?

- How and when do we get missing stakeholders involved?

- Have we considered all our outside interest: customers, suppliers, partners, contractors...?

- Can everyone participating make necessary commitments: people, facilities, money, time, materials, technology...?

2. Decide on the format and content of the process plan

The design team must begin with a clear concept of the work ahead of them. They must ensure that their process design integrates with and supports the other "design for" plans. They must also agree on all communications protocols to be used in creating and coordinating the plan:

- Are the project leader's authority and responsibilities clear?

- Does anyone have any issues that will cause problems now or in the future?

• Are the specifications received from management clear?

• Is everyone familiar with the design process used in developing a proposal for management's approval?

• Are there any special procedures or accommodations needed to enable this group to work as a team: communications, coordination, distribution, time constraints, physical constraints, cultural problems, language?

3. Analyze management's specifications

This is perhaps the most important step of the design process -- making sure that we know exactly what management requires from this work effort, and knowing what a successful conclusion looks like. The team must pay equal attention to what is not specified as well as what is:

• What do management's specifications MEAN, and do we all agree?

• What are the business related goals and objectives dependent on this project?

• What results are really important to management?

• How will management measure results: cost, time schedules, utilization of resources?

• What are the real constraints that can influence the results?

• Are there any persistent differences of opinion or perceptions about what must be done (these won't go away and must be consistently foregrounded)?

• Are there any political games or agendas going on that will endanger the success of this project, no matter how well planned?

Up to this point the focus has been to define and scope the problem to create a clear and shared understanding of what management's expectations and requirements are. Clarity at this level is the responsibility of the project leader and the key stakeholders. Now that we know the "what," the design focus shifts to the design of the specific work task and it is time to bring the actual "doers" of these tasks and activities into the dialog.

4. Identify key tasks and dependencies

We need an overview of the key task and processes critical to meeting management's specifications to use as a starting point for identifying virtual opportunities:

- Are we satisfied with our process overview? Does it include

    -- all the major tasks needed to complete the project

    -- critical dependencies

    -- our confidence level concerning successful completion

    -- the tasks that are critical to success

    -- areas that have high risk

    -- areas that have high management interest

    -- areas that need special attention?

- Does the overview indicate physical locations for where work will be done?

- Does the overview indicate who controls the resources committed to each task?

- Does the overview indicate special events or activities such as

    -- management reviews

    -- progress reviews

    -- training/learning events

    -- budget/financial reviews

    -- marketing events

    -- customer events?

5. Brainstorm for the virtual spin

Examine the key elements of the processes selected. If these are on-going traditional activities, map the existing processes to identify each step, work locations, and essential dependencies. This will expose the virtual aspects of the work. Identify opportunities for creative spin application. For complex processes, select two or three key results along the value network and brainstorm to determine alternative virtual workflow patterns that will improve performance and replace serial with parallel activity·

- Do we know why we do it (task, process, activity) this way?

- Is this activity dependent on

  -- something

  -- someone?

- Does the activity create dependencies? What would happen if we didn't do it?

- Can we do it differently?

- Who cares and why?

- What options do we have?

- Can we re-design the process using the capabilities provided by applying virtual techniques?

A variety of system analysis, modeling techniques and process mapping or diagramming are available. Use what's available and comfortable for the participants.

With virtual work task design underway, it's time to begin the virtual teaming system.

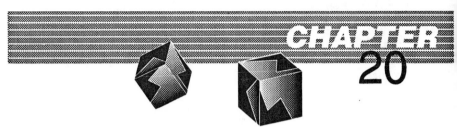

CHAPTER 20

DESIGNING VIRTUAL TEAMING

The design process we suggest here builds on the results of the organizational sensing evaluation described in Part V. The insights into the current state of the organization and the project team will provide the designers with an overall sense of the organization's readiness to initiate and sustain virtual teaming operations and the prototype initiative. The teaming design process, as with the other designs, can be self-directed or employed by an outside facilitator.

These teaming design checklists are only suggestions. The leader/ facilitator knows specific teaming goals and capabilities from earlier sensing exercises and should expand or revise the prompts as needed to derive the most effective teaming plan.

The important thing is to ensure that the group focuses on those special issues that are important for their virtual operations -- the virtual spin. It is especially import to pursue with passion the hard questions, the ones that are politically sensitive or not fully understood. Problems not addressed here in the design stage can surely sink the team as the work pace quickens.

Competency and Skill Requirement Assessment

This first step is used to start the design process and provide the leaders and stakeholders with a macro view of the skills and competencies the project requires. These first few items also provide the leader with a sense of how well the participants understand virtual operations and the terms and concepts used in the design process.

• Construct a high level list of primary and support functions, processes, and tasks that all stakeholders agree must be included to meet the project specifications. Be careful to consider tasks that are

-- required to prepare facilities and workers to start work: planning, facilities, logistics and supplies, communications and information system support, training, contracts, and other legal support

-- required to launch the project: project design, management approvals, kick-off activities, announcements, publicity

-- associated with the active, operations phase of the project

-- necessary to complete and shut down the project: final reports, learning activities, briefing, rewards, contractual and legal activities.

• Using the high level task list as a base line, identify required competencies for tasks in each stakeholder area:

-- Is it necessary to contact and coordinate with managers who are not included on the design team to make sure resource estimates are accurate?

-- Do some tasks require competencies that are not part of the organization, and are these areas represented?

• Using all inputs, construct a personnel resource table that includes all required skills and competencies, their availability, their location, their controlling management, and identify all shortfalls that must be resolved prior to project launch. (*This table should be used for input into the Design for Learning.*)

• Using the personnel resource table, estimate the number of resources needed.

• Individual stakeholders should complete a team resource survey for their functional area. In this survey they should

-- identify by name the most qualified individuals available for this project

-- note where are they located

-- cite conflicts created by assigning these individuals to this project

-- state whether their participation requires virtual access. If so do they have the skills, tools and experience they'll need? How will they get them?

-- consider alternative team participants who may be available? Who? Where?

-- ask whether all the best outside competencies been considered?

Teaming Environment Assessment

Most of these items are similar to those used for high level organizational sensing. They are used here to provide a general overview for the leaders and stakeholders to begin their detailed work:

• Establish and sketch the "chain of command" that will have a direct impact and influence on the project team. Identify all management and cross-functional/competency stakeholders, nominated or selected team leaders, and key team members.

• Create a matrix that reflects management approval and decision processes for technical, administrative, and support requirements expected for this project.

• Determine whether everyone understands the following:

-- Management's expectations for this project including the strategic business goal and objectives

-- The need to ensure dedicated leadership for the full project schedule

-- The concept of electronically enabled work processes, and the need for virtual process design to optimize the productivity of virtual teams

-- The need for dynamic, real-time change management

-- Special training and preparation for virtual teaming will be provided; including distributed meeting techniques, concurrent electronic work, documentation and knowledge transfer, metrics and rewards, and other unique and specialized virtual teaming techniques and practices

-- The responsibility of the stakeholder team to create teaming input to the project proposal that will respond to management specifications. The proposal will include stakeholder commitments to support all team based activities.

Teaming Barrier Identification and Assessment

It is necessary for the stakeholders to assess their initial team selections to determine potential barriers that will compromise the virtual teaming initiative. Not all barriers can be addressed up front but actions and plans should be put in place to thwart the show-stoppers:

- Identify situations that would inhibit virtual teaming.

-- Do individuals oppose participation in joint efforts?

-- Do individuals or groups resist taking direction from outside

their established chain of command?

-- If resistance is indicated, how is it displayed?

- Are the stakeholders committed to providing clear directions and purpose?

-- How do they insure clarity within their area of responsibility and communicate purpose and direction to subordinates?

-- Do they receive feedback? How?

- Are there established values, expectations, or history influencing team/teaming activities?

- Are there indications of overarching organizational or individual values/motivations existing; for example, stovepiped loyalties, political associations, personal ambitions, rewards, recognition, image, etc?

Stakeholder Empowerment

This segment determines the responsibility and authority of each key stakeholder or agent. Because of the fast pace of a virtual teaming project, stakeholders must be clear about their relationships with their parent groups. The goal is to ensure project management team representation so that the majority of decisions can and will be made at the operations level:

• Does each stakeholder or assigned leader have the authority to fully represent the parent group?

-- Does this authority include the assigning of group resources consistent with the needs of the project plan?

-- Are selected team leaders fully trained in their speciality and in the techniques and technical support requirements of virtual teaming?

-- Do team leaders have authority over their team members within the scope of the project?

-- Does team leader authority extend to individuals from cross-functional groups or members that are recruited from outside the organization?

• Does each stakeholder and team leader have the technical support necessary to access all project information? Is the technology needed for access or participation in electronic information exchange available?

Attitude Toward Change

Virtual teaming generates significant changes to established processes, behavior, and individual work habits and performance. If there is strong resistance to change within the organization, virtual teaming will be difficult. Where organizations are more comfortable with a changing environment, establishing teaming processes can be streamlined.

• Is management reactive or pro-active toward change? Consider examples of recent change and try to document the process which brought the situation to the attention of management. Determine if the example was a problem and management reacted; or an opportunity and management took action.

• How will change be managed in this project?

-- What are the formal and informal change processes?

-- Will any of these compromise virtual teams?

-- Are there recommendations we should make to improve change management in the team environment?

• Is there an "early warning system" to help teams identify potential or future situations that will require change?

• Are change management techniques appropriate for various organizational levels: worker, management, executive?

Team Profile

This segment is used to create a profile of the teams selected for the project. This will help to determine how best to manage the virtual teaming concept:

• Identify and rank major work environment patterns that each team will operate: production oriented, professional services, developmental, support services.

• Determine ratios within each team for skilled/unskilled, professional contributors, management.

• Characterize teams by education level, professional training, mix of specialities of functions, gender, age, any other attribute that appears significant.

• Identify other potential political situations that might affect the performance of teams: culture, language, equipment, dissimilar process applications, critical resource shortages.

• Identify other important concerns and activities: labor issues, financial concerns, job security, political stress, and so forth.

Teaming Environment

This segment is used to determine the current status of teaming within the organization. Most organizations have experience in the use of dedicated teams, but few have adapted their teams to be effective in virtual, electronically supported environments. Further, the increasing complexity of the tasks teams must address under compressed time constraints requires special training and support.

• Is there a formal team training process in place?

- Is there any training available for virtual teaming?

-- Have the individuals selected for this project attended?

-- How is the training offered? How long? Is it available now?

• Determine the results of previous team efforts. *(Look for audited results, activities to capture learning about the teaming process as the project matured, check if these teams published final reports. Note the distribution of team reports.)*

• Were past leaders of successful teams assigned to new team responsibilities where they could use their teaming skills? Examine the follow-on assignments of successful teams.

• Is team performance called out in performance reports?

• Is team building and leadership formally included in the planning of new projects?

• Are there specific recognized rewards or incentives for participation in teams?

Knowledge Building and Information Access

Knowledge sharing is perhaps the most effective way of building trust and cohesiveness in virtual teams. It is critical to determine the value that an organization places on knowledge and knowledge sharing:

• Are there formal processes in place that focus on building, preserving, and accessing organizational knowledge and group intelligence?

• Are there training programs to establish knowledge building techniques and processes?

• How is information identified as organizational knowledge and distributed throughout the organization? Determine if the flow is both up and down and across functional divisions.

• What approval and review process is used to validate information as organizational knowledge?

• How is knowledge changed, or removed? How is the organization informed of these changes?

• Do workers have access to organizational knowledge in forms that will enhance their job performance? Determine if there are technology constraints impeding information access.

• Is information currently controlled or managed? Determine what process is used and where the control decisions are made. Determine if control decisions include rationale, or if they are simply general policies.

• Will all teams have full access to all project information?

• What are the procedures to deal with information security, information overload, information access, and user navigation through information and knowledge resources?

Decision Making Processes

The decision processes practiced in the organization can have critical impact on the pace required to sustain effective virtual teaming:

• How are issues resolved, decisions made? Determine if the decision process is open, a process where all stakeholders are aware of the issues and options and have the opportunity to influence the outcome; or conversely, where decisions are made unilaterally by individuals or special interest groups.

• What is the decision culture: dictatorial, democratic, or nonexistent so that issues are resolved over time or not at all?

• Do issues and decisions require formal review? By whom?

• Are issues and decisions recorded? Are they distributed? How? To whom?

• Are decisions permanent, or are they viewed as tactical expedients and revised as required by changing circumstances?

Metrics and Rewards

Virtual teaming and the accelerated schedules associated with widely distributed work projects generates intense stress and pressures. These operations require total commitment from managers and workers, and team leaders must determine how the organization identifies and values results and contributions:

• Is the focus on

-- Output measured in terms of quality or quantity

-- Contribution to process, planned or ad hoc

-- Commitment to quality as an overarching goal

-- Individual or team accomplishments

-- Commitment to process improvement or product development

-- Adapting to changing environments or processes?

• Is interaction with individuals and groups outside the organization valued?

• Do all levels of the organization participate in a reward/recognition process?

• Are the conditions and criteria for reward formal and widely publicized?

• Are there formal standards for measuring team activity and results?

• Are there special incentives for experienced team leaders and members to seek out and experiment with new teaming opportunities?

Team Empowerment

These issues should be addressed early on to reduce confusion at start-up. Virtual teams are particularly vulnerable to start-up confusion because the members are not in physical contact. Additionally, this segment is used to begin the trust building process essential to success:

• Have the program manager and responsible stakeholders prepare a tasking document that accomplishes the following:

-- Identifies each member of the various teams, their location, their area of expertise, and their specific responsibilities. If possible, relate responsibilities to specific segments of the project. It is also useful to include any personal information about the team members that may be available. Photographs also help bridge the distance gap by giving the virtual team members a graphic image that puts a face with a voice or text.

-- Identifies team leaders. Include a brief summary of the team leader's authority and responsibilities, and a chart showing the team's relationship to other elements engaged in the project.

-- Provides a team schedule. The key dates will be those effecting the delivery of committed tasks, but also include dates and times for reviews, visits, and any other event important to the project. If possible schedule a start-up meeting where the team members can have the opportunity to meet people they will interact electronically face-to-face.

-- Lists all tasks for which the team is committed. Relate the tasks to the management proposal.

-- Provides a communications matrix. Relate the communications matrix to the communications design and the schedule. Use this document to check on the availability and functionality of technical systems, and the competency of team members in using various media. If required, arrange training.

• Has the team leader scheduled a project launch meeting for all team members? (If some team members are at distributed locations and cannot travel to a central site, they can be included electronically.)

-- Do all team members understand their responsibilities to the tasking and the schedule?

-- Is the communications matrix understood, and can each member meet requirements?

-- Do any team members require special training?

-- Do any changes need to be made? (Make sure that changes are communicated to the project leader indicating potential impact on the schedule.)

-- Do any members have recommendations that could improve the efficiency of the team?

-- Are any special communications or learning procedures required?

Over time virtual teams begin to behave like communities, or sub-cultures. Communication protocols become implicit, trust is expected, knowledge and information sharing is the norm. With experience, mutual expectations are more easily understood and the process of building the cohesive "converged culture" goes more quickly. Teaming participants no longer worry about sharing incomplete information, constantly changing their work to meet collaborative goals, or working electronically. But every new virtual team needs to address these teaming issues at the start. These checklist items can be used more as sensing, rather than design instruments.

Now to virtual communications.

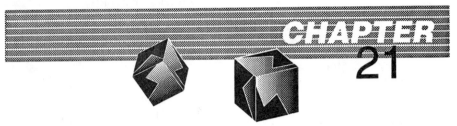

DESIGNING VIRTUAL COMMUNICATIONS

The communications design addresses the interactive protocols that embody the processes and commitments that enable teams to work virtually. The activity also defines the technologies and systems that support the information and knowledge exchange, flow, and access. In the design/planning exercise the project leader, stakeholders, and other members of the design team use their collective expertise and experience to establish an effective electronic infrastructure to support the flow of information and work. The design will help leaders and workers understand and accept the virtual options because it will help make their work easier, better, and more personally rewarding. The design process constantly investigates what's traditional and available, what's innovative, and what's desirable but not possible because of technology gaps or people-competency shortfalls.

Communications Design Guidelines

1. Timing

The communications design effort should be scheduled as soon as possible after

- Key management and team leadership assignments have been made

- Preliminary work by the process and teaming designers has identified the essential tasks

• Distributed team members are identified. It is a good idea for the management team to augment the communications design group with representatives from essential technical support groups: telecommunications, data processing, telecommunications service providers, and from dispersed locations and other organizations, including any virtual partners involved in the work process. However, remember that all participants must be empowered to make decisions and commitments. If people need to go ask their management for approval on every decision, schedules will be irrelevant.

2. Goals

The communications design team is goaled to create documents and graphics that will inform and train virtual teams in the communication protocols, technologies, and techniques of virtual work. These include the following:

• A communications map that indicates the physical location of all the virtual teams and the network resources that can be used to link them together

• A communications schedule that lists the formal events that all or most of the teams will participate in such as progress reviews

• A list of communications and networking software applications available at each location

• A communications contingency guide that provides instructions for unexpected situations or system failures that require deviation from normal procedures.

3. People and place

These prompts are intended to help ensure that the right people are participating in the design effort and that they have the support they will need to complete the communications design.

• Have all members and/or skill requirements required for the project team been identified?

• Is the entire management team representing all key stakeholder functional areas nominated/represented prior to the beginning of the communications plan design process?

• Does the team include stakeholders from outside the organization? Are these members represented? (Customers, suppliers, partners)

- Are alternates empowered by their principles to make decisions?

- Are team member locations known?

- Can each member commit the time needed to complete the first draft of the plan?

- Is a room available to the team for the entire period needed for the first draft?

- Does the room have

    -- Drawing surfaces

    --Access to telephone, Fax, Scanner, network access, duplication equipment?

- Can necessary information/materials be secured overnight?

- Is access to the facility available for extended periods?

4. Purpose and policy

- Has management provided a clear statement of purpose (Speci fication Document) for the project? Has each participant been pro vided a copy prior to the first meeting? Also:

    -- Are the specifications clear?

    -- Should anything change?

    -- Is anyone aware of barriers that could compromise the communications design process: physical, political, interpersonal, conflicting agendas, etc.?

    -- Is there a specified goal that eludes design?

- Does the management team have access to network information that includes all locations?

- Can the team communicate directly with each individual nominated for the project team with information support staffs at each team member's location?

- Has management committed to a review/action schedule for the communications design proposal?

- Has the management team developed a schedule for completing the communications design proposal? Can all members of the design team meet the schedule?

5. Design considerations

This activity will determine the overall communications needs of the project team. Stakeholders will draw on their previous experiences in similar situations, and should have the results of the process and teaming designs to work with. From these documents they can identify the events that will drive communications activity and technical support. A matrix can be used to organize communications requirements.

Participants should consider existing processes, events, or tasks that are used by the organization primarily for the exchange of information -- meetings, reviews, announcements of changes -- and determine if they are adequate for the current project, or if they can be altered to meet the conditions generated by virtual operations, or need to be totally redesigned. The discussants should rely extensively on personal experiences with both virtual work processes and their hands-on experience with the communications and information infrastructure currently in place. They should consider which systems and applications work for them, which don't, and which require extraordinary effort to use and keep working. These last are to be avoided if possible.

6. Design process

• Create a list of the essential tasks/events that need to be accomplished if the project is to succeed; for example, progress reviews, change processing, problem alerts, problem analysis, etc.

• For each task/event listed, identify appropriate primary and alternate communication media requirements: discussion only, discussion with graphic augmentation, full graphic presentation.

• Identify the primary audience for each communications task/event.

• Determine timeliness of required communications: real-time, near-real-time (specify time boundaries), regular published schedule.

• Identify the appropriate response required from each participant: become informed, creatively discuss, approve/take action.

• Determine task/event documentation requirements.

• Determine if task/event has secondary audience.

• Determine how the secondary audience will be informed.

7. Selection criteria

The following tasks, events and sub-processes are good candidates for support by virtual communications:

• Primary and alternate communications channels and the applications needed to support teams and teaming

• Scheduled interactions in which electronic meetings could substitute for face-to-face meetings

• Continuous and periodic processes and events that have high communications content

• Parallel sub-processes

-- Assessment of available communications support resources and essential training requirements

-- Determining the justifications for capital investment

-- Procedures for managing changes, additions and other normal operational activities

-- Processes to be used for the collection and processing of project data and information.

• Support for special communications roles such as

-- "Technographer," an individual trained to record and summarize the activities and results of electronic meetings

-- Project documentation manager responsible for electronic journals and notebooks

-- "Circuit riders" who physically travel between dispersed groups and provide a channel for face-to-face personal interaction

• Contingency communications options and procedures

• Pertinent information controls necessary for security

• Emergency procedures

• Training.

8. CommunicationS Link Design

This is the most complex task for the design team. The team may need to be augmented with technical experts who have detailed knowledge of the existing communications infrastructure and the information support systems. In virtual situations this may require participation of experts from outside the organization. Once a format is established and the basic geography and team particulars are known, the technical design can be completed virtually, using the infrastructure under design.

• Create a map that physically and logically identifies each participating location that will support project team activity.

• Using the task/event list, select the primary telecommunications channel for each. For example:

Task Progress Reviews	
Schedule	Weekly
Format	Audio discussions with a schedule graphic available for reference
Audience	Project management team with task leader
Secondary audience	Management team
Support	Meeting minutes and voice recording of discussion.

Issue Resolution	
Schedule	Continuous
Format	Problem presented as a statement for discussion
Audience	All team members to have access and contribute commentary in near real time
Support	Electronic conferencing

• Using the completed task/event list, summarize the communications media requirement for each location on the communications map. Consider the available telecommunications technology and conventional communications techniques. For example:

-- Face-to-face meetings

-- Audioconferencing

-- Computer conferencing

-- Shared data base access

-- Shared screen

-- Videoconferencing (Desktop or dedicated room)

-- Circuit riding.

• Determine the technical resource availability for each location's requirement needs.

• Determine, by location, communications resource shortfalls.

• Re-evaluate requirements list to find possible alternative communications options.

• Revise shortfall list and determine project impact.

• Complete communications map indicating each available and required communications link.

• Calculate investment needs.

9. Team communications skills assessment

This segment focuses on the ability of individual team groups and members to use the communications electronic infrastructure to maintain the virtual links needed for continuous information flow. Some of this information will have been generated by the sensing activities that preceded the design processes (see Chapter 14).

• Using the requirements detailed on the communications map, determine if each team member has the requisite skills and experience needed to meet communications requirements.

• Determine whether each team member has access to required communications applications.

• Determine if each team member can access network facilities for each required transmission media.

• List shortfalls for each team member.

• Identify group and/or individual communications training needs.

• Determine if required training is available, and if team members are available for training.

- Determine if there are schedule conflicts that would cause training delivery to interfere with project schedules.

- Calculate the cost of providing team members with required training.

10. Communications change management

The communication infrastructure must be able to continuously adapt to the dynamics of change. Having a change management protocol serves to reduce time and error in processing changes. Assume that a change process exists and can be used or adapted if necessary. If no process exists use the following as a guide for developing a change management procedure:

- Is there an established procedure for initiating technical and process communications change requirements in the organization?

- Are all team leaders familiar with the change plan? Are third parties aware of and agreeable with the change plan?

- Does the change plan specify change request/approval procedures?

- Does the plan identify responsible individuals?

- Does the plan specify time limits for processing changes?

- Does the plan insure appropriate technical oversight for requested/recommended changes?

- Does the change plan specify documentation requirements?

- Does the plan include instructions for the publication of changed procedures?

- Does the plan include procedures for resolving disagreements and protest?

11. Special communications activities

This segment addresses special communications requirements that cannot be satisfied by electronic media. These requirements may be political, driven by security needs, or exceed the boundaries established in the management specifications design.

- List special communications requirements.

- Select an appropriate communications technique for each requirement on the exception list: face-to-face meeting, special visits, etc.

- Determine for each requirement if special skills or functions of knowledge are required.

- If the requirement requires the intervention of an individual, is there a qualified individual available?

- Is training required/available for selected individuals to meet specialized communication needs?

- Estimate cost for special training needs.

Consider these guidelines a minimum set of considerations for developing the communications design. The approach here has been generic, while each situation requires unique design elements. The important thing to keep in mind is that communications is the key to successful virtual operations, at all levels. As an extremely complex amalgam of beliefs, skills, behaviors, and technologies, virtual communications will not happen by accident. You must design communications; there are many options for how you can do it. These guidelines represent one such option.

Last in order but not importance, we turn to designing virtual learning.

CHAPTER 22

DESIGNING
VIRTUAL LEARNING

If we take the design processes in this section serially, then this, the Design for Learning comes last. But we have urged that the design process be simultaneous not serial, so learning is not an afterthought, but a systemic part of the project, the initiative, the organization. Designed-in with the other virtual operations, learning becomes the instrument of creating the Virtual Learning Organization.

To recap a bit, in Chapter 18 we introduced the Strategic Learning Model (SLM) as a framework for the Design for Virtual Learning. The model can be instrumental in all four aspects of this, or any design process:

1. Establishing needed competencies

2. Making an inventory of current competencies

3. Identifying gaps

4. Identifying systemic, pedagogically sound ways of developing the knowledge needed to fill the gaps and ensure future capability for virtual operations.

The learning design methodology is generally the same as the other virtual designs. There is no need to repeat the basic process. Instead, in this chapter we will focus entirely on the key learning attributes that must be designed into the prototype project to meet the learning needs of the virtual initiative.

The Design for Learning Process

Review the Strategic Learning Model to help keep the design process focused on real needs and possibilities. The SLM can be tailored and represented in a variety of ways to provide a visual representation of the problem space and a guideline for designing the learning system.

In this example of the SLM, the data points represent relative stages of knowledge, knowledges, or competencies in a virtual initiative.

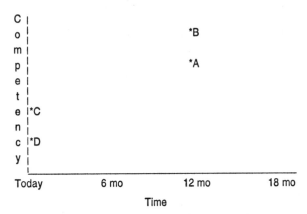

Figure 22.1   Knowledge Points-Application

The vertical axis represents increasing levels of competencies required/in place, and the horizontal axis represents linear time in a project cycle.

The data points indicate the following:

A= What you (the team) think you need to know

B= What you really need to know

C= What you think you already know

D= What you really already know.

1. Benchmarking the organization's readiness to engage in virtual learning

The following prompts should help you better understand your organization's current virtual learning capabilities and shortfalls. This process will help you create a rich definition of SLM Point D, as opposed to being misled by the more casual assumption that you are at Point C!

• Has your organization made a strategic *commitment* to continuously re-evaluate and provide for its people's needs for new

-- information

-- knowledge

-- skills

-- perspectives and beliefs?

• Are all *virtual stakeholders* participants in your strategy

-- your own parent organization's representatives, top to bottom

-- customers

-- alliances

-- benchmark competitors?

• Is your organization putting into place the *virtual processes and infrastructure* to meet those needs?

-- remote information access (Internet, network databases and public information bases, electronic project handbooks)

-- interactive, network learning systems (audio-, computer-, videoconferencing)

-- self-paced training infrastructure (multi-media, client-server based workstations)

-- cross-organizational/cultural networked conversation systems (computer conferencing)

• Are there learning plans in place to provide training and support? Do they encourage experimentation and innovation in using technology to support learning?

• Have you incorporated *processes* for

-- identifying the competencies your organization needs for new initiatives

-- deciding whether to *buy* or *build* those competencies?

• Are training and organizational development staff and consultants granted full stakeholder status in line initiatives?

• Does your learning system address *virtual teaming* competencies as well as domain knowledge and technical skills?

-- understanding electronic communication processes

-- maintaining people-relationships electronically

-- sustaining high-performance, concurrent, electronic information work.

• Does your approach to learning encourage you to confidently assess learning needs and approaches for the *"next"* and *"next next"* projects?

• Do you have in place processes for measuring

-- levels of competency

-- probability of achieving learning goals

-- personal and team learning

-- correlations between learning and current/future project successes?

• Do you *reward* people for learning as part of performance? Do you reward team, as well as individual learning?

2. Assessing competencies

Competencies needed to accomplish the goals set forth in the project specification and indicated in the other designs should be explicit. Each competency should be approached from the perspective of the following skills:

- Skills

- Knowledge

- Beliefs and Perceptions

- Behaviors

The set of competencies identified should be robust but not neccessarily complete. Actually, the set can't be complete because new needs will be discovered as the project progresses.

In assessing competencies, be sure to include operational as well as specialty competencies:

• At the management, leader, and knowledge worker levels operational competencies could include

- How to make build or buy decisions

- Using virtual communications technologies

- Working in a collaborative, virtual design team

- Managing the stress of simultaneous work.

• Specialized competencies include such areas as

- Object oriented programming

- Virtual leadership

- Biochemistry

- Active modelling

- Desktop publishing.

Also, pay special attention to developing the capabilities needed to overcome barriers to virtual operations.

In other words, proceed to a definition of Point B in the SLM: What you really need to know to succeed in the virtual project.

3. Assessing learning gaps

Use the framework of the SLM to help make an accurate assessment of the learning gaps: ΔDB. Use whatever metrics you are comfortable with, decide what shortfalls are most important to address, and design-in how you plan to close the gaps using the tolls of virtual learning themselves whenever possible.

• Have individual development plans and virtual team DPs been started?

- Are objectives clearly stated?

- Are metrics assigned?

4. Determining Completeness of the learning design

While the Design for Virtual Learning is a living, evolving document, it should cover as much of the learning situation as possible in its first instance.

• Does the design of the virtual learning system actually meet the team's needs?

• Have all possible options to initiate, support and sustain the learning system and the team been considered? Review the virtual learning process and technology options:

Learning Processes	Learning Technologies
Traditional Classroom and Computer Assisted Training	Seminars
	Workshops
Distance Learning	Courses
Networked Learning	Audioconferencing
Electronic Classroom	Videoconferencing
Situated Learning	Electronic Mail
Action Learning	Computer Conferencing
Constructive Learning	Data, Information, and Knowledge
Hyperlearning	Access Tools
Computer Assisted Learning	FAX
Computer Mediated Networked Learning	Animation, Imaging, Modelling and Simulation
Structured Learning	
Random Learning	
Learner Centered Computer Assisted Curricular Learning	
Discovery Learning	
Innovative Learning	

At this point there should be enough in the learning plan to begin using existing process and technologies, designing new processes where technologies exist, and investigating new technologies that appear to have the potential of helping meet the team's learning needs. The learning design should continue to evolve to meet new needs and new conditions, as should innovative learning processes. The complexity and competency axes are infinite; no steady state will ever be reached. Besides, what then would be the challenge?

EPILOGUE:
VIRTUAL REALITIES

In the middle of the journey of my life,
I found myself in a dark wood,
Where the straight way was lost.
        The Divine Comedy, **Dante**[1]

In this book we have followed an almost too neat, too sequential approach to transitioning to virtual operations. We've done this for a purpose; to present the concepts, activities and behaviors involved in the transition in a coherent context. Unfortunately, reality is never so neat: The map is not the territory.

Writers of epics such as the *Divine Comedy*, and more recently *Star Wars* and *The Godfather*, know that real epics start *in medias res*: in the middle of things. Just as Dante's pilgrim found himself at midlife in a dark wood, organizational managers like MRA's Ray McCann, often find themselves starting out amidst the virtual journey rather than at the beginning. Usually they experience the virtual epiphany while struggling to accomplish virtual teaming goals without the support of virtual operations processes or technologies. Often the shock of recognition is captured in a loud, spontaneous exclamation:

- "But your describing exactly what we're doing in our new joint project with Gandex Corporation!"

- "Hold it! By your definition everything we do is virtual, but we don't know it!"

[1]Dante Alighieri, *The Divine Comedy: Inferno.* Translated by Charles S. Singleton. (Princeton University Press, 1970) p. 3.

• "We use outside resources all the time. Maybe the reason it's getting tougher and tougher is that we're trying to do virtual work without virtual tools!"

These managers need salvage plans, not blueprints; lifeboats not shipyards.

In this section we'll offer some mid-stream guidance for those already adrift in the virtual sea. The guidelines will be pragmatic, consisting of observations we think will be useful to executives, stakeholders, and knowledge workers already engaged in virtual missions, consciously or not. The point here is that there are actions you can take with work-in-progress that will begin to integrate the virtual perspective and virtual operations into your organization's activities. The mid-stream remedies will have additional value as a basis for the eventual planning and design of a full scale virtual effort. It will give the organization a head-start when there is an opportunity to plan and design a full-cycle virtual project.

We will keep our remarks short, using as context the reader's understanding of virtual challenges and operations built through reading the earlier chapters. Again we will focus on people, the three constituencies of the organization: executive management, stakeholders, and knowledge workers.

Executive Management

To bring to light the virtual opportunity, you need to provide your managers and workers with a vision of the future that involves virtual operations. While this kind of vision is not something that is easily crafted and articulated, it is absolutely necessary and can be developed in parallel with the ongoing work. Visioning is very much a state of mind and it starts with you. Encourage participation through the entire organization. In this way everyone will be exposed to the virtual perspective and will share ownership of the vision.

Besides setting strategic direction, your most important responsibility is to identify project situations in which the team is trying to accomplish virtual work with traditional perspectives and tools. You need to work closely with project management. For example, help project leaders create and manage relationships and commitments with the top executives of partners in the project. Do this by working with them in the

team, not as top-guns occasionally summoned to help out when all else
has failed. If you can settle a resource issue with a counterpart in
another company over lunch, do it. It could consume all of your leader's
time carrying messages between executive suites and moderating political agendas between executives who have not established or exercised
relationships with their peers.

Here are some questions you can ask yourself as prompts to help
your midstream transition:

• Does our vision reflect the reality of our future virtual situation? Have we (executives) made every possible effort to make sure
that everyone in the organization knows that our vision includes a
formal and deliberate transition to virtual operations? Do they
know what this means? Do they know what we expect them to do,
and what we commit to do for them to make this transition effective
and as painless as possible? If not, why not?

• Does everyone understand the business reasons that justified
our decision to engage in virtual operations? Are we all still in
agreement? If not what are we doing to reach consensus?

• Are we looking at our current projects for virtual potential?

• Have we identified future projects as prototypes for formal
transitioning to virtual? Have we planned and designed that transition (See Part VI)?

• Are we communicating with the current project leadership? Do
we know about problems that might indicate virtual entry points?
Likely places to look are internal and external communications,
managing simultaneous tasks, systems interoperability, meeting
resource commitments, building external relationships and acquiring outside competencies. Have we offered our help in a way that
preserves and enhances the leader's position?

• Are we able to monitor team activities? Do we know about problems before they become crises?

• Are we rewarding effective leaders and teams? Does the whole
organization know it when a team makes a breakthrough? Do they
know it when one of our virtual partners makes a significant contribution?

• Do we value, encourage, and support the learning efforts current teams are making? Are we accelerating our path to becoming a
learning organization, however we choose to define it?

• Are we setting a virtual precedent for investment in the information infrastructure? Are we satisfied that our investments are consistent with our vision? Are we practicing what we preach -- using the information support systems ourselves?

• Are we already doing whatever it takes to continuously improve our organization's core competencies? Are we doing everything we can to improve our own competencies as executives?

• Do we search out exceptional performance, creativity, and other examples where individuals turn our initiatives into successes?

As these prompts indicate, there are plenty of actions executives can take to help current projects begin to take advantage of virtual opportunities and build momentum for the virtual transition. Today is not too early to start.

Stakeholders

As an external stakeholder in a current project, you are probably dwelling in that amphibian state between job-shopper and empowered virtual partner. Your expectations for a voice in the project, and the lead virtual organization's expectation on you for full resource commitment will be tempered by the reality that your own management still sees "inside" work as having top priority. Your ability to firmly commit resources as a full partner may be limited.

You are faced with the triple challenge of managing the virtual team leadership, your own resources, and your own management. You know that the project leader trusts stakeholders to honor their resource commitments. Your most important job, then, is to understand how well you can respond to that trust. You need to know the full extent of expectations placed on you in the virtual stakeholder role, and the degree of support you can count on from your management and your resources.

Here are a few questions you can ask yourself to better understand the potential you have for helping the project team go virtual:

• Am I (any stakeholder) absolutely certain that I know the extent -- and limits -- of my responsibilities and authority? When I delegate someone to act for me, are they fully empowered to make firm decisions in my name?

• Am I clear on the purpose of the project? Can I fully support the effort? If not, am I willing and able to provide my full support if my objections are overruled by executive management?

• Do I have a system that helps me keep track of the commitments I made to the team?

• Does my management system enable me to inform teams of changes I must make that impact my commitments? Does my system provide enough lead time to avoid creating crises? Can I spot problems that might be alleviated through virtual processes; for example, bringing in more outside resources to augment or provide competencies not available in the current team?

• Do I work effectively with the project leader? If not, why not? Should I nominate someone to act for me to ensure that the project will not be affected by my personal feelings?

• Am I giving full attention and support to the learning agenda?

• Am I meeting my commitments to expedite decisions that effect the project? Have I provided and empowered alternative decision makers in the event that I am not available?

• Am I fully participating in the reward and recognition program?

Leaders

The leader of a current project is probably also the project manager. As organizations "sub-clinically" go virtual, as the worlds of traditional and virtual work collide, the leader's job becomes more difficult. The project team gradually has more and more members from outside the "host"organization. These folks may or may not be co-located with the rest of the team. Certainly there will be cultural, communications, and reporting issues.

• The competency model will not be fully understood; organizational loyalties will collide with getting the best competencies.

• Competencies will be distributed, but electronic processes and technologies will not be robust enough to support distributed work.

• The opportunity for parallel task performance will be masked by the habits of serial work.

There is no way to avoid these tensions, but they certainly be alleviated, even turned to advantage if leaders know how to tune their perspectives and activities to capture virtual potential. The following questions may help you do just that:

- Do I know enough about the virtual paradigm to spot opportunities in this project? Do I know my team, my stakeholders well enough to sense when problems come up, especially problems that can be addressed through virtual means?

- Do feel comfortable leading virtual work? I know the stresses, do I know the rewards? Do I understand all the business reasons why it's important to begin thinking virtual?

- Do any aspects of virtual operations bother me: electronic communications, constant learning, the use of outside competencies? Can I secure necessary investment capital for technology or training?

- Is there a management champion for virtual operations? Is there someone I can trust and work with?

- Do I anticipate or have any problems with any of the stakeholders? Are they in for the duration?

- Am I able to keep the teams together for the duration? Am I satisfied that they have the necessary competencies? Is finding replacements a problem?

- Do I have the authority to recruit outside resources if they can deliver better, faster, cheaper?

- Can I maintain the constant communication with the team so necessary for virtual work?

- Can I spot and respond to stress and other individual and group problems in a pro-active manner?

- Do I need to replace individuals who cannot or will not work in our evolving virtual environment, will not expose potential and real problems to management, acknowledge mistakes, ask for (even demand) help, value and encourage learning, and accept responsibility for themselves, their team, and the outcome of their tasks?

- Am I recognizing and giving credit to teams and individuals who deliver results? Am I making sure that these successes are publicized to the entire organization, enterprise, industry, community?

Knowledge Workers

Knowledge workers are the first to feel the strain of working virtual with traditional tools. Even before putting a name on the thing, the folks in the team doing the work know that something is amiss with the management model, the communications protocols, resource allocations, or the progress of work. They're the first to feel the high stress and low morale that accompanies frustration in getting work done.

The good news is that as a knowledge worker you can begin to address this transitional gridlock, even if unenlightened management prefers to churn through denial, bombast, and blame before listening to the troops. Ask yourself these questions about the work situation, and act as you can to begin the bottom-up transition to virtual operations:

• Do I understand the concept of virtual operations, and how virtual objectives and practices affect the way I work? If not, do I know how and where to get this knowledge?

• Am I paying attention to the work being done in my "boundary" areas? Do I know the expectations of my teammates, so that I add value to their work and receive value from them? Do we behave as a team rather than a network of individual contributors?

• Are we a network, a community? Do we take advantage of the electronic infrastructure to build our value added?

• Do I think of problems as "team problems," or do I consider a problem as "my" problem or "their" problem? Do I look for team problems that could be alleviated through better communications, virtual task design, or learning?

• Am I clear about the nature of the commitments I will be asked to make? Can I live with these commitments?

• Do I understand the purpose of the team to which I am assigned? Do I feel that my competencies complement the team? Do I think the rest of the team can support my needs? Can I depend on management to support our needs?

• Do I understand the communications protocols? Am I clear about the communications capabilities available to me?

• Do I understand all the technologies that I could use: for electronically representing my competency? for communicating? for accessing information? for modelling? If not, can I acquire necessary skills and help the team participate in the learning?

• Can I identify valid personal reasons why I should make the effort to change the way I work? Are these reasons enough?

• Am I comfortable sharing information?

• Do I understand the importance of sharing ideas, work in progress, constructive criticism, problem alerts, collateral knowledge, or any other information that will benefit my team? With peers? With management? With outside collaborators? Am I capable of this level of sharing?

• Do I know what to do if I get in trouble? Whom to inform? What to expect? How to insist that I get the help I need, when I need it?

• Can I work effectively in spite of continuous changes?

• Do I have a problem with trust? Can people trust me?

• Do I know of competencies that are better suited to this situation than those currently committed? Am I able, willing, to do something about it?

There's no need to give equal time to all these reflective questions. Some will hit home immediately; work at turning those to action. You may be particularly sensitive to communications problems in your team. These may be traceable to issues of technology gaps, lack of trust, or just habit. Open the dialog with your peers and leadership on the issues that affect you emotionally; you'll be surprised at how often others will agree with your assessment and contribute to solving the problem.

Final Advice to All Mid-Streamers

The point of this chapter has not been to convince you to ignore the structured designs suggested in Part VI, but to find ways to implement those designs while work is in progress. In this first project peruse the formal designs for what you can use immediately; incrementally bring in the rest as you progress. If you believe in the 80/20 rule, go right to communications sensing and design. With some virtual communications in place you can more easily build the process, teaming, and learning infrastructures. It's better to do something than nothing, and all designs, plans, and actions are revisable.

We hope that by reading this book you will have personally prepared to go virtual. Now if you are convinced of and committed to virtual operations, get to work and spread the word. Find tasks to reengineer with the virtual spin, aim for success, and announce that success when it comes. We think that by doing this you will be contributing to your own and your organization's future achievements.

BIBLIOGRAPHY

A Team, The. NBC Television. ca. 1980.

Ackoff, Russell L. *Creating the Corporate Future: Plan or Be Planned For* (New York: John Wiley, 1981).

Alexander, Christopher. *Notes on the Synthesis of Form* (Harvard University Press, 1964).

Alighieri, Dante. *The Divine Comedy: Inferno.* Translated by Charles S. Singleton (Princeton University Press, 1970).

Austin, J.L. *How To Do Things with Words* (Oxford University Press, 1962).

Berlin, Isaiah. *The Hedgehog and the Fox: An Essay on Tolstoy's View of History* (New York: Simon & Schuster, 1953).

Boschmann, Erwin, ed. *The Electronic Classroom: A Handbook for Education in the Electronic Environment* (Medford, New Jersey: Learned Information Incorporated, 1995).

Campbell, Jeremy. *Grammatical Man: Information, Entropy, Language and Life* (New York: Simon & Schuster, 1982).

Checkland, Peter. *Systems Thinking, Systems Practice* (New York: John Wiley & Sons, 1981).

Crane, Stephen. "The Open Boat," in *Men, Women & Boats* (Freeport, NY, 1972).

Dartmouth College Alumni Magazine, August 1994.

Davenport, Thomas H. *Process Innovation: Reengineering Work through Information Technology* (Boston, MA: Harvard Business School Press, 1993).

Davidow, William H. & Michael S. Malone. *The Virtual Corporation: Structuring and Revitalizing the Corporation for the 21st Century* (New York: Harper Business, 1992).

De Mente, Boye Lafayette. *Chinese Etiquette & Ethics in Business*. NTC Business Books, 1994.

Detroit Edison 1992 Annual Report. 2000 Second Avenue, Detroit, Michigan.

Drucker, Peter. "The Age of Social Transformation," in *The Atlantic Monthly*, November 1994. pp. 53-80.

---------- *The Effective Executive* (New York: Harper & Row, 1966).

Engelbart, Douglas C. *The Bootstrap Institute*, Fremont, CA.

Frost, Robert. *In the Clearing*, "How Hard It is to Keep from Being King When It's in You and in the Situation" (New York: Rinehart and Winston, 1955).

Garfinkel, Harold. *Studies in Ethnomethodology* (New York: Appleton-Century-Crofts, 1967).

Gates, William. Keynote Address to the Electronic Mail Association, Anaheim, CA, April 19, 1994.

Gingrich, Newt. Conference address at the Mayflower Hotel, Washington DC, January 10th, 1995.

Grenier, Raymond and George Metes. *Enterprise Networking: Working Together Apart* (Maynard, MA: Digital Press, 1992).

Gundry, Dr. John. Unpublished papers for *Knowledge Ability, Ltd.*, Malmesbury, Wiltshire, U.K.

Hammer, Michael & James Champy. *Reengineering the Corporation: A Manifesto for Business Revolution* (New York: Harper Business, 1993).

Hampden-Turner, Charles, and Fons Trompenaars. *The Seven Cultures of Capitalism.: Value Systems for Creating Wealth in the United States, Britain, Japan, Germany, France, Sweden and the Netherlands* (London: Piatkus, 1994).

Hoban, Russell. *Riddley Walker* (New York: Summit Books, 1980).

Hobson, J. Allan M.D. *The Chemistry of Conscious States: How the Brain Changes its Mind* (New York: Little Brown 1994).

Index Corporation and Michael E. Treacy. *The Costs of Network Ownership* (Cambridge, MA: Index Group, Inc., 1989).

Kesey, Ken. *One Flew Over the Cuckoo's Nest* (New York: Penguin, 1976).

Kincaid, D. Lawrence. "The Convergence Theory and Intercultural Communication," in *Theories in Intercultural Communication* ed. Young Yun Kim & William B Gudykunst (Newbury Park: Sage, 1988).

The Last Temptation of Christ. By Paul Schrader, based on the novel by Nikos Kazentzakis. Directed by Martin Scorcese. Produced by Barbara De Fina. Universal Pictures & Cineplex Odeon Films, 1988.

Lipnack, Jessica & Jeffrey Stamps. *The TeamNet Factor: Bringing the Power of Boundary Crossing Into the Heart of Your Business* (Essex Junction, VT: Oliver Wight Publications, 1993).

Morris, Jan. *Manhattan '45* (London: Penguin Books, 1969).

O'Hara-Devereaux, Mary & Robert Johansen. *GlobalWork -- Bridging Distance Culture & Time* (San Francisco: Jossey-Bass, 1994).

Perelman, Lewis J. *School's Out: A Radical New Formula for the Revitalization of America's Educational System* (New York: Avon Books, 1992).

Petroski, Henry. *To Engineer is Human: The Role of Failure in Successful Design* (New York: Vintage, 1992).

Rheingold, Howard. *The Virtual Community: Homesteading on the Electronic Frontier* (Reading, MA: Addison-Wesley, 1993).

Roth, Philip. *Portnoy's Complaint* (New York: Vintage Books, 1994).

Salinger, J. D. *The Catcher in the Rye* (Boston: Little, Brown Company, 1951).

Senge, Peter. *The Fifth Discipline: The Art and Practice of the Learning Organization* (New York: Doubleday/Currency, 1990).

Shneiderman, Ben. *Software psychology: Human factors in Human and Information Systems* (Cambridge, MA: Winthrop, 1980).

Short Cuts. A film directed by Roger Altman. Screenplay by Robert Altman and Frank Barhydt. Based on the writings of Raymond Carver. Fineline Features in Association with Spelling Films International, 1994.

Schrage, Michael. Shared Minds: *The New Technologies of Collaboration* (New York: Random House, 1990).

Suchman, Lucy A. *Plans and Situated Actions: The problem of human machine communication* (Cambridge University Press, 1987).

Taubes, Gary. *"Surgery in Cyberspace," Discover,* December 1994. pp.84-94.

32 Short Films about Glenn Gould. A film directed by Francois Girard. Screenplay by Francois Girard and Don McKellage, Canada: Max Films, 1993.

Tolstoy, Lev. *Anna Karenina* (Moscow: Progress Publishers, 1978).

INDEX